Angels of the Lord
365 Reflections on Our Heavenly Guardians

Angels of the Lord

365 Reflections on Our Heavenly Guardians

CATHERINE M. ODELL
& MARGARET A. SAVITSKAS

Our Sunday Visitor

www.osv.com
Our Sunday Visitor Publishing Division
Our Sunday Visitor, Inc.
Huntington, Indiana 46750

Contents

Introduction

In *Angels of the Lord: 365 Reflections on Our Heavenly Guardians* you will discover many of the ways God has sent his glorious angels into our world. Every day for a year, you will find a Scripture passage, Church teaching, quote, or story about an angelic encounter. Also included in this book are readings that share the wonderful way that angels have inspired the world's greatest writers, painters, sculptors, and musicians.

In recent years, many Christians have either forgotten about the reality and role of angels, or have reduced them to sweet and harmless imitations of human beings. In fact, angels are so much more! They are the greatest of God's creatures. They are powerful heavenly beings who were made by God before he created the world. Their intelligence is second only to God's, and each angel has a unique personality. Angels serve God in all things, and in doing so, they reflect the glory of God — light from Light. They adore, praise, and honor God completely and eternally.

The angels were made through and for Christ. They are his angels even as they are charged with the mission to assist, protect, and guide human beings and all of God's creation. The word "angel" (Latin *angelus*; Greek *aggelos*) is from the Hebrew for "one going" or "one sent"; a messenger). "Angel" refers not to their nature, which is pure spirit, but to their ministry of being a messenger. The phrase "the angel of the Lord" was used as a way of describing how God sometimes came to people in human form.

One role of the angels is to be sent into our world with a message for mankind, and sometimes to individuals with a message for all of us. Though the angels in the Bible and the lives of the saints appear as human beings in order to communicate with us, angels do not have, and never had, bodies. A creature made of only will and intellect is hard for us to imagine. Yet angels have been depicted in art for thousands of years — sometimes as ethereal beings far beyond the reach of humans, sometimes as ordinary persons to emphasize their closeness to us. But angels are pure spirits — no bodies, no wings, no halos.

Throughout the Old Testament and New Testament, from Genesis to Revelation, there are two hundred and twenty-seven references to angels. Saint Gregory the Great (540–604) said, "Nearly every page of Scripture testifies to the fact that there are angels and archangels." A pope, Scripture scholar, and one of the Doctors of the Church, Gregory would also point out that his belief in the angels didn't come only from his studies and from the testimony of the Bible. You will learn about one of his personal experiences with angels in the reading for his feast day, September 3.

You will also read the stories of early martyrs who received courage and consolation from angels. These stories inspired other Christians to be steadfast in their faith. You will hear from the great Fathers and Doctors of the Church who shaped what the Church believes and teaches about angels. (By the way, Doctor of the Church is an official title given by the pope for the outstanding contribution a person has made to the Church in the understanding and/or development of Scripture, theology, and doctrine. There are presently thirty-five Doctors of the Church — four are women.) You will smile at the anecdotes about Saint (Padre) Pio of Pietrelcina (1887–1968), who saw and spoke to angels as old friends and received prayer requests from guardian angels on behalf of others. You will be amazed at the accounts of ordinary people who had encounters with angels.

You will also recognize throughout the weeks and months ahead that angels can inspire your reflections and prayers. Thinking about their constancy, their orientation to God above everything else, can impact the way you see your life and your journey to God. The Church assures us that angels definitely do exist and that every person has an angel guardian "to light and guard, to rule and guide" as the Guardian Angel Prayer says. "Make yourself familiar with the angels, and behold them frequently in spirit; for, without being seen, they are present with you," wrote Saint Francis de Sales, a seventeenth-century bishop.

On October 2, 2014, on the Feast of the Guardian Angels, Pope Francis reminded us that guardian angels are primarily concerned with helping us reach heaven, their home and our true home, where we will join them in eternally praising God. Warning us not to ignore the angels among us, Pope Francis said, "Guardian angels are not the stuff of fantasy. They are really present as wise travel companions. Nobody walks alone, and none of us can believe we are alone. All of us have an angel who watches over us and lets us hear — deep inside — wise words meant to help us make the right choices…. It's the voice of your travel companion helping you to navigate life's journey. Be confident that this advice will take you through to the end of your life." The Lord said, "See, I am sending my angel before you, to guard you on the way and bring you to the place I have prepared. Be attentive to him" (Exodus 23:20–21).

May your year of encounters with *Angels of the Lord* be full of blessings and new knowledge of God's amazing love.

"The Angel of the Lord Declared unto Mary"

 When Pope Francis greeted three million young Catholics in Rio de Janeiro, Brazil, for World Youth Day 2013, he was setting the tone for his papacy. He prayed the Angelus with the young people and then explained why. "The Angelus prayer is a beautiful popular expression of the faith," Pope Francis said. "It is a simple prayer, recited at three specific times during the day. It thus punctuates the rhythm of our daily activities: in the morning, at midday, and at sunset. It reminds us of the luminous event that transformed history: the Incarnation, the moment when the Son of God became man in Jesus of Nazareth. Every time we pray the Angelus, we recall the event that changed the history of mankind forever."

As this brand new year begins, consider putting prayer into the rhythm of your day. Let it become a normal, natural, necessary part of your life. Consider praying the Angelus in the traditional way — in the morning, at midday, and at sunset (see the appendix, page 377). "Pray for us, O holy Mother of God, that we may be made worthy of the promises of Christ." [1]

January 2

Saint Basil the Great (c. 330–379)

Angels on Alert

 Saint Basil valiantly defended the teachings of the Church from heresy but also encouraged fellow Christians by writing about the angels God sends to support and protect us. "Beside each believer," Basil said, "stands an angel as protector and shepherd, leading him to life." He also said that "an angel is assigned, who guards the soul like an army on alert." That guardian angel "will not retreat from us, unless we drive him away." Basil did not mince words about sin and repentance: "Sin turns away angels as smoke turns away bees and a nasty stench puts doves to flight." [2]

Angel of mine, protect me from the destruction of sin. Mount a strong defense of my soul, and lead me to eternal life. Amen.

The Angel of the Lord Appeared in a Dream

 In order to safeguard the newborn Lord, Joseph and Mary cooperated with angelic warnings and messages. The Gospel of Matthew tells us that "the angel of the Lord appeared to Joseph in a dream." The angel told Joseph to take the child and his mother and flee to Egypt to escape the soldiers Herod sent to slaughter all of the male infants. When Herod died, the angel again "appeared in a dream to Joseph in Egypt" and told him that it was safe to return with his family to the land of Israel (Matthew 2:12–13, 19–20).

Lord Jesus, help me to hear and heed your messages and to follow your directives. Mindful that angels appear in mysterious and wonderful ways, I pray that you will enable me to always be open to your designs for me.

January 4

Saint Elizabeth Ann Seton (1774–1821)

ANGELS TAKING WATCH

 Elizabeth Ann Seton is the first American to be canonized. After her husband, William, died, she converted to Catholicism, but struggled against religious prejudice and found it difficult to support her family. A deep love for her Catholic faith shaped Elizabeth's vision. "If we beheld a soul after baptism with the eyes of faith," she wrote, "we would see angels taking their watch around it." Her strong faith grounded her. Despite hardship and setbacks, Elizabeth established the first Catholic school in the nation at Emmitsburg, Maryland, and founded the first American congregation of religious women, the Sisters of Charity. [3]

Although you have not seen him you love him; even though you do not see him now yet believe in him, you rejoice with an indescribable and glorious joy, as you attain the goal of your faith. (1 Peter 1:8–9)

Wings of an Angel?

 Although artists have often portrayed angels with wings, angels don't have wings — or bodies. They are created spirits who love, think, make choices, and have free will. They can appear in any form but have usually appeared as humans. Angels known as cherubim and seraphim were sometimes represented with wings in Scripture. But, early Christians did not picture angels with wings. In catacomb frescoes in Rome, the angel Gabriel is shown appearing to Mary at the Annunciation in human form. No wings. In the fourth century, however, Christianity was legalized. Emperor Constantine authorized the building of Christian shrines and churches, where angels were often shown with wings to explain their instantaneous speed, freedom, and power. [4]

As the Ark of the Covenant was being built, God told the Israelites to portray the angels protecting it with wings: "The cherubim shall have their wings spread out above, sheltering the cover with them; they shall face each other, with their faces looking toward the cover" (Exodus 25:20).

January 6
Saint André Bessette (1845–1937)

HONORING SAINT JOSEPH

Saint André Bessette, a Holy Cross brother from Montreal, saw that Christmas scenes typically featured Mary, Baby Jesus, angels, and shepherds. Saint Joseph, the foster father of Jesus was often in the background. Like the angels, God's messengers, Brother André had something important to tell the world. Saint Joseph should be properly honored. When people were healed through André's prayers, he gave all credit to Saint Joseph. When the beloved ninety-two-year-old brother died, all but the dome of Saint Joseph's Oratory had been built to honor "the man in the background" and the power of prayer. [5]

> *"Those who give themselves to prayer should in a special manner have always a devotion to Saint Joseph; for I know not how any man can think of the Queen of the angels, during the time that she suffered so much with the Infant Jesus, without giving thanks to Saint Joseph for the services he rendered them then."*

> — Saint Teresa of Ávila [6]

In the Society of Saints and Angels

Blessed John Henry Newman, a prominent Catholic convert of the nineteenth century, reflected on the reassuring presence of the spiritual world in our lives. "Though a member of this world, you have but to kneel in prayer and you are at once in the society of saints and angels. Wherever you are, you can, through God's incomprehensible mercy, in a moment bring yourself into the midst of God's holy Church invisible.... Are you lonely? Does the day run heavily? Fall on your knees and you are at once relieved by the reality of your unseen companions. Are you tempted to sin? Fix at once your eyes upon those pure and shining witnesses in God's dwelling place." [7]

Is there no border between visible and invisible, except perhaps in our own minds? A small leap of faith takes us into the presence of the saints and angels. How can they help me today?

January 8

Transported by Angels

 In October 1962, Pope Saint John XXIII knelt to pray in the home of the Virgin Mary — not in Nazareth, or Jerusalem, or even Bethlehem. The pope went to Loreto, a small village in Italy, to seek the blessing of the Mother of the Church on the upcoming Second Vatican Council. He was in the house where tradition holds Mary was born, where the Archangel Gabriel greeted her and Christ was conceived, and where the Holy Family lived in Nazareth. An inscription on the wall of the humble dwelling reads: "Angels conveyed this house from Palestine." The belief is that in the years 1291 and 1294, the house was miraculously carried by angels out of the Holy Land, first to a place of safety in Dalmatia (present-day Croatia) and after three years to Loreto, where it remains a place of pilgrimage.

In 1595, Pope Clement VIII had the story inscribed on the Holy House of Loreto, concluding with: Pious Pilgrims, worship with devout affection the Queen of Angels, our Gracious Mother, so that through her merits and prayers, she may obtain for you from her beloved Son, the forgiveness of sins, health of body, and the happiness of eternity. [8]

HOMELESS ANGEL

 Angels are all around us. We just need to see and listen with our hearts. Barbara Romanowski shared her experience. "I was standing outside a department store when an older woman approached me and asked if I could give her change for a cup of coffee. I reached into my pocket and pulled out the only bills I had on me — $3.00. 'Thank you,' she whispered. 'I'm an angel, you know, and I will watch over you.' And she walked away. Only then did I realize that I had no money to get my car out of the parking lot. I stood there wondering how the heck I was going to get home. Starting to panic, I began checking my pockets for a train ticket I might have. When I put my hand into the pocket from which I had pulled the $3.00 I gave to the angel, I found three dollar bills in that pocket!" [9]

We are already strangely related, even acquainted, with the angels during our earthly lives. Once we attain to their company, to heaven, to the space of the heart of Christ, we shall no longer ask: "Who are you?" We shall probably call out in final recognition: "So it was you all the time!" [10]

January 10

AIRLIFTED BY AN ANGEL

 Now the prophet Habakkuk was in Judea. He had boiled pottage and had broken bread into a bowl, and was going into the field to take it to the reapers. But the angel of the Lord said to Habakkuk, "Take the dinner which you have to Babylon, to Daniel, in the lions' den." "I have never seen Babylon," the prophet excused himself, "and I know nothing about this den." The angel of the Lord took Habakkuk by the crown of his head, lifted him by his hair and, with the rushing speed of the wind itself, set him down in Babylon, right over the den. Within moments, Daniel had his meal. Read this Old Testament angel story in more detail in Daniel 14:33–41.

"You have remembered me, O God," said Daniel. "You have not forsaken those who love you." When the king who had condemned Daniel found him still alive, he cried aloud: "You are great, O Lord, the God of Daniel, and there is no other besides you!" (Daniel 14:38–41)

BELIEF IN ANGELS

 A 2011 poll conducted right before Christmas by the Associated Press and Gallup pollsters revealed some surprising statistics. Many people who never went to church believed in angels! Overall, 77 percent of adult Americans then believed that "angels are for real." Among all Christians in the United States, the percentage of believers was even higher — 88 percent. A majority of non-Christians claimed belief in angels, and four in ten Americans who didn't attend religious services said they did, as well. Additionally, pollsters found that women were more likely than men to believe in angels. And adults over thirty tended to believe in the heavenly messengers more often than younger adults. [11]

"The existence of the spiritual, non-corporeal beings that Sacred Scripture usually calls "angels" is a truth of faith. The witness of Scripture is as clear as the unanimity of Tradition."

— Catechism of the Catholic Church, 328

January 12

ANGELS SERVE AS WITNESSES AT BAPTISM

 The Church celebrates the Baptism of the Lord on the Sunday after Epiphany. The feast closes the Christmas season with Jesus asking John the Baptist for baptism. The sinless Son of God did not need baptism, but the event prefigures the sacrament of Baptism. Jesus was plunged into the water of the Jordan, while a Christian is immersed in the water of Baptism. Tertullian, a Father of the Church, taught that an angel serves as the "witness of baptism" and prepares the newly baptized to witness to Christ. "Thus the angel set in charge of baptism makes ready the way for the coming of the Holy Spirit by the washing away of sin." [12]

Scripture reminds us that the angels rejoice when Creation glorifies God. Imagine how overjoyed the angels are when baptism acknowledges that we are sons and daughters of God and members of Christ's body, the Church.

An Angel's Light

 During the dark days of winter, some people suffer with SAD (Seasonal Affective Disorder), a type of depression related to seasonal changes, particularly less daylight. Light therapy helps, because light naturally lifts our spirits. We need light! It's the way we're made! No wonder that angels — when they appear to us — are bright and shining beings. An angel's light is always a reflection of God's awesome light and holiness. When the angel Gabriel appeared in blinding radiance to Daniel to encourage him, the terrified young man fainted (Daniel 8:16). But Daniel's fear was soon followed by joy.

Now this is the message that we have heard from him and proclaim to you: God is light, and in him there is no darkness at all (1 John 1:5). Even if today is a cloudy day, thank God for the wonderful gift of light. And let yourself be drawn to the Greater Light.

January 14

Snowflakes and Angels

 What do angels and snowflakes have in common? No two are alike. While children are fascinated by the frozen wonder of snowflakes, winter-weary adults are seldom amazed that each snowflake is unique. Perhaps they should be. Think of it! Millions of snowflakes form, fall, and melt, yet each is one-of-a-kind. Saint Thomas Aquinas recognized that each magnificent angel is also unique. He said that each angel has distinctive characteristics, a unique name and personality. Every angel reflects a specific attribute of God to the highest degree possible for a created being. Because God is limitless, there are more angels than all the snowflakes. [13]

Angels of the Lord, bless the Lord, praise and exalt him above all forever.... Frost and chill, bless the Lord; praise and exalt him above all forever. Ice and snow, bless the Lord; praise and exalt him above all forever. (Daniel 3:58, 69–70)

Needed: An Angel to Guide Us

 We're already two weeks into the New Year. Those well-intentioned "New Year's Resolutions" now seem too hard or impractical. We want to do what we should do, but it's hard to do on our own. Where can we find help? Throughout the Old Testament, God told his Chosen People that he wouldn't abandon them. God sent Moses to lead them out of slavery in Egypt to freedom in the Promised Land. God also sent his angel to guide them through the desert. Their journey out of Egypt and slavery took many years and wasn't easy. It proceeded day-by-day — just like yours and mine.

"See, I am sending an angel before you to guard you on the way and bring you to the place I have prepared" (Exodus 23:20). God's angel guided the Israelites. God also has a plan for you. Ask often for direction in your life during this year.

January 16

Angel Therapist: "Not to Worry!"

 Once, the faith-filled Pope Saint John XXIII struggled with insomnia. He shared his own story with a visiting bishop who wasn't sleeping very well himself. Concern over new pastoral responsibilities was consuming the new bishop. "The very same thing happened to me in the first few weeks of my pontificate," the pope nodded with understanding. "Then, one day, my guardian angel appeared to me in a daydream and whispered, 'Giovanni, don't take yourself so seriously!' Ever since," Pope John smiled, "I've been able to sleep." [14]

Can you see your job and your responsibilities in a different perspective — God's perspective? Can you take yourself less seriously?

INSTRUCTED BY AN ANGEL

As a young man, Saint Anthony gave his large inheritance to the poor and retreated from the world to a life of solitude, penance, and prayer in the desert. But he found that without the distractions of the material world, the challenges of the spiritual life were stronger. One day he begged God, "What shall I do? How can I be saved?" Then Anthony saw a man like himself braiding a rope, rising from his work to pray, returning to his work, and getting up again to pray. Then Anthony understood that the Lord sent an angel to answer his prayer. When he heard the angel say to him, "Do this and you will be saved," Anthony was filled with joy and courage. [15]

Many people were drawn to Anthony in search of spiritual healing and guidance. His biographer, Saint Athanasius, wrote that "strangers knew him from among his disciples by the joy on his face." That joy may well have come from following the instruction of an angel: Work and pray dutifully and you will be saved. [16]

January 18

An Angel Stirred the Water

 In Jerusalem there was a pool called Bethesda where the ill and infirm gathered. They believed that an angel of the Lord would come down into the pool and stir the water so the first person to get into the pool after the stirring of the water was healed. One day Jesus went to this pool and saw a man lying there who had been ill for thirty-eight years, because he had no one to put him into the water. Jesus said to him, "Rise, take up your mat and walk." Immediately the man was able to get up and walk (see John 5:2–9). Early and current biblical translations make no mention of the angel who came to stir the waters. However, for centuries the angel was an integral part of the biblical account, because the presence of the angel explained how the water imparted the healing power of God.

Think of some healing that you are longing for. Then pray: "Lord Jesus, thank you for the gift of your life that I received in the holy water of Baptism. Cleanse, heal and renew _____ with the power of your living water."

THE ANGEL OF THE WATERS

In the middle of Central Park in New York City, a graceful eight-foot bronze angel hovers over Bethesda Fountain. The Angel of the Waters extends her right hand over the water in a gesture of blessing. In her left hand, the angel carries a lily to symbolize the purity of the water. Bethesda Fountain was commissioned to commemorate the 1842 opening of the Croton Aqueduct, which was built to supply New York City with fresh water. The new, pure water was like a miracle following a cholera epidemic that devastated the city. Emma Stebbins, who created the beautiful sculpture, likened the clean, healthy water that cascaded from the fountain to the healing properties of the biblical pool of Bethesda.

Jesus said to the woman at the well, "Whoever drinks the water I shall give will never thirst; the water I shall give will become in him a spring of water welling up to eternal life" (John 4:14). Lord, you know me; you know everything I have ever done. Wash away my sins in the wellspring of your grace. Heal me with your love, and I will live forever.

January 20
Saint Sebastian (died c. 250)

AN ANGEL'S GENTLE TOUCH

 As a high-ranking officer in the Roman army, Sebastian was able to secretly lead others to belief in Christ and encourage fellow Christians in their faith. When Sebastian's faith and evangelization was discovered, his fellow soldiers bound him to a tree and shot him with arrows. He survived this ordeal, only to be beaten to death. This unusual martyrdom became a popular subject for Renaissance artists. Giovanni Baglione painted Saint Sebastian in 1603, showing an angel gently removing an arrow from the martyr's body. This scene depicted a popular belief that Christ sent an angel to untie Sebastian and tend to his wounds. Soon after his death, Christians began to venerate his tomb on the Appian Way outside of Rome. Today this underground burial area is named for him, The Catacombs of Saint Sebastian, and is a popular destination for visitors.

Lord, fill us with that spirit of courage that gave your martyr Sebastian strength to offer his life in faithful witness.

ANGELIC BODYGUARD

 Saint Agnes loved her Savior above all else. Just as she refused the young men who wanted to marry her, Agnes refused to offer incense to the imperial gods. Bribes of wonderful gifts did not tempt her. Threats of torture did not break her resolve. Though she was young — only twelve or thirteen years of age — and from a noble Roman family, the prefect ordered that Agnes be placed in a brothel. Waiting for her there, however, was an angel of the Lord ready to protect her. The light of the angel's presence surrounded her like a shield and blinded all who tried to approach her. Finally, Agnes was sentenced to death and beheaded.

"Rejoice with me, and be glad, for I am espoused to him whom the angels serve. I have taken my place with all the saints in the kingdom of light; sun and moon stand in wonder at his beauty."

— Antiphons from Morning Prayer
for the Feast of Saint Agnes

January 22
Saint Vincent of Saragossa (died 303)

ANGELS SENT TO COMFORT

 Saint Vincent, archdeacon of the church at Saragossa, Spain, was arrested under the persecution of the Roman emperor Diocletian. His unswerving faith under extreme torture inspired Christians throughout Gaul and as far away as Africa, where Saint Augustine preached about his courage. When it became clear that he would never deny his faith, Vincent was thrown into a dungeon. The earliest account of Vincent's martyrdom is a hymn written by the poet Prudentius around 400. The poem recounts how Christ sent his angels to assure Vincent that his trial would soon be over and he would join them in heaven. Later, the guard stationed outside the dungeon testified that he saw brilliant light breaking through cracks in the door and heard the prisoner singing, and beautiful voices praying with him.

How can you find peace amid pain and loss? In prayer, unite your suffering to the suffering of Jesus. He will be with you through it all. He will give you light in the darkness and his holy angels will console and strengthen you.

SAINT PAUL'S GUARDIAN ANGEL

 Saint Paul was being transported to Rome to stand trial before Caesar when a violent storm at sea heavily damaged the ship and threatened the lives of all on board. Paul encouraged the sailors: "I urge you now to keep up your courage; not one of you will be lost, only the ship. For last night an angel of the God to whom (I) belong and whom I serve stood by me and said, 'Do not be afraid, Paul. You are destined to stand before Caesar; and behold, for your sake, God has granted safety to all who are sailing with you.' Therefore, keep up your courage, men; I trust in God that it will turn out as I have been told" (Acts 27:22–25).

Many times in the Gospels we hear the words, "Do not be afraid," spoken both by Jesus and by his angels. Paul placed his trust in the message of an angel. And so it came to pass: only the ship was lost. Grant me, Lord, not to succumb to fear when my life is buffeted by storms. Help me to place my trust in your word.

January 24
Saint Francis de Sales (1567–1622)

THE GUARDIAN ANGEL OF A PRIEST

Saint Francis de Sales was only thirty-five when he became the bishop of Geneva and began ordaining young men to serve the Church during a challenging era. Francis reminded them and everyone else that their guardian angels were always nearby. After ordination, one young priest told his bishop that he'd seen his guardian angel. He sensed his angel wanted him to know that he should serve the Church and its people boldly, without hesitation. "Before my ordination," he told Bishop de Sales, "my guardian angel was always on the left, and he always preceded me." After he became a priest, the young man said, his angel was always on his right, following him and showing respect for his priesthood. [17]

Saint Francis de Sales knew that angels are sent from God to guide us. He advised: "Make yourself familiar with the angels, and behold them frequently in spirit; for without being seen, they are present to you." [18]

January 25

ANGELS IN CHARGE

 Gathering rain clouds. An ancient Redwood tree. A chicken scratching for food. Saint Augustine wrote that these and every other "visible thing in this world is put in the charge of an angel." Augustine's belief was rooted in his study of Scripture, Judaic teachings, and in the order God created in the universe. Angels are created beings, but they are also extensions of God's care and authority. They were given authority to watch over planets, nations, seasons, animals, everything that grows — and us. Although science can reveal the mechanics of natural processes, we should also recognize that God's hand has set them all in motion. [19]

"Behind every blade of grass is an angel whispering: 'Grow, grow, grow.'"

— The Talmud [20]

January 26

Biblical Names for Angels

 The Bible is full of angels. From the first book — Genesis — to the last — Revelation — we read of their creation and role as messengers of God and guardians of his people. Both the Old and New Testaments have many different names for these shining and amazing celestial creatures. In the Book of Job, they are called "sons of God" (Job 1:6), and in the Book of Daniel, they are described as "watchers" (Daniel 4:14). In the Psalms, angels are called the "holy ones" (Psalm 89:5), "hosts of the heavens" (Psalm 33:6), and "mighty ones who do his bidding" (Psalm 103:20). The Letter to the Hebrews in the New Testament calls angels "ministering spirits" (Hebrews 1:14).

Bless the LORD, all you his angels,
mighty in strength, acting at his behest,...
Bless the LORD, all you his hosts,
his ministers who carry out his will.
(Psalm 103:20–21)

A VISION OF ANGELS

Until age ten, Saint Angela Merici had a happy childhood. But within a few years, her little world in Brescia, Italy, collapsed. First, her father died. Then, her only sister and her mother died. Angela grieved because her sister hadn't received the sacraments right before her death. Aptly named for the angels, Angela was beautiful and compassionate. She served the needy and taught uneducated, poor girls. In 1506, she had a life-changing vision. She saw angels and young women descending from heaven. Her own sister was among them. Shortly after, she founded the Company of Saint Ursula, which became the Ursuline Sisters. Today, their excellent high schools and colleges are found around the world. [21]

"The more you love them, the more you will care for and watch over them. And it will be impossible for you not to cherish them day and night ... for this is how real love acts and works."

— Saint Angela Merici [22]

January 28

Saint Thomas Aquinas (1225–1274)

INSTANT MESSAGING, ANGEL STYLE

 The word "angel" means "messenger," and believers know that angels are God's special messengers. Saint Thomas Aquinas wrote and taught extensively about angels. He explained that speech between angels is never a matter of sounds or words. In his *Summa Theologica,* he said angel-to-angel communication means the direct communication of knowledge. Angels can also "speak" to God by consulting his divine will. Time or distance does not affect "angel talk." An angel can communicate with just one other angel, with many, or with all. It is simply a matter of the will. It's "instant messaging" — angel style. [23]

"We are like children who stand in need of masters to enlighten us and direct us; and God has provided for this by appointing his angels to be our teachers and guides."

— Saint Thomas Aquinas [24]

January 29

ASK THE ANGELS

 Author Mike Aquilina proposes a very practical and easy way to tap into the awesome power of the angels who are present to us at all times and in every circumstance. He advises: "Think of all the people who most need your Christian witness: a son or daughter? a son-in-law? a daughter-in-law? an estranged friend? a former colleague? What's the best way to begin to reach them? Well, each of them has a guardian angel who's eager to help." He advocates this approach in your daily interaction with your spouse, or children, your coworkers, neighbors — your adversaries. First ask your own guardian angel to help you do or say the right thing. If you need more help, remember that your spouse's or child's guardian angel is there to help. The main thing is to be aware of the angels around you and to get in the habit of calling on them often. [25]

The angels are in God's presence. That means that they are present everywhere. In the area of human existence an angel is universally pervasive and penetrative. [26]

January 30

TV's Award-Winning Angels

 From 1994–2003, millions of people watched *Touched by an Angel*, an award-winning CBS television series about angels interacting with ordinary people. Angel trainee Monica (Roma Downey) and supervisor Tess (Della Reese) brought hope and the assurance of God's love to those who needed it. Traveling in their 1972 red Cadillac Eldorado convertible, they encouraged fractured families and communities to reunite. Wounded, marginalized people found healing. Although the series never claimed to teach complicated theological truths, the basic message was fundamentally biblical. *Touched by an Angel* touched — and inspired — many viewers.

"There are angels near you to guide you and protect you, if you would but invoke them. It is not later than we think; it is a bigger world than we think."

— Archbishop Fulton J. Sheen, an American television "star" during the 1950s and 1960s [27]

WHEN WE'RE TEMPTED

"When tempted, invoke your Angel. He is more eager to help you than you are to be helped!" That's what Saint John Bosco, the Italian founder of the Salesians, told homeless youth in Turin. He cared for hundreds of boys and was like a father to them. The boys called him "Don Bosco," the traditional and familiar title for Italian priests. Bosco worked day and night supporting and educating them. He too had grown up in poverty. He knew how tempting it was to take things when you grew up with very little. "Ignore the devil and do not be afraid of him," he reassured his boys. "He trembles and flees at the sight of your Guardian Angel." [28]

Saint John Bosco, your advice to homeless boys is just as good for me. When I am tempted, let me remember to call upon the angels for help.

February 1

Saint Brigid of Ireland (c. 451–525)

AN ANGEL OF GENEROSITY

 Brigid of Ireland often showed over-the-top generosity. When she emptied her pantry to feed the poor, it was miraculously restocked. When she gave her father's battle sword to a beggar, she said no gift was too precious to give to Christ. Brigid's vision of happiness was generous, as well. Her prayer is for all of us.

> I would like the angels of heaven to be among us.
> I would like the abundance of peace.
> I would like full vessels of charity.
> I would like rich treasures of mercy.
> I would like cheerfulness to preside over all.
> I would like the friends of heaven to be gathered
> around us from all parts.[29]

What is my vision of happiness? What do I want in abundance? Why is it sometimes so hard to let go of the things I do have? Is it because I am afraid I won't have enough for myself? I want to understand that in you, God, I have all I need and plenty to share.

ANGELS REFLECT GOD'S LIGHT

In obedience to the Law of Moses, Mary and Joseph took the forty-day-old Jesus to the Temple to consecrate him to the Lord and to fulfill the purification sacrifice. Simeon, an old man waiting to see the promised Messiah, called Jesus "a light for revelation to the Gentiles" (Luke 2:32). Because this day falls about midway between winter and spring, it is associated with the increase of natural light in our world. It has also been called Candlemas. With the blessing of candles, we welcome Christ, the Light of the World. We also welcome his angels who are a dim — yet true — reflection of the pure light of Christ. Today, light a candle as you say this prayer:

May this candle remind me, Lord Jesus,
that You are my Light in darkness,
my Protector in danger,
and my Savior at all times.
I praise You and give You glory,
With all of the angels in heaven
for You are Lord, forever and ever. Amen.

February 3

Go, Angel, Tell the News

 More than a century ago, ninety-year-old Penny Jessye sang as she prepared to go to her "Good Lord in that Heaven." She called on her Guardian Angel to fulfill an angel's primary mission — to be a messenger. Her granddaughter, Eva A. Jessye, transcribed Penny Jessye's deathbed spiritual, her last prayer.

Good Lord
In that Heaven,
Good Lord
In that Heaven,
Good Lord,
In that Heaven,
I know I gotta home at last!

Go, Angel, and tell the news,
Go, Sister, and tell the news,
Go, Elder, and tell the news,
I know I gotta home at last. [30]

Go, Angel, go and tell the news that I am on my way. Someday, someday, I will be going home. Stay, Angel, stay and help me find my way.

February 4

ANGELS — NEITHER MALE NOR FEMALE

 A young woman receiving the Sacrament of Confirmation wanted to honor Michael the Archangel by taking Michael as her Confirmation name. When she told the bishop her chosen name, he said that "Michael" is not a girl's name. "Neither is it a boy's," she replied softly, with a smile for the bishop. She received the name. And she had a point. The angels, even the ones who have masculine names such as Michael, Raphael, and Gabriel, are not male. Angels — spiritual, not physical, beings — have no gender. [31]

"At the resurrection they neither marry nor are given in marriage but are like the angels in heaven" (Matthew 22:30).

Our lives after the final resurrection will be essentially different from our life here on earth. The relationships of this world will be transformed, transcended; the risen body will be "a new creation" (2 Corinthians 5:17).

February 5

Saint Agatha (c. 231–251)

ANGELS TO HEAL ME

 Saint Agatha is one of the seven women martyrs of the early Church named in Eucharistic Prayer I. Agatha grew up in a Christian family in Sicily. During the persecutions of Christians under the Roman Emperor Decius, the governor of Sicily tried to force Agatha to renounce Christ. Agatha defended her faith: "If you threaten me with wild beasts, know that at the Name of Christ they grow tame; if you use fire, from heaven angels will drop healing dew on me." Agatha endured cruel tortures and a month in prison before she died. [32]

Lord, our Creator, heal the hearts of all women who suffer from sexual assault, verbal threats, and physical abuse. We beg you to send your angels to protect them. Saint Agatha, help us to exorcise this evil in our society.

RELEASED BY AN ANGEL

 Peter was in prison in Jerusalem, under heavy guard, awaiting execution at the order of King Herod. During the night before his trial, the angel of the Lord stood by him and a light shone in the cell. The angel woke Peter and told him to get up quickly and put on his belt and sandals. At that, the chains fell from Peter's wrists. As Peter followed the angel out of the prison, the guards took no notice of them, and the iron gate of the prison courtyard opened of its own accord. They hurried through the gate and into an alley where the angel suddenly left him. Only then did Peter understand that his escape was not just a dream (Acts 12:1–11).

In you, LORD, I take refuge;
let me never be put to shame.
In your righteousness deliver me;
incline your ear to me;
make haste to rescue me!
Be my rock of refuge,
a stronghold to save me.
(Psalm 31:2–3)

It Is His Angel

 After his release from prison, Peter went to the house of Mary, the mother of John Mark, where many had gathered in prayer. Peter knocked on the gate, and a maid named Rhoda came out and asked who was there. When she recognized Peter's voice, she was so overjoyed that she ran back into the house, leaving Peter standing at the gate. She announced to those assembled that Peter was outside. They told her she was crazy! Over their objections, Rhoda insisted that Peter was really there. "It must be his angel," they said, to explain who was knocking and speaking. When they finally opened the gate, they were astounded to find Peter there (Acts 12:12–16).

It was a popular Jewish belief that guardian angels were our doubles and represented us personally. Jesus cited this as a sign of our great worth to God, "See that you do not despise one of these little ones, for I say to you that their angels in heaven always look upon the face of my heavenly Father" (Matthew 18:10). Today, keep in mind that you are in the presence of God.

An Avenging Angel

 The death of King Herod follows the account of Peter's escape from prison in the Acts of the Apostles (Acts 12:21–24). This story gives us an entirely different image of an angel. King Herod addressed the people of Tyre and Sidon, wearing royal robes to display his authority over them. Some admirers in the crowd called out, "This is the voice of a god, not of a man." Herod accepted their praise. Because he did not give the honor to God alone, the angel of the Lord struck him down. This is the avenging angel more often encountered in the Old Testament.

To you we owe our hymn of praise,
*   O God on Zion;*
To you our vows must be fulfilled,
*   you who hear our prayers.*
(Psalm 65:2–3)

February 9

Angels of Gates and Doors

 Writers and artists often portray angels as guardians of doors and gates. "Angels are the ones who carry us from one realm to another," wrote F. Forrester Church. Moving from one world to another entails crossing a threshold, recognizing that there are different realities on either side. Jacob's vision of a stairway with angels ascending and descending symbolizes this kind of transition (Genesis 28:12). The distance between heaven and earth, between God and man, is connected by angels moving effortlessly between the two realms. The doorway to heaven is open for us. [33]

Father Agostino returned from Naples at about three o'clock in the morning. Arriving at Padre Pio's house, he was surprised to find the door open. When Father Agostino asked Padre Pio why he didn't lock his door, the saint replied, "I have the guardian angels of the house keeping watch through the night. There is no reason to fear." [34]

February 10
Saint Scholastica (480–542)

Thunderstorms and Angels

 Like many twins, Saints Scholastica and Benedict were close. They were also united in their faith. Scholastica established a convent near Monte Cassino, Italy, where Benedict founded the first monastic community of men. Scholastica and Benedict visited just one day a year. In 542, Scholastica sensed death was near. When Benedict prepared to leave, Scholastica begged him to delay. And she prayed. Did Scholastica's angel rush her request to God? Possibly. A violent thunderstorm began, delaying his departure. The next day, Scholastica died. Benedict saw a white dove rising into the sky, and he knew that angels were escorting his sister to heaven. [35]

Has God sent you any storms special-ordered by an angel? Could they have been sent your way for a larger, greater purpose?

February 11

Our Lady of Lourdes

ENVYING THE ANGELS

 Long before she died at thirty-five in 1879, Bernadette Soubirous envied the joy of the angels in God's presence. As a poor, illiterate fourteen-year-old, Bernadette peeked into heaven's mysteries. On February 11, 1858, the beautiful Virgin Mother of God began to appear to her in a rock grotto near Lourdes, France. Our Lady asked Bernadette to pray for sinners and to have a church built. Bernadette was happy to obey the Virgin, but it attracted attention that she didn't want. People begged "the saint" to bless their rosaries. Bernadette entered a convent for peace and to give her life to God. When she developed painful tuberculosis of the bone, she praised God, longing for heaven and the Virgin's smile. Bernadette had learned what the angels know: we're never truly happy until we live with God. [36]

"I shall do everything for Heaven, my true home. There I shall find my Mother in all the splendor of her glory. I shall delight with her in the joy of Jesus himself in perfect safety."

— Saint Bernadette Soubirous [37]

February 12

Angel Facts and Fiction

 Fact: "Angels" are mentioned 273 times in some editions of the Bible. Only three angels are named in Catholic Bibles. They are Michael, Gabriel, and Raphael and are also called archangels. Michael's name means "Who is like God." His name appears most often. "Gabriel" means "God is my strength." Gabriel, the herald of Good News in the New Testament, announces the coming of a Savior. Raphael's name means "God has healed." Raphael appears only in the Book of Tobit. What's an example of angel fiction? Believing that angels know the future of those they guard or the future of the world. Only God is all-knowing. [38]

And suddenly there was a multitude of the heavenly host with the angels praising God and saying: "Glory to God in the highest and on earth peace to those on whom his favor rests." (Luke 2:13–14)

February 13

ANGELS IN THE SNOW

 On a snowy winter night in Chicago in the late 1870s, two boys went to the rectory of Holy Family Church to ask a priest to visit their dying grandmother. Father Arnold Damien, S.J., immediately accompanied the boys to a chilly apartment building where they thanked him and left. After anointing and giving the dying woman the Eucharist, Father Damien praised her faithful grandsons. "Father," she whispered weakly, "I had two grandsons, but they died many years ago. They were altar boys at Holy Family Church." Suspecting that his young visitors were angels, the pastor commissioned statues of altar boys to stand as sentinels in the church sanctuary. [39]

Are they not all ministering spirits sent to serve, for the sake of those who are to inherit salvation? (Hebrews 1:14)

February 14

Saint Valentine (died 269)

Champion for Love

 Although three different Saint Valentines were once celebrated together on this date, it's the third-century bishop of Terni, Italy, who became our patron saint of love. According to tradition, Valentine illegally officiated at the marriage of Christian couples. Emperor Claudius had banned marriage, believing that unmarried men made better soldiers for his army. Valentine also became known for healing. When he healed the sick child of a wealthy family in Rome, the news spread like wild fire. Because Roman authorities couldn't tolerate Christian heroes, the elderly Valentine was arrested, jailed, and sentenced to death. He wrote a last loving note to Terni, signing it "your Valentine." [40]

O God, let my words, work, and prayers serve as valentines, carrying a message of love to others. Let the angels, your holy messengers, help carry and deliver my valentines.

February 15

An Entrance for Angels

 We all do it: "Why?" we ask. "Why is this happening?" "Why did this happen to me?" Maybe we should look at it in a very different way. English writer Mary Cholmondeley (1859–1925) suggested that our sorrows allow us to live more fully. "If you had not undergone an agonized awakening, all the great realities of life — love, hatred, temptation, enthusiasm — would have remained for you merely words to string on light conversation. But the sword that pierced your heart forced an entrance for angels, who had been knocking where there was no door — until then." [41]

Can I allow heartbreak to become an entrance for angels? Help me, Lord, to admit your angels to sustain me throughout the great realities of my life and to show me the deeper reality of your providential love for me.

LET US HONOR THE ANGELS

Saint Bernard of Clairvaux (1090–1153) elevated devotion to the angels to new heights in the Church. Preaching on Psalm 91:11, "For God commands the angels to guard you in all your ways," Bernard said, "The angels are not only with you, but for you. They are with you to protect you, they are with you to help you. Nevertheless, although it is He who gives His angels charge over us, yet it is they who with such love obey his bidding, and assist us in all our needs, which are so great. Let us therefore cultivate a pious and grateful spirit towards our noble guardians; let us love and honor them as much as we can and as is fitting." [42]

"Yes, holy angel, God has given you charge of me. Take my hand and bring me to the path that leads to salvation. Protect me during the night and keep me safe. Intercede for me with the Lord; ask him to make me love him more and more, and to enable me to give him the service his goodness deserves. Amen."

— Saint Macarius of Egypt [43]

February 17

My Angel without Wings

 Ordinary people sometimes act as angels, bringing healing messages from God. Mary William shared her story, "I have a lot of friends and a lot of good friends, too. But when my marriage was in trouble, when I was so depressed, not one of my close and good friends noticed it. I thought God had abandoned me, too, and I was becoming angry with God, when I felt comforting hands upon my shoulders. They belonged to a man named Norman, 'my angel without wings.' It seemed like God was saying, 'I am extending my hands to touch you, why are you shying away?' Norman talked to me first and then invited my husband and me for tea, and we talked all afternoon. I found out more about my husband than I did in our 15 years of marriage. It was this angel's gentle touch that opened my heart for healing." [44]

"How consoling it is to know that near us is a spirit who, from the cradle to the tomb, does not leave us even for an instant.... And this heavenly spirit guides and protects us like a friend, a brother," wrote Padre Pio to a spiritual daughter. [45]

February 18

Blessed Fra Angelico (1395–1455)

Painted by an Angel

 His parents named him Guido, and he received the name Giovanni when he joined the Dominican order. But the brothers who knew him best called him Fra Angelico, as the whole world does today. He was Angelico because of his kindness to others, his simplicity and holiness, and because the frescos he painted on the monastery walls looked as if angels painted them. C. S. Lewis said that the angels that appeared in Fra Angelico's brush strokes "carry in their face and gesture the peace and authority of heaven." [46]

Fra Angelico's art was his prayer and his life. He said that "anyone who creates works involving Christ ought always to reside with Christ." Is my work a prayer? [47]

February 19

Angels Awaken Us

 Angels are always there for us, in every need and in every opportunity. As gifts of God they bless us at every moment. "Angels awaken us to the wonder and mystery of being God's creatures. They laugh at us when we take ourselves too seriously, and gently try to help us to see the joke. They surprise us with the beauty of their strangeness, their amazing commitment to our lives and welfare. They knock on our doors to deliver messages of death and birth — of every kind. They are salt when we lose our savor, joy and pain when we've forgotten how to feel." [48]

"A characteristic of the great saints is their power of levity. Angels can fly because they take themselves lightly."

— G. K. Chesterton

What is weighing on you today? What is hampering your angel's desire to lift you up into the tremendous love of God? May the angels awaken you.

Blesseds Francisco and Jacinta Marto (1908–1919; 1910–1920)

THE ANGEL OF PEACE

 In the spring of 1916, an angel appeared to three children, Francisco and Jacinta Marto, and their cousin Lucia Santos. They were tending their family's sheep near Fatima, Portugal. Lucia described the encounter: "A strong wind began to shake the trees.... And then we saw, in the distance, above the trees, a light whiter than snow in the form of a young man, quite transparent, and as brilliant as crystal in the rays of the sun. As he came near we were able to see his features. We were astonished and absorbed and we said nothing to one another. And then he said: 'Do not be afraid. I am the angel of peace. Pray with me.'" The children didn't know it yet, but the angel was preparing them for the appearance of the Virgin Mary on May 13, 1917.

> *The angel knelt and placed his forehead on the ground. The children did the same, and repeated the words they heard him say: "My God, I believe, I adore, I hope, and I love You. I ask pardon for those who do not believe, do not adore, do not hope, and do not love You."* [49]

February 21

Saint Peter Damian (1007–1072)

SOMEONE WATCHING OVER US

 There must have been many angels guarding Peter Damian — especially in his early years. Born into a large Catholic family in Ravenna, Italy, Peter was orphaned while still very young. An older brother took Peter in but fed him scraps and treated him like a slave. Another brother, Damian, a priest, intervened, rescued and raised Peter. Damian really cared for Peter. Peter was so grateful. When he grew up, he changed his last name to Damian. Peter Damian became a happy priest, a brilliant teacher, a Benedictine monk, and finally, the cardinal-archbishop of Ostia.

God sends many people to act as our earth-bound "guardian angels." Call to mind the people who have lovingly protected and guided you. Pray for them. Thank God for them. Look for ways that you can "be an angel" for others.

ANGEL "DENIERS"

Not everyone who believes in God believes in angels. Even some modern theologians are angel "deniers." Blessed John Henry Newman (1801–1890), the leading Roman Catholic theologian of his day in England, regretted that many scholars saw belief in angels as superstitious or medieval nonsense. There was danger, Newman said, in "resting in things seen and forgetting unseen things," such as angels. A century later, French Catholic philosopher Jacques Maritain (1882–1973) echoed Newman. More and more theologians were questioning belief in angels and devils. According to Maritain, these theologians were unknowingly becoming "public relations men of the Old Liar" (Satan). [50]

"The world of spirits then, though unseen, is present, not future, not distant. It is not above the sky, it is not beyond the grave; it is now and here, the kingdom of God is among us."

— Blessed John Henry Newman [51]

February 23

Saint Polycarp (69–155)

SURROUNDED BY ANGELS

 At the beginning and end of his life, angels surrounded Saint Polycarp. Tradition says an angel told Kallista, a Christian woman, to adopt Polycarp when his parents died. A student of Saint John the Evangelist, Polycarp had great pastoral gifts. When he became bishop of Smyrna (in present-day Turkey), the Church grew quickly. Rome hated "the father of all the Christians." As Roman persecution of Christians increased, Polycarp's flock hid him. Finally, Polycarp was arrested and sentenced to be burned alive. At first, angels surrounded him, shielding him from the flames. Then, the angels apparently heard the Lord calling Polycarp home. The eighty-six-year-old bishop was stabbed repeatedly as he died a martyr. [52]

Before his death, Polycarp prayed, "Lord God Almighty, Father of your beloved and blessed Son Jesus Christ, through whom we have received the knowledge of you.... I give you thanks for judging me worthy of this day, this hour." [53]

February 24

Making a Case for Angels

 Though it's impossible to prove the existence of angels, philosophers say a good case can be made for them. In our universe, there are undeniable hierarchies. In the animal kingdom, human beings are clearly superior to all living animals. Below us are less intelligent species like dolphins or apes, then plants of various kinds. With bodies and rational minds and souls, human beings are obviously higher in the order of living creation. Angels are created beings with greatly superior intellects, but don't have bodies. If angels didn't exist, there would be a step missing between God and us. It makes perfect sense that pure spirits bridge the gap between our Creator and us. [54]

Lord, from your glorious angels to the simplest amoeba, the order and beauty of everything you have created is overwhelming! Help me to see and honor it — and you — every day.

February 25

Undercover Angel

 In the Book of Tobit, one of the most delightful books of the Old Testament, a main character is an angel — operating undercover. Raphael, whose name means "God heals," is sent by God to help Tobit, a faithful Jew who is blind. Posing as a young man, Raphael also frees a young woman, Sarah, from a demon's influence. With Tobit's son, Tobiah, Raphael journeys to retrieve family money. At journey's end, Tobit's blindness is cured. Tobiah and Sarah are happily married. The Book of Tobit is the only place in Scripture where the Archangel Raphael is mentioned by name.

"Now when you, Tobit, and Sarah prayed, it was I who presented the record of your prayer before the Glory of the Lord…. I am Raphael, one of the seven angels who stand and serve before the Glory of the Lord." (Tobit 12:12, 15)

February 26

Gabriel Awards

 Each year, the Catholic Academy of Communications Professionals gives the Gabriel Award for excellence in film, television, radio, and social media. Award winners have produced media that entertains but also affirms human dignity and virtue. The award is a silver angel that holds high a globe encircled by electrons. Of course, the award is named for the Archangel Gabriel who carried the most joyful news ever heard on earth. Gabriel came to Nazareth to tell Mary that Jesus, the Son of God, would be born to her. [55]

Share God-centered, happy news in your world today. The world really needs good news, and you will be collaborating with the Archangel Gabriel.

February 27

Who Are the Fallen Angels?

 Where did fallen angels — or demons — come from? Fallen angels do exist, the Church teaches, and have great power in the world. Both Scripture and the Tradition of the Church affirm the existence of Satan or the devil (see *Catechism of the Catholic Church* 391). Saint Augustine maintained that fallen angels, created with free will, rejected God out of pride because they were brilliant and glorious creatures themselves. Old Testament prophets referred to Satan, leader of the fallen angels, as the adversary of God. In the New Testament, the coming of Jesus is explained as God's answer to Satan's destructive work on earth. "Indeed, the Son of God was revealed to destroy the works of the devil" (1 John 3:8).

Although many people no longer believe that fallen angels or demons exist, that's not what Scripture says. Saint Peter warned, "Your opponent the devil is prowling around like a roaring lion looking for [someone] to devour." (1 Peter 5:8)

Angels and Islam

 Along with Christianity and Judaism, Islam teaches that God (Allah) created angels. According to Islam, however, the angels did not have free will. They were created to obey and worship Allah. They were also bound to carry out Allah's commands. Although the Koran refers to angels having wings, Muslims believe it is blasphemous to depict angels in any way. Islam also says that an angel named Jibreel (Gabriel) appeared to Mohammed as well as to Mary, the Mother of Jesus. Because angels lack free will, Islam says that there are no fallen angels or demons. [56]

"When a man dies, those who survive him ask what property he has left behind. The angel who bends over the dying man asks what good deeds he has sent before him."

— The Koran [57]

March 1

The Angel's Violin

One night, Saint Francis of Assisi prayed that God would grant him a small taste of the joys of eternal life. Then an angel appeared holding a violin and bow. While Francis was still amazed at the sight, the angel placed the violin to his chin and drew the bow across the strings a single time. Francis heard a melody so sweet that it filled his soul with immeasurable joy, as if he no longer had a body, and could know no sorrow. Francis told the Brothers afterward that if the angel had drawn the bow back across the strings of the violin a second time, his soul would have left his body from uncontainable happiness. [58]

Lord, fill me with a desire for the joys of eternal life. Let me find just a small taste of that joy in a peaceful moment, in a sweet musical note, in a new opportunity, in an ordinary day — in the gift and receipt of your grace.

March 2

Angels of Mercy

President Abraham Lincoln proclaimed that the Catholic Sisters who nursed the wounded soldiers during the Civil War (1861–1865) were Angels of Mercy. "Of all the forms of charity and benevolence seen in the crowded wards of the hospitals, those of some Catholic Sisters were among the most efficient.... As they went from cot to cot, distributing the medicines prescribed, or administering the cooling, strengthening draughts as directed, they were veritable angels of mercy. Their words were suited to every sufferer. One they encouraged, another they calmed and soothed … by their presence and their words!… How often has a soldier been refreshed, encouraged and assisted along the road to convalescence by the home memories with which these unpaid nurses filled his heart." [59]

Blessed are the merciful,
for they will be shown mercy.
Blessed are the clean of heart,
for they will see God.
Blessed are the peacemakers,
for they will be called children of God.
(Matthew 5:7–9)

March 3

Saint Katharine Drexel (1858–1955)

SAINTS AND ANGELS WORK TOGETHER

 Jan Judge believes that angels and saints are working together on our behalf. "Six years ago," she wrote, "I developed a rare chronic disease. Not long after, I visited the National Shrine of Saint Katharine Drexel near Philadelphia. I prayed at Saint Katharine's casket and then I went to fill out some prayer request forms. As I was writing, a distinguished black woman approached me and said she was sent there that day to find me. I immediately felt very nervous. We talked and she told me that I would never be rid of my illness unless I lost my anger. Together we prayed Psalm 102 (Prayer in Time of Distress) and Psalm 103 (Praise of Divine Goodness). We hugged and then she was gone. I was not cured, but I am at peace. I truly believe that she was an angel sent to me from Saint Katharine." [60]

Bless the LORD, all you angels,
mighty in strength, acting at his behest,
obedient to his command.
Bless the LORD, all you hosts,
his ministers who carry out his will.
Bless the LORD, all his creatures,
everywhere in his domain.
Bless the LORD, my soul!
(Psalm 103:20–22)

Like an Angel

On June 18, 2015, gang members in Guatemala City threw twelve-year-old Ángel Ariel Escalante Pérez off a bridge because he refused their order to murder a bus driver. Although the branches of the trees and the underbrush in the area cushioned Ángel's fall, rescuers found him with two fractured legs. After fifteen days in intensive care, Ángel died at Saint John of God General Hospital. Ángel was in the sixth grade and liked drawing, music, and soccer. Angel's courageous decision to stand up to gang pressure left his grieving family and friends convinced that his guardian angel took Ángel directly to heaven. [61]

You see or hear about bullying and gangs every day, but what can you do about it? You can be sure that your guardian angel would tell you to stand up to evil and injustice. There really is no other right choice, is there?

March 5

Angels Ministered to Jesus

 In the sixth century, on the First Sunday of Lent, Pope Gregory the Great gave a sermon on the temptation of Jesus in the desert. Gregory said that we can recognize ourselves in this Gospel because Jesus was tempted as a man. After the devil left Jesus, angels ministered to him. In this we see the two natures of the One Person. "For it is a man the devil tempts; and the same Person is God to whom angels minister. We recognize then our own nature in Him; for unless the devil saw Him as man he would not have tempted Him. We venerate in Him His own divinity; for unless He was God of all, angels would not have come and ministered to Him." [62]

Temptation is a rallying place for angels. We can count on their help twenty-four hours a day. Morning, noon, and night. Weekends and holidays. Lead us not into temptation, and deliver us from evil. Amen.

Do Angels Really Sing?

Do angels really sing? It seems they do in monasteries! One night, in the Benedictine monastery of Saint-Riquier in northern France, the abbot and a number of monks heard angels chanting harmoniously in their midst. They also reported that the entire sanctuary was filled with a sweet fragrance along with the celestial voices. Saint John Gualbert, founder of the Vallombrosan order of monks, was surrounded by angels who continuously sang songs of praise to God for three days before his death. And, for six months before he died, Saint Nicolas of Tolentino was blessed every night with the joyous sound of angels singing. This strengthened his desire for heaven and his anticipation of seeing God as the angels do. [63]

In the liturgy of the Church it is always the whole cosmos which takes part in the worship of God. The angelic hymn is never absent from our earth-bound worship. Human existence is transcended in it and joins with the praise offered by the angels. We must also remember that one of the essential characteristics of a monk — in the original sense of the word — was his imitation of the existence of angels, and his practice of an "Angelic liturgy." [64]

March 7

Saint Perpetua and Saint Felicitas (died 202)

BORNE BY FOUR ANGELS

 Perpetua and Felicitas were young Christian mothers who gave their lives for their faith in Carthage, North Africa. During their imprisonment Perpetua kept a diary that provides an authentic record of their suffering and martyrdom. She wrote that one of their companions, Saturus, related a vision he had. "We were gone forth from the flesh," he said, "and were borne by four angels into the east; and their hands touched us not. We floated upwards, as if ascending a gentle slope, until we saw boundless light; and I said, 'Perpetua, this is what the Lord promised to us.' Then even brighter angels appeared who cried out with admiration, 'Here they are! Here they are!' And the angels said to us, 'Come, enter and greet your Lord.'" [65]

When Perpetua was awaiting the gladiator's sword, she said to her brother, "Stand fast in the faith and love one another; and do not be discouraged by our sufferings." She would say the same to us today. Our faith and love and, yes, our sufferings will someday be met with the words, "Come, enter, and greet your Lord."

RAPHAEL TO THE RESCUE

 John was already past middle age when he dedicated his life to helping the destitute and defenseless people living on the streets of Granada, Spain. He was especially devoted to those suffering from mental illness. What John had lost in years he made up with immense passion. He set up a house where he tended the sick, and at night he went out to beg for money and medical supplies. It is said that the Archangel Raphael (the name means "God Heals") visited him with advice and encouragement in this ministry. In time, he received human help as well. Twenty years after John's death, his followers formed the Brothers Hospitallers of Saint John of God. It is now a worldwide religious order. To this day, many of their facilities are called "Raphael Centers" in honor of the angel who aided their founder.

The Archangel's message to John of God — and us — is this: "I am Raphael, sent by God to assist you in your works of charity. The Lord has given me custody of your person and along with you all who will serve the Lord." [66]

March 9

Saint Frances of Rome (1384–1440)

The Angel Beckons Me

 After the death of her young son, an archangel who became her guardian and spiritual guide accompanied Frances for twenty-four years. The angel was, she said, about the size of an eight-year-old child. The brilliant light that emanated from the angel guided Frances at all times, keeping her safe from hazards. It was so bright that Frances reported that she could never look directly at the angel's face. Four years before her death, Frances received an even more beautiful and majestic angel companion. This one exerted great power over the evil around her and helped her to advance in virtue and holiness. Her last words were, "The angel has finished his task — he beckons me to follow him."

"An angel can illume the thought and mind of man by strengthening the power of vision, and by bringing within his reach some truth that the angel himself contemplates."

— Saint Thomas Aquinas

Angels of Martyrs

 In 316, forty new Christians gave their lives for Christ. The martyrs were Roman soldiers in Sebaste, Armenia. Their conversion to Christianity had embarrassed Rome, and they were condemned to death. On a bitterly cold night, they were stripped naked and forced onto a frozen lake. Onshore, a tub of warm water was set up to entice them to change their minds. One soldier did weaken and hurried to the heated tub. A guard witnessing the agonies of the remaining soldiers then saw angels descending from the sky to bring them comfort and "crowns of martyrdom." Instantly converted, he stripped off his own clothing and joined the thirty-nine. [67]

Giving up one's life for any reason takes courage. Angels must rush to strengthen those who give up their lives for the love of God or for the sake of others.

March 11

Converted through an Angel

 The Acts of the Apostles portray Cornelius the Centurion as God-fearing and generous (Acts 10:1–33). Nonetheless, he was also a Roman soldier charged with keeping the peace in a conquered land — a difficult assignment. A courageous veteran of many battles, Cornelius was nevertheless terrified when an angel appeared one day. The heavenly visitor told Cornelius to send for Peter, who was in Joppa. Meanwhile, Peter also received a message from heaven. He was told to teach the Gentile Cornelius about Jesus. Cornelius and his family heard Peter's testimony, received the Holy Spirit, and were baptized. According to tradition, Cornelius the Centurion later became a bishop of Caesarea.

When an angel visits, life is going to change. Romanian-born Jewish writer Elie Wiesel said, "Whenever an angel says 'Be not afraid!' you'd better start worrying. A big assignment is on the way." [68]

Angels of Judgment

Angels do more than guide and protect human beings. Scripture reminds us that these heavenly creatures can be instruments of God's judgment. In Genesis 19, two angels visited Lot, Abraham's nephew. Lot was living in Sodom, a city that was already very displeasing to God. Upon seeing the young visitors, men from Sodom told Lot to hand them over. But Lot protected his guests, risking his own life. The Lord became angrier than ever with Sodom and Gomorrah and determined to destroy the cities. The angels warned Lot to take his family and escape from the coming devastation. After they left, sulfurous fire rained down upon the cities, killing the inhabitants and leaving the cities in ashes.

Angels will accompany Christ when he comes for the Last Judgment. "And he will send out his angels with a trumpet blast, and they will gather his elect from the four winds, from one end of the heavens to the other" (Matthew 24:31).

March 13

SAINT MICHAEL ON THE CATHEDRAL WALL

 Religious art can draw us closer to God. It may do the same for the artists who create it. In 1957, renowned Jewish sculptor Jacob Epstein was at the end of his career. The American-born British sculptor was asked to depict Saint Michael the Archangel for Coventry Cathedral, which was almost destroyed by German bombing in World War II. By the time his breath-taking, nineteen-foot-high bronze sculpture of Saint Michael and the Devil was completed in 1960, the artist had died. Each year, transfixed visitors stop to view the cathedral's imposing exterior piece. A triumphant Michael stands, massive wings gloriously outstretched, holding a spear, with Satan eternally bound and defeated at his feet. [69]

The great Michelangelo knew that creating art was holy work. "I saw the angel in the marble and carved until I set him free," he said.

March 14

SAVED FROM A TIGER'S TEETH

In Billy Graham's popular book *Angels: God's Secret Agents*, he shared an angel story from his wife Ruth who was born in China to Christian missionaries. Ruth told about a peasant woman who was making her way one day through the foothills with her baby and toddler. Suddenly, she heard a terrifying growl as a snarling female tiger attacked her. "She had never seen a Bible," Graham wrote. "But a year or two earlier, a missionary had told her about Jesus, 'who is able to help you when you are in trouble.'" The woman shrieked as the tiger clawed her, but she also managed to shout "O Jesus, help me!" Instantly, the tiger ran. Jesus, she later insisted, had sent her help. [70]

"If we had open, spiritual eyes, we would see not only a world filled with evil spirits and powers — but also powerful angels with drawn swords, set for our defense."

— Billy Graham

March 15

Cities Named after Angels

 Receiving someone's name sends honor in both directions. The one being named is honored to receive the name of someone wonderful. The one who gives or shares a name is honored too. Something of the giver's gifts and qualities may be reborn and live in another person. Catholic explorers who visited and later settled in different regions around the world often named communities after the angels. Los Angeles (The Angels), settled by Spanish settlers in California in 1781, was originally named for Our Lady of the Angels. Among the many other cities named for the angels are: Angeles City, Philippines, Bangkok, Thailand, Kiryat Malakhi, Israel, Torun, Poland, and Tilburg, the Netherlands.

Through the blessing of the upright, the city is exalted. (Proverbs 11:11)

Lord, please bless all the cities of the world with upright and loving people and protect them through your angels.

March 16

ANGELS NEVER FORCE US

 Many people fondly remember a teacher or coach who brought out the best in them — without pushing, pulling, threatening, or promising huge rewards. The best mentors let us act freely. They understand that real love means giving others real freedom. That's the approach of our guardian angels. Theologians say that angels don't know our secret thoughts but can suggest things to our imagination. Their influence on our minds and hearts is subtle and gentle. Sometimes, people are spontaneously inspired to act in a generous way or to say something that needs to be said. Did the idea come "out of nowhere?" A guardian angel may have pitched that great idea.

Thank you, God, for blessing me with such great freedom and for an angel you sent who inspires and guides me so gently, so respectfully.

March 17

Saint Patrick (387–461)

PATRICK'S ANGEL CAME IN DREAMS

 Saint Patrick, born in Britain, was kidnapped and taken as a boy to Ireland. He worked for six lonely years as a slave, herding cattle and sheep. But, on Ireland's windy hills, he also met God. According to his autobiography, Patrick escaped slavery through the assistance of his angel, whom he called "Victoricus." In a dream, the angel told Patrick to walk to the coast where he was to board a ship. Years later, in another dream, Victoricus shared a message from the Irish. "We beg you, holy youth," it said, "that you shall come and walk again among us." Patrick responded. He became a priest and bishop and returned to bring Christ to Ireland. [71]

The Breastplate of Saint Patrick, a prayer of Ireland's great patron saint, poetically lists many ways to ask for God's protection. Patrick prayed, "May the angels of God guard us — against the snares of the evil ones, against the temptations of the world." [72]

THE ANGELS' HYMN OF PRAISE

 As the bishop of Jerusalem, Cyril prepared catechumens for Christian Initiation. When explaining the Eucharistic liturgy, he said, "We make mention of heaven, and earth, and sea; of sun and moon; of stars and all the creation, rational and irrational, visible and invisible; of Angels, Archangels, Virtues, Dominions, Principalities, Powers, Thrones; of the Cherubim with many faces. We make mention also of the Seraphim … standing around the throne of God, with two of their wings veiling their face, and with two their feet, while with two they did fly, crying *Holy, Holy, Holy, is the Lord of Hosts* (Isaiah 6:2–3). Our reciting this confession of God … is so we may be partakers with the hosts of the world above in their hymn of praise." [73]

Lift up your spirit to praise the Lord of Hosts. With the great powers of God's creation, pray: "As in the angels your will is done, O Lord, so likewise be it done on earth in me."

March 19

Saint Joseph

TRUSTING AN ANGEL

 Joseph is mentioned four times in the second chapter of the Gospel of Matthew. Each time, Joseph either receives a message from the angel of the Lord in a dream, or carries out the angel's instructions. Each time, the message is surprising — preposterous! The angel's words turn his world upside down; they strain his faith to the very limit. Mary, his betrothed wife, is with child! Don't divorce her — this is God's plan! Herod is trying to kill the child! Flee to Egypt — tonight! Joseph, however, did not dismiss these crazy dreams. Each time, Joseph trusted the message of the angel, and he was not led astray.

When your angel is prompting you — repeatedly — to go, to do, to accept, to seek — listen! Listen in the quiet of a dream, in ten seconds of silence, in a prayer, in a sigh. Then trust! Trust that God's will is accomplished through your response. Finally, obey. Do what your angel is telling you to do. Not as simple as it sounds. Not easy. But your angel will never lead you astray.

My Angel Is with You

When the army of Nebuchdnezzar took the people of Israel into captivity in Babylon, Jeremiah the prophet sent God's message to them. He told them that they were taken captive for the sins they had committed before God. Jeremiah said: "When you reach Babylon you will be there many years, a long time — seven generations; after that I will bring you back from there in peace. And now in Babylon you will see gods of silver and gold and wood, carried shoulder high, to cast fear upon the nations. Take care that you yourselves do not become like these foreigners and let not such fear possess you. When you see the crowd before and behind worshiping them, say in your hearts, 'You, Lord, are the one to be worshiped!' For my angel is with you, and he will keep watch on you" (Baruch 6:1–6).

We are like exiles longing to return to Heaven, our true home. Our sinfulness leaves us vulnerable to the temptations of our culture. Yet our hearts call us back to the one true God. The angel of the Lord is with us, to keep watch over our hearts.

March 21

ANGELS IN MORTAL COMBAT

 Abba Moses (330–405) was a reformed thief who went into the desert to do penance. Once, he found himself fighting an overpowering temptation. He implored Abba Isidore for help. Abba Isidore took him out onto the open plain and said, "Look toward the west." Moses saw a horde of demons circling in the air and shrieking viciously. Then Isidore said, "Now look toward the east." Abba Moses turned and saw a vast multitude of angels resplendent in glory. Abba Isidore said, "The Lord sends his angels to help us, while the demons fight against them. Those who are with us are greater than those who are against us." [74]

The Psalmist prayed, "Come quickly to help me; Do not let my heart incline to evil, or yield to any sin" (Psalm 141:1, 4, 8). What a consolation to know that powerful angels aid our battle against temptation.

God Will Send Us His Angels

As Lent wears on, take solace in the wisdom of Saint Pio of Pietrelcina, who was a spiritual counselor for thousands. He assured people that "God, whom we desire to see and hold before us, is always ready to come to our assistance. Always faithful to his promises and seeing us fighting valiantly, he will send us his angels to sustain us in the trial." [75] So take heart. Persevere in penance, in prayer, and in almsgiving. Live your Lent with faith-filled determination, knowing that you can grow in strength and holiness. Trust in the angels to lead you closer to God.

"The angels rejoice and celebrate with Christ over the return of the Lord's sheep. He sought us on earth; let us seek Him in heaven."

— Saint Peter Chrysologus

March 23

Saint Toribio of Mogrovejo (1538–1606)

BETWEEN HEAVEN AND EARTH

 In a courtyard of the Museum of Salamanca, Spain, a stone carving by the Spanish sculptor Luis Salvador Carmona depicts *The Miracle of Saint Toribio of Mogrovejo*. As a young man, Toribio felt called to join the strictly cloistered Cistercian community. The statue shows the Virgin Mary and Saint Bernard, the founder of the Cistercians, appearing to Toribio. An angel, serving as the intermediary between heaven and earth, hands Toribio a college scholarship, a sign that he should serve God in the world rather than in the monastery. Toribio became a professor of law and a judge. Then, the king appointed him Archbishop of Lima, Peru. There, Toribio tirelessly defended the rights of the native people who were oppressed by the ruling Spanish upper class and largely ignored by the Church. Toribio was where God wanted him to be.

"Saints rise up from time to time in the Catholic Church like angels in disguise, and shed around them a light, as they walk on their way heavenward."

— Blessed John Henry Newman [76]

SAINT MICHAEL THE ARCHANGEL
AND EL SALVADOR

 On this date in 1980, Blessed Archbishop Oscar Romero was shot to death while saying Mass in El Salvador during his country's civil war. To everyone's surprise, including the priests of his archdiocese, Romero had become an outspoken critic of the right-wing, militarist government. He spoke out for his people who were poor and powerless. The government supported assassinations and terrorist attacks against the people. To Romero's shock and grief, his country was receiving no help. Not even the United States would intervene. In a homily, the archbishop promised his people that heaven would not forget El Salvador. Saint Michael the Archangel, he said, would help the powerless and the persecuted.

"Michael serves only God and bends to Jesus Christ and all who serve him. He has fought and stays with those who struggle to be faithful until once again all things will be subject to Jesus Christ, the Lamb of God whose blood is testimony to our life."

— Blessed Archbishop Oscar Romero [77]

March 25

The Annunciation of the Lord

AN ANGEL'S REVERENCE

 We should look at the Annunciation from an angel's point of view, suggests Catholic author Mike Aquilina. The Archangel Gabriel, he wrote, "showed Mary deference, as though he, the angel — archangel, in fact — was in awe of a humble Jewish woman who was hardly more than a girl." Gabriel greeted her with reverence: "Hail, full of grace, the Lord is with you." This glorious and magnificent archangel was overwhelmed by Mary's great holiness and beauty. She had been conceived free of sin. God had prepared her to be the mother for his only Son, Jesus. Mary agreed. The Word became flesh within her. The future of humanity shifted toward hope and heaven. [78]

"In the set noon of time shall one from heaven,
An angel fresh from looking upon God,
Descend before a woman, blessing her
With perfect benediction of pure love."

— Elizabeth Barrett Browning

ANGELS IN THE DESERT

In Anne Rice's novel *Christ the Lord: The Road to Cana*, angels comfort Jesus when he falls from a desert cliff during a sandstorm. Rice's depiction of the Savior's forty desert days moves beyond the Gospels. "I heard the flapping, the fluttering, the muffled beating of wings," Jesus says of the angelic visit. "All over me came the soft touch as if of hands, countless gentle hands, the even softer brush of lips — lips against my cheeks, my forehead, my parched eyelids." Jesus resisted Satan's temptations, but he was surely hot, tired, hungry, exhausted, thirsty and sun-burnt. Both the Gospels of Matthew and Mark say that angels ministered to him. [79]

Scripture assures us that the life of Jesus was filled with angels — from his birth until his Death and Resurrection. Angels surround you, as well!

March 27

The Priest Mistaken for an Angel

 In the summer of 2013, Father Patrick Dowling of the Diocese of Jefferson City stopped on an eastern Missouri highway to see if he could help car accident victims. Dowling learned that nineteen-year-old Katie Lentz was conscious, but trapped inside her virtually demolished car. Though not a Catholic, Lentz asked the priest to pray for her and her rescuers. Despite previous failed attempts, rescuers soon cut through the mangled car to free Katie. Later, two rescuers insisted that they heard a man's voice urging calm and giving directions. Since Father Dowling seemed to disappear unnoticed and unidentified, early accident reports referred to the priest as an angel. [80]

Father James Martin, S.J., a well-known national media consultant and author said, "There are angels, of course, but we tend to ascribe to angels anonymous acts that we find incredibly loving — when in fact human beings do incredibly loving things in hidden ways every day." Ask God to show you where to do loving things in hidden ways. [81]

March 28

C. S. Lewis and the Angels

 The author of *The Chronicles of Narnia* and other books on Christianity never doubted the existence of angels — or devils. During World War II, C. S. Lewis (1898–1963), a Cambridge University professor, wanted to lift the spirits of his war-weary countrymen. So, Lewis wrote *The Screwtape Letters,* a hilarious series of letters from a senior devil named Screwtape. Screwtape instructs his bumbling nephew, Wormwood, on strategies to tempt a man and lead him to hell. Wormwood learns to encourage his client's vices, murmuring little words of discouragement and promoting his selfishness. English readers chuckled, but they got Lewis's point. The battle between good and evil is real, relentless, and all around us. [82]

"I believe in angels, and I believe that some of these, by the abuse of their free will, have become enemies to God, and as a corollary, to us. These, we may call devils. They do not differ in nature from good angels, but their nature is depraved."

— C. S. Lewis, Preface, *The Screwtape Letters*

March 29

Angels Shadowing Us

 Saint Augustine taught that angels are always nearby. They're a bit like our shadows, connected to us on the ground. Whether we are in a sunny place in our lives or a cloudy one, they never leave us. Augustine said, "The angels go in and out with us, having their eyes always fixed upon us and upon all that we are doing. If we stop anywhere, they stop also; if we go forth to walk, they bear us company; if we journey into another country, they follow us; go where we will, by land or by sea, they are ever with us all day long and all night long, and during every moment of our life." [83]

"Watch, O Lord, with those who wake, or watch, or weep tonight, and give your Angels and Saints charge over those who sleep."

> — Night Prayer of Saint Augustine (see the complete prayer in the appendix, page 378)

March 30

Bodyguard in the Forest

 One winter evening in the 1940s, a German minister was walking back to his village alone. When he reached a forested area in Bavaria, an unexplainable dread filled him. He prayed and a deep peace quickly replaced his fear. That night, in a dream, he saw his battered body on the forest floor. A voice said, "That's what you would look like if I hadn't protected you." Months later, the minister learned that some young men had planned to kill him that night. They hated him because his Bible classes were influencing their girlfriends. The men insisted that a bodyguard suddenly appeared and walked on the minister's right all through the forest. Then, the protector vanished. [84]

Psalm 34:8 assures us, "The angel of the LORD encamps around those who fear him, and he saves them." Pray for an angel at your shoulder when fear of any kind fills you with dread.

March 31

ANGELS SPREADING THE GOSPEL

 After the first Pentecost, the Church received angelic help to spread the Gospel. One instance of angels on the job is about an Apostle and an Ethiopian Jew. On his way home from Jerusalem, the Ethiopian was puzzling over a reading from Isaiah. At the same moment, an angel spoke to the Apostle Philip who was nearby. The angel told Philip, "Get up and head south on the road that goes down from Jerusalem to Gaza, the desert route." So, Philip set out and caught up with the Ethiopian's carriage (Acts 8:26–27). Riding along in the carriage, Philip talked about Jesus. The prophecies of Isaiah, he said, were about Jesus. Convinced, the Ethiopian stopped the carriage when they came to some water and was baptized.

Then I saw another angel flying high overhead, with everlasting good news to announce to those who dwell on earth, to every nation, tribe, and people. (Revelation 14:6)

Like Philip and the angels, you too can carry the Gospel's Good News to the world around you.

April 1

THE ANGEL OF RIGHTEOUSNESS

 The Shepherd of Hermas, a second-century Christian writer, described a vision of a man with two angels — an angel of righteousness and an angel of iniquity. The man asks the Shepherd, "How, sir, am I to know the powers of these, for both angels dwell with me?"

"Hear," said the Shepherd, "and understand them. The angel of righteousness is gentle and modest, meek and peaceful. When, therefore, he ascends into your heart, immediately he talks to you of righteousness, purity, chastity, contentment, and of every righteous deed and glorious virtue. These are the deeds of the angel of righteousness. Trust him and his works." [85]

Today, take time to meditate on the Shepherd's advice: When you trust the angel of righteousness, and do his works, you live in God. Furthermore, if you refuse to do the works of the angel of iniquity, you will live in God.

April 2

The Angel of Repentance

 The Shepherd of Hermas used a common image of wine jugs to warn Christians about the devil. As this ancient story goes, a man filled good wine jars with good wine, but left a few jars empty. Later, he didn't look at the full jars because he knew they were full. But he did look at the empty jars because he feared they had become sour. If they become sour, they can't be used for good wine. Similarly, the Shepherd explained, the devil goes to the servants of God to try them. Those who are full of faith can resist him. So, he withdraws, having no way to enter them. Then the devil goes and enters the empty jars. He produces whatever he wishes in them, and they become his servants.

But I, the angel of repentance, say to you, "Fear not the devil; for I was sent to be with you who repent with all your heart, and to make you strong in faith. Trust God, then." [86]

AN ANGEL OF CONSOLATION

 It is easy to read familiar Scripture stories quickly and superficially. Instead, take a deep breath and then read this familiar story slowly, letting each word live within you: After eating the Passover Meal together, Jesus and his disciples went out, as they often did, to an olive grove called Gethsemane. There, knowing what was going to happen that same evening, Jesus told them to pray that they would not be tested beyond their limit. Jesus himself then withdrew about a stone's throw from them and, falling to his knees on the rocky ground, opened his heart to his heavenly Father. "Do not have me drink this cup of suffering," he prayed, "yet, not my will but yours be done." He was in such agony and his prayer was so intense that his sweat became like drops of blood falling on the ground. And his Father, with infinite love, sent a consoling angel to strengthen him in his passion and death. (Based on Luke 22:39–44.)

Father, it is not possible for me to imagine the tremendous love that compelled Jesus to accept the cross for our sake. It is even harder to fathom the love required to sacrifice your only Son to atone for our sins. Strengthen my faith in your boundless love.

April 4
Saint Isidore of Seville (c. 560–636)

The Essence of Angels

 Saint Isidore, archbishop of Seville, Spain, was considered the most learned man of his time, and has been suggested as an appropriate patron saint for the Internet. Isidore had a vast collection of sources and he studied and wrote on a great variety of subjects.

His major work *Etymologies* consisted of twenty books. In Book VII, Isidore reflected on the *essence* of angels:

> Angels ... announce the will of God to people. The word angel is the name of their function, not their nature. They are always spirits, but when they are sent, they are angels. Through artistic license, painters give them wings.... Just as in the fables of the poets, the angels are said to have wings because of their velocity. Where also the Holy Scriptures say: "Who walks upon wings of the wind" (Psalm 104:3). [87]

"Learning unsupported by grace may get into our ears; it never reaches the heart. But when God's grace touches our innermost minds to bring understanding, his word which has been received by the ear sinks deep into the heart."

— *Book of Maxims*, Saint Isidore of Seville [88]

Saint Vincent Ferrer (1350–1419)

THE ANGEL OF THE APOCALYPSE

 Saint Vincent Ferrer, a Dominican priest, had a vision of Jesus accompanied by Saints Dominic and Francis. They told him to go through the world preaching and calling people to Christ. At the time, the Church in Europe was in total disarray — three men claimed to be pope. Each had his loyal supporters. People, governments, and even the clergy didn't know who or what to believe. In contrast to this upheaval, Vincent became a messenger of penance and preparation for judgment — the real business of the Church. For the next twenty years, he crisscrossed Western Europe preaching repentance and conversion — and drawing huge crowds. He called himself the Angel of the Apocalypse, referring to the angel with the seventh trumpet in Revelation 11:15–19, who proclaimed victory over the forces of evil and the coming of God's reign.

The nations raged, but your wrath has come, and the time for the dead to be judged, and recompense your servants, the prophets, and the holy ones and those who fear your name, the small and the great alike, and to destroy those who destroy the earth. (Revelation 11:18)

April 6

The Guardian Angel of Barcelona

 One day, as Saint Vincent Ferrer approached the north gate of the fortified city of Barcelona in Spain, he saw an angel holding a sword aloft. The angel told Vincent that he was there at God's command to guard the city. Meanwhile, a crowd had assembled in the cathedral to hear the famous preacher's sermon. Speaking from the pulpit, Vincent said that he had just met the most beautiful person in Barcelona. He then told the people about his conversation with their guardian angel. Surprised and pleased, the people built a shrine near the north gate with a statue of the angel as Vincent had described it. Today, the busy avenue nearby is called The Gate of the Angel, and a replica of the statue remains there.[89]

Because we can't see them, it is easy to forget that angels are always with us, actively with us. Develop the habit of invoking the help and prayers of your guardian angel whenever you need assistance. See what a difference it makes.

ANGELS AT THE RESURRECTION

 All four evangelists joyfully tell about the Resurrection of Jesus. However, details about the angels at the Resurrection vary. In the Gospels of Matthew and Mark, just one angel appears. Shining and wearing clothing that is white as snow, the angel of the Lord sits in the empty tomb waiting to share the good news. In the Gospel of Luke, "two men in dazzling garments" appear to the friends of Jesus. And in John's version of the Resurrection, Mary of Magdala finds "two angels in white sitting there, one at the head and one at the feet where the body of Jesus had been." In all of the Gospels, angels are messengers of the fundamental truth of our faith.

"Do not be amazed! You seek Jesus of Nazareth, the crucified. He has been raised; he is not here" (Mark 16:6), the angel told the living followers of Jesus and all of us who were to come.

April 8

Saint Julie Billiart (1751–1816)

AN ANGEL OF TRUTH

 Julie Billiart loved to teach others the truths of the faith she held so firmly. This was a dangerous thing to do after the French Revolution (1789–1799). The Church was officially suppressed, and teaching religion was a crime. Julie had to take great care to evade arrest. When a priest loyal to the state took over her parish church, Julie saw the people as a flock without a shepherd. She maintained that it would be better to have no priest. "All those good people, who find it utterly impossible to get into touch with their legitimate pastors, will not be punished for it," she said. "God will send an angel from heaven to them rather than allow them to perish forever." [90]

Despite all of the challenges she faced, Saint Julie Billiart's motto was "How good is the good God!" Bring this thought to mind often today.

ANGEL OF PURE JOY

 An angel of the Lord descended from heaven, approached the tomb where Jesus was buried, rolled back the stone, and sat upon it. His appearance was like lightning, and his clothing was white as snow (Matthew 28:2–3). Everything about this angel — his appearance, his actions, and his words — has meaning, said Saint Gregory the Great. "The angel appeared clothed with a white robe because he has announced the joys of our Great Feast [Easter]: for the shining whiteness of the garment proclaims the splendor of our solemnity." Saint Jerome agreed: "The enemy now put to flight, and the kingdom restored, the shining white garment is that of pure joy: for the King of Peace is sought and found and never given up. This young man [angel] therefore reveals the nature of the resurrection to those who fear death." [91]

Have mercy on me, God, in accord with your merciful love; in your abundant compassion blot out my transgressions.... Cleanse me with hyssop, that I may be pure; wash me, and I will be whiter than snow. You will let me hear gladness and joy. (Psalm 51:3, 9–10)

April 10

Angels of the Light

 Saint Ambrose (340–397) was the archbishop of Milan, Italy, and an influential Church Father. In an Easter Sunday sermon he focused on one line from Saint Matthew's Gospel: *Then the angel said to the women.... "I know that you are seeking Jesus the crucified."* (Matthew 28:5). Ambrose advised, "If you wish to find Him, *the sun being now risen*, then come as these women came; that is, [in the light]. Let there be no darkness of evil in your hearts; for the desire of the flesh, and works that are evil, are darkness. They in whose hearts there is darkness of this kind see not the light, and understand not Christ; for Christ is the Light."

God is light, and in him there is no darkness at all. If we say: "We have fellowship with him," while we continue to walk in darkness, we lie and do not act in truth. But if we walk in the light as he is in the light, then we have fellowship with one another, and the blood of his Son Jesus cleanses us from all sin. (1 John 1:5–7)

ANGEL MAIL DELIVERY

 Gemma, a lovely, quiet girl, grew up in Lucca, about two hundred miles from Rome. Because of poor health, she quit school early. By the time she was nineteen, her parents had died and she was caring for her seven younger siblings. But the daily demands on her time didn't end her prayer life or mystical experiences. Since childhood, Gemma had been talking with her guardian angel. This relationship was so close that Gemma asked her angel to take letters to her confessor in Rome. She had no money for postage! The priest confirmed that he would simply find Gemma's unstamped letters on his desk. No one witnessed their arrival. [92]

Angels are called ministering spirits (Hebrews 1:14). Lord, nothing should surprise me about the amazing help you send us through your angels. Keep me watchful.

April 12

THE ANGEL OF GRIEF

 In cemeteries around the world, granite angels watch over the graves of believers. Families who are missing loved ones, especially infants and young children, are consoled by angel monuments. Angels are perceived as loving and protective, and Scripture supports this view. Scripture also confirms that angels are connected with the Resurrection, the day of Judgment, and escorting the dead to paradise. A famous angel memorial is the "Angel of Grief" carved by the nineteenth-century American sculptor William W. Story. The beautiful life-sized angel is draped in grief over a four-sided pedestal at the gravesite of Story's wife, Emelyn, in Rome. Story completed the statue shortly before his own death in 1894. He was buried with his wife.

"O God, by whose mercy the faithful departed find rest, send your holy Angel to watch over this grave. Through Christ our Lord, Amen."

— Prayer said at graveside [93]

April 13
Saint Martin I (d. 655)

ANGELS IN BATTLE

 Though he didn't die violently, Pope Martin I is honored as a martyr. Many Eastern Christians believed that because he was God, Christ had no human will. Pope Martin opposed this heresy. Jesus has two natures — human and divine. Having free will was part of Christ's human nature. Because he upheld this doctrine, Pope Martin was arrested, tortured, and exiled to Crimea by the infuriated emperor of Constantinople. According to theologian Megan McKenna, angels "minister especially to those whose actions and lives have import far beyond their own concerns. They are especially near to those who do battle." As Martin died defending the Truth, he surely had the special comfort of the angels. [94]

Saint Martin stayed strong and faithful to his beliefs and to the teachings of the Church. Ask for help from the angels to stand up for the beliefs you hold most dear.

April 14

ANGEL'S TRUMPETS

 In the spring, people wait expectantly for flowering plants to bloom. During the Easter season, flowers that emerge from bulbs in the ground or appear on bare branches are signs of new life, and symbols of the Resurrection. Though it flourishes only in the southern, coastal regions of the United States, Angel's Trumpet is a flower that makes us think of the joyful music of the angels. The bell-shaped blooms are six to twenty inches wide and hang delicately from sturdy branches. Appropriately, the Angel's Trumpet comes in an array of colors — peach, white, yellow, orange, red, and green. The flowers even produce a "heavenly" fragrance on warm evenings. No wonder they are typically the pride and joy of gardeners in the South.

God, the variety, beauty and color of things that grow must delight even your angels. During this season, I pray for growing respect and protection for the gardens, forests, and farmlands of our earth.

April 15

Lincoln's Hope for "Better Angels"

 On this date in 1865, President Abraham Lincoln died after being shot the night before. He and Mrs. Lincoln had been celebrating the end of the Civil War. Four years earlier, Lincoln had hoped and prayed that war would never begin. At his first inaugural address in 1861, Lincoln conceded that the demons of war were at work. He knew that the southern states would fight to preserve their economy and way of life. But, the president prayed for peace, "We are not enemies, but friends. We must not be enemies," he said, admitting that deep differences had strained the friendship. He ended by predicting that the nation would ultimately choose peace, moved by "the better angels of our nature." [95]

The angels couldn't have given us a better prayer for peace than the one named for Saint Francis of Assisi: "Lord, make me an instrument of your peace. Where there is hatred, let me so love, where there is injury, pardon…." Look for ways to be an instrument of God's peace today.

April 16
Saint Benedict Joseph Labré (1748–1783)

CARRIED AWAY BY ANGELS

 Though born to a prosperous French shopkeeper, for most of his adult life, Benedict Joseph Labré was poor and homeless. He hoped to join a religious order, but fragile health, insufficient trade skills, and his unusual personality worked against him. Instead, he became a secular Franciscan and adopted a hard life of pilgrimage and prayer. He visited most of Europe's shrines but later lived in Rome. There, he slept in the Coliseum and frequently attended Eucharistic adoration at different churches. Benedict died in a borrowed bed. Everyone who knew him agreed that angels carried the holy beggar heavenward just like the poor man Lazarus had been in Luke's Gospel story (Luke 16:22). [96]

"This poor one cried out and the LORD heard, and from all his distress he saved him" (Psalm 34:7). How is God calling you to hear and answer the cry of the poor?

April 17

Dancing Angels

 "How many angels can dance on the head of a pin?" This silly question about angels is said to have preoccupied medieval scholars. They were fascinated by angels, but there's no evidence that they were posed the "angels-on-the-head-of-a-pin" question. However, the great Doctor of the Church Saint Thomas Aquinas (1225–1274) did ask: "Can several angels be in the same place?" He concluded that angels can move anywhere instantaneously but don't occupy space. Historians say that students tried to stump teachers with difficult riddles. Aquinas didn't mind, though, because honestly considering questions helped lead him to the Truth. [97]

God, there are so many mysteries about angels and creation that I can't solve or understand. Help me focus on what you really want — my love and trust.

April 18

THE CHERUBIC HYMN

 The Cherubic Hymn, or Song of the Angels, has been part of the Divine Liturgy of Saint John Chrysostom since about A.D. 573. The cherubim, angels of the first hierarchy, guard and support God's throne. They also surround and protect sacred spaces. Images of the Cherubim adorned the Ark of the Covenant and the tabernacle built by the Israelites. The hymn, sung in the Eastern Catholic Church as well as the Eastern Orthodox Church celebrates the prayerful union of those who partake in the liturgy on earth and the holy angels who praise God in heaven.

> Let us, who mystically represent the Cherubim,
> And sing the thrice-holy hymn to the Life-giving Trinity,
> Lay aside all worldly cares
> That we may receive the King of all,
> Invisibly escorted by the angelic hosts.
> Alleluia, alleluia, alleluia! [98]

My God, help me to set aside my concerns and worries so that I may immerse myself in your presence, here and now. Help me to appreciate that my anxieties are made insignificant when cast into the fire of your love or flung with abandon into the depths of divine mercy.

An Angel Named José

 Brazilian Archbishop Dom Hélder Câmara (1909–1999) believed in the existence of angels and the traditional teaching of the Church that we each have a guardian angel. In fact, he had a close friendship with his guardian angel, whom he named José after the childhood nickname his mother had given him. He depended on José for protection in times of danger and assistance when he needed strength. He looked to his angel for solace, encouragement, and courage to defend the oppressed. Dom Hélder said that he had never seen an angel — not even his guardian José — but he was convinced with all certainty that angels exist and that they are near us, protecting and helping all of us. [99]

"For, as it is written in the book of the Prophets: 'And the angel that spoke in me, said to me....' [The prophet] does not say, 'Spoke to me' but 'Spoke in me.'"

— Saint Augustine

April 20

ANGELS ASCENDING AND DESCENDING

 Jacob had deceived his father Isaac and angered his brother Esau. Fearing for his life, Jacob fled to his uncle's home in the land of Haran. When the sun set, he stopped for the night, laid down and placed a stone under his head. Then he dreamed of a stairway reaching from the ground to the heavens, with the angels of God ascending and descending. The Lord stood beside him and promised this land to Jacob's descendants who would spread throughout the earth with his blessing. In the morning, Jacob took the stone and built a pillar to mark the place that was the gateway to heaven. In spite of Jacob's shortcomings, God's plan would be accomplished, step by step, as the angels hurry to do his will on earth. (See Genesis 28:10–28.)

To the spiritually aware, windows are always open to heaven and the Lord. The angels of the Lord are always present to help us in our journey. And as we all know, sometimes that journey can be as lonesome and harrowing as Jacob's. [100]

THE HAPPINESS OF THE ANGELS

 Many people have asked if angels can sin. Anselm, a brilliant theologian, thought about that. He reasoned that freedom is a power *for* something. God gave the angels both the will for happiness and the will for justice — giving God what is rightfully his, such as obedience. The rebellious angels chose happiness for themselves over justice. The good angels chose justice over their own happiness. As a result of their free choices, the rebellious angels forfeited their happiness. The good angels gained all the happiness they could possibly want. Since there is no further happiness left for them to will, their will for happiness can no longer tempt them to trespass the boundaries of justice. For this reason, the good angels are no longer able to sin. [101]

"It is a great gift of the mercy and love of God for us that our Lord Jesus Christ became Incarnate — He identified Himself completely with us by sharing fully in our human nature. He did not do this for the angels!"

— Saint Anselm [102]

April 22

When Angels Grieve

 "Then the Lord God stationed the cherubim and the fiery revolving sword east of the garden of Eden, to guard the way to the tree of life" (Genesis 3:24). Saint John Chrysostom thought that the angels took on this assignment with heavy hearts. "Though the Cherubim stood guard before Paradise, the angels yet sorrowed for our unhappiness; just as a servant taking a fellow servant at the bidding of his master, and putting him in prison guards him, yet moved by compassion for his fellow servant he is distressed because of what has happened to him. So did the Cherubim undertake the duty of excluding men from Paradise, while they grieved for their return.... For when you see men having compassion on their fellow servants you cannot doubt that the same is true of the Cherubim. For these heavenly powers are more kind than men." [103]

"There will be rejoicing among the angels of God over one sinner who repents" (Luke 15:19), just as the angels both rejoice or grieve over your personal choices.

THE COSMIC BATTLE

 According to Tradition, George was raised in a Christian family in Palestine and became a tribune in the Roman army. When the Emperor Diocletian ordered the arrest of all Christian soldiers, George went to him and publicly declared his worship of Jesus Christ. George was tortured and died a martyr. The legend of Saint George slaying the dragon and the biblical account of Michael the Archangel expelling Lucifer from heaven (Revelation 12:79) are, in a sense, the same story. They valiantly battle and defeat dragon and devil — both powerful images of evil. Speaking of them as stories does not deny their truth. The story is about every angel and every saint. All faced the test, and all chose good/God. For when evil is slain, sanctity may be attained.

In life, we all confront demons and dragons, temptations and trials. Minor or mighty, each battle requires courage, heroic faith, and perseverance. Our final victory comes when we enter God's presence for eternity. Lord Jesus Christ, let nothing separate me from you. Amen.

April 24

The Archangel Uriel

 The Archangel Uriel (or Phanuel) doesn't appear in the Catholic Biblical canon. But this angel is often mentioned in the Book of Enoch, an important text in the first Christian centuries. Several Fathers of the Church, including Augustine, considered the Book of Enoch inspired. Uriel is named along with Michael, Raphael, and Gabriel in 1 Enoch. In her book *Angels Unawares* theologian Megan McKenna devotes a chapter to Uriel, the "angel of death and conversion." McKenna suggests that through his angels God cares about us from the beginning until the end of our lives — and beyond. "The Angel of Death serves God as any other angel does," according to McKenna, "obeying the will of the Holy One." [104]

"I came to know their names, which the angel who came with me revealed to me ... and the fourth, who is set over all actions of repentance unto the hope of those who would inherit the eternal life, is Phanuel (Uriel) by name" (1 Enoch 40:2–10). As a follower of Jesus, re-evaluate your beliefs and attitudes toward death.

DRAGGED BY PAGANS, EMBRACED BY ANGELS

Saint Mark, author of the first Gospel, knew it was dangerous to tell the world about Jesus. He was an early disciple of Christ and learned about the Savior's persecution, suffering, and death from Peter. Sent by Peter to Egypt, Mark founded the Church in Alexandria. During the reign of Emperor Nero, persecution of Christians was becoming common — and acceptable. One spring day in A.D. 68, pagans seized Mark, bound him, and dragged him through Alexandria behind an ox cart. In prison that night, Mark suffered intensely from many injuries and broken bones. Angels visited; and he heard the comforting voice of Jesus. He died the next day, while being dragged again through the city he had called to Christ.

Afterwards, Jesus himself, through them, sent forth from east to west the sacred and imperishable proclamation of eternal salvation. Amen.

— Conclusion of the Gospel according to Mark

April 26

Shakespeare's Cast of Angels

 This is the birthday of one of the greatest writers of the English language. Some scholars claim Shakespeare was Catholic and secretly married in a Catholic Church during Queen Elizabeth's anti-Catholic reign. His work reflects belief in angels and in God-given human dignity. In *Romeo and Juliet*, Romeo calls Juliet an angel, saying that she is "as glorious to this night, being o'er my head as is a winged messenger of heaven." In *Macbeth*, Malcolm warns of Macbeth's hidden treachery, adding that "Angels are bright still, though the brightest fell." For centuries, audiences for *Hamlet* have been moved by one of the playwright's most beautiful concluding lines. Hamlet's friend Horatio ends the drama with prayer for the dying Hamlet. "Good night, sweet Prince, and flights of angels sing thee to thy rest." [105]

Shakespeare's prayer for Prince Hamlet can be every believer's prayer for the dying: May flights of angels sing them to their rest.

April 27

ANGEL FACTS AND FICTION, PART II

 Angel fact: Christ is the center of the angelic world. Though Jesus was born after the creation of angels, he was always at the heart of their mission. He is the Second Person of the Trinity and always existed. The Creator foresaw the need for angelic help in the world Jesus would redeem. Angel fiction? There is the belief that angels appear only to holy people. In the Old Testament, an angel repeatedly appeared to the donkey of Balaam, a conniving pagan prophet who planned to curse the Israelites. Initially, Balaam didn't see the angel blocking the road. But Balaam's donkey did (Numbers 22:21–35). An angel also appeared to terrified Roman soldiers guarding Christ's tomb after his Resurrection (Matthew 28:4).

"When you close the doors to your dwelling and are alone, you should know that there is present with you the angel God has appointed ... he sees all things and is not hindered by darkness."

— Saint Anthony the Great

April 28

Angels and the Solar System

 In the Middle Ages, people imagined that angels were "steering" the planets and keeping them in proper orbits. After all, planets revolved around the sun in very predictable paths. The laws of gravity as applied to moving objects were not yet fully understood. So, it seemed logical that the Creator had assigned angels to this immense task of solar-system management. Centuries earlier, some of the ancients held views about God's heavenly creatures that were even less scientific. Many people thought that the stars and angels were expressions of the same thing. Stars and planets, it was believed, never changed and would exist forever — just like the angels. [106]

Praise him, all you his angels;
give praise, all you his hosts.
Praise him, sun and moon;
praise him, all shining stars.
Praise him, highest heavens,
you waters above the heavens.
Let them all praise the Lord's name;
for he commanded and they were created.
(Psalm 148:2–5)

April 29
Saint Catherine of Siena (1347–1380)

LOVE AND THE ANGELS

Though the youngest children in a large family may be overlooked, little Catherine Benincasa wasn't. She and twin Giovanna were the twenty-third and twenty-fourth children. Giovanna soon died, but Catherine was healthy, happy, and so outgoing that people nicknamed her "Joy." Catherine loved prayer and often saw guardian angels near those they protected. As a teen, Catherine became a Dominican tertiary, living a life of prayer at home. At twenty-one, surrounded by angels, she was mystically engaged to Jesus. Then, she began serving Siena's poor and homeless. Near the end of her short life, she worked hard to reconcile political and Church conflicts. She helped convince Pope Gregory XI to return to Rome from French exile. Since her writings are spiritual classics, she was named a Doctor of the Church in 1970.

Saint Catherine of Siena's spiritual advice couldn't be more modern. Does one of her statements about God's love resonate with you?

- *"Love transforms one into what one loves."*

- *"Be who God meant you to be and you will set the world on fire."*

- *"Love does not stay idle."* [107]

April 30
Saint Pius V (1504–1572)

ANGELS SHALL SUPPORT YOU

 As a Dominican priest, Pope Saint Pius V taught theology and Scripture and must have known many Psalms by heart. When he became pope at sixty-two, he needed the consolation and support of angels that Psalm 91 promises. Pius had to implement many reforms ordered by the Council of Trent. That included better seminary training, a new missal, new catechism, and children's religious education programs. But everything was set aside when Europe faced invasion from the Ottoman Turks. The pope organized a coalition to defend Europe. He also asked everyone to pray the Rosary to beg for Mary's help. On October 7, 1571, the Turks were decisively defeated near Greece. Bells rang out everywhere; Europe rejoiced.

Psalm 91 has given believers hope for thousands of years. Make it your prayer too when someone needs angelic support and protection. "For he commands his angels with regard to you, to guard you wherever you go. With their hands they shall support you, lest you strike your foot against a stone" (Psalm 91:11–12).

Queen of the Angels

A popular celebration during May, a month traditionally dedicated to the Blessed Virgin, is a May Crowning. This ceremony includes prayers and hymns, presentation of flowers, and crowning a statue of Mary with a wreath of flowers. The hymn "Bring Flowers of the Rarest" is a traditional favorite, and the chorus reminds us that Mary is also Queen of the Angels.

Bring flow'rs of the fairest,
Bring flow'rs of the rarest,
from garden and woodland
and hillside and vale;
Our full hearts are swelling,
our glad voices telling
the praise of the loveliest
Rose of the vale.

O Mary! we crown thee with blossoms today,
Queen of the Angels, Queen of the May,
O Mary! we crown thee with blossoms today,
Queen of the Angels, Queen of the May.

May 2

ANGELS LEAD US TO CHRIST

 As we walk with the angels throughout this year, keep in mind that the journey is not only forward, but also inward. Writer Judith Lang points out: "The angels lead us to Christ, and in him we shall most truly find them. As we are promised his presence with us at all times, here on earth, so the angels are all about us, every day, in, through, and with him, but we should never take them for granted;... Christ and his angels would overcome us totally were they to appear before us in all their power; even so, he himself, and the angels, come down to us in our lowest need." [108]

"When our eyes are opened the angels' light can illuminate the present moment."

— Judith Lang

The Revelations of an Angel

At the age of seventeen, Saint Margaret of Cortona (1247–1297), both beautiful and reckless, ran off with a nobleman and began a nine-year relationship as his mistress and the mother of his son. The scandalous affair ended when he was murdered by his enemies. Profoundly shocked, Margaret began a life of penance. She sought refuge with the Franciscan friars at Cortona, Italy, where she supported herself by nursing elderly women. God was happy with Margaret's repentance and granted her an intimate friendship with her guardian angel. During this time, Margaret's guardian angel consoled and reassured her. Gradually, the angel revealed the depths of God's divine love for her.

"I have been darkness; I have been darker than night!" Margaret cried, to which Christ replied: "For love of you, new light, I bless the little room where you live concealed in my love." Lord, grant me your love and mercy. [109]

May 4

ANGELS REJOICE AT HIS ASCENSION

 "As [the disciples] were looking on, [Jesus] was lifted up, and a cloud took him from their sight.... Suddenly two men dressed in white garments stood beside them" (Acts 1:9–10). Why did the angels wear white garments at the Lord's Ascension, but not when he was born? Pope Saint Gregory the Great said that the *white garments* reveal to us a festive state of mind. They indicate that there was great rejoicing among the angels when the Lord entered into heaven. "For when the Lord was born the divinity seemed to be brought low. But at the Lord's Ascension humanity was exalted. And white garments were more becoming for exaltation than for humiliation … for He who at His birth appeared as God made lowly is seen in His Ascension as Man exalted."

Saint Gregory reminds us that the Ascension of Christ is our triumph too, as God-made-man takes his throne in heaven. "From now on," he said, "make fast to your eternal home the anchor of your hope, and fix the course of your soul by that True Light." [110]

Pray for Your Angel

 In the Liturgy of the Eastern Orthodox Church, the Litany before the Communion of the Faithful includes a petition for an angel: "For an angel of peace, a faithful guide, a guardian of our souls and bodies, let us entreat the Lord." Nicholas Cabasilas, a fourteenth-century theologian, commented on this surprising petition and put it into proper context: "We pray for a guardian angel, not that one may be given to us, since each of us has one from the moment of birth, but that it may be active and may fulfill its task, that it may protect us and lead us in the right way, and may not, angered by our sins, desert us." [111]

Great, therefore, is the dignity of the human soul, since each has an angel assigned to it as its attendant.

— Saint Jerome

May 6

ANGELS ON THE TRAIL

 On a bright, sunny day in May, several boys went to the woods to pick berries. When they came to a small stream, they decided to wade across rather than cross on the bridge. As the stream appeared to be shallow, it was a shock when the leader suddenly disappeared beneath the water! He had stepped into a deep hole and was unable to regain his footing. The other boys managed to return to the bank. At that moment, two hikers stepped out of the woods on a nearby path. One of them reassured the boys, while the other, without a word, descended into the water up to his head, and pulled the struggling boy to safety. Surprisingly, the clothes of the hiker who had rescued the boy seemed perfectly dry when he and his companion resumed their hike. [112]

Fear not, for I have redeemed you;
I have called you by name: you are mine.
When you pass through the water, I will be with you;
in the rivers you shall not drown.
When you walk through fire, you shall not be burned;
the flames shall not consume you.
For I am the Lord, your God,
the Holy One of Israel, your Savior.
(Isaiah 43:1–3)

ANGELS OF THE LORD, BLESS THE LORD

 The Old Testament's Book of Daniel offers one of the Bible's most interesting accounts of angelic protection. Three young Jews — Shadrach, Meshach, and Abednego — refused to worship the golden statue that King Nebuchadnezzar of Babylon had made. Enraged, the king threatened to throw them into a fiery furnace, taunting them, "Who is the God who can deliver you out of my hands?" He ordered the furnace heated seven times hotter than usual, and the three men were cast into the white-hot furnace. They walked about, singing and blessing the Lord. Then the angel of the Lord went into the furnace and reduced the fiery flames. When Nebuchadnezzar saw this, he demanded: "Did we not cast three men bound into the fire?… I see four men unbound and unhurt, walking in the fire, and the fourth looks like a son of God" (Daniel 3:91, 92).

> *"Blessed be the God of Shadrach, Meshach, and Abednego, who sent his angel to deliver the servants that trusted in him; they disobeyed the royal command and yielded their bodies rather than serve or worship any god except their own God. For there is no other God who can rescue like this." (Daniel 3:95–96)*

May 8

CATHEDRAL CAVE FOR THE ANGELS

 This date celebrates apparitions of Saint Michael the Archangel that had a strange beginning in 490. One day, near Siponto, in southeastern Italy, a wealthy landowner heard that his prize bull couldn't be lured from a large cave. Archers were told to shoot the animal, which was becoming dangerous. When arrows turned around on the archers, the terrified landowner consulted with the bishop. Prayer and fasting were advised. Saint Michael soon appeared to the bishop. God wanted this mountaintop cave consecrated to Michael and all angels for prayer and pardon. When the bishop came to celebrate Mass, an altar with a red altar cloth and cross were already in place. Over the centuries, many saints, popes, and pilgrims visited this cave shrine to Saint Michael at Monte Gargano. [113]

For thousands of years, Saint Michael has appeared offering heavenly protection and guidance. May the world remain open to Michael's help and protection!

ALL ABOUT ANGELOLOGY

 Angelology is a branch of theology focused on the study of angels. "Angelologists" are scholars of Scripture, Church history, and teachings about angels gathered over many centuries. There is a great deal of literature about these celestial creatures. Saint Thomas Aquinas is widely acknowledged as Christianity's most important angelologist. He wrote extensively about angels in his *Summa Theologica* and is known as the "angelic doctor." Aquinas often used truths about the angels — created spirits — to teach about human beings, creatures with bodies and souls. Thomas also believed that learning more about angels, God's splendid messengers, would help us to better understand our Creator.

Many brilliant and educated people have believed in angels and routinely called for their assistance. Saint Francis de Sales, pausing momentarily in the pulpit before he began his sermons, would always pray to the guardian angels of the congregation to soften their hearts to his words. [114]

May 10
Saint John of Ávila (1500–1569)

STAYING STRONG AND JOYFUL — LIKE THE ANGELS

Saint John of Ávila may not have seen angels, but he knew those who did. A diocesan priest and popular teacher, he was a friend and spiritual advisor to Saints Teresa of Ávila, Francis Borgia, and Ignatius Loyola. In their lives and in his, he saw that problems and persecution could serve God's purposes. As a young priest, he gave his inheritance to the poor, expecting to become a missionary in Mexico. Instead, his bishop asked him to serve in Spain. John didn't hesitate to denounce wrongdoing by rich and powerful people. So, he was falsely accused of heresy and imprisoned temporarily by the Inquisition. Like the angels, John remained joyful, knowing the message he was sharing was God's message.

"To those who suffer wounds in fighting his battles, God opens his arms in loving and tender friendship."

— Saint John of Ávila

Let John's reassuring observation encourage you when you are wounded in battles fought for God or his children. [115]

WHEN WE OVEREAT, ANGELS RETREAT

 When Pope Francis canonized Jesuit priest Peter Faber in 2013, few people had heard of this close companion of Jesuit founder Saint Ignatius Loyola. Yet, Loyola himself claimed that Faber was the expert in leading others in the Spiritual Exercises — prayers and spiritual practices developed by Loyola to help people grow closer to God. Father Faber believed that it was important for each person to be open to the inspiration and good influence of the angels. Some choices and bad habits left people vulnerable to evil spirits. For instance, Faber believed that eating or drinking too much harmed not only one's body, but also one's spirit. This holy Jesuit practiced moderation, and advised the same for others. [116]

"The devils enter uninvited when the house stands empty. For other kinds of guests you have to first open the door."

— Dag Hammarskjöld [117]

May 12

AN ANGEL'S QUIET VISIT

 Sometimes, angels appear in terrifying majesty. At other times, angels have come as ordinary people who disappeared once their mission was complete. Caesare Angelini (1886–1976), an Italian priest and spiritual writer, described a different sort of visit. At an abbey one evening, he was strangely moved by the abbot's closing prayer. "Come to this hearth, Lord," the abbot prayed, "and may your angels dwell here and keep us at peace." Back in his room, Angelini sensed that an angel was present — just for him. A deep joy filled him. Though there was no visible manifestation, he later wrote, it was greater than any joy he had ever felt. [118]

"The angel said to them, 'Do not be afraid; for behold, I proclaim to you good news of great joy that will be for all the people'" (Luke 2:10). Angels and joy come together.

KNOWING WHAT THE ANGELS KNOW

"All shall be well, and all shall be well, and all manner of thing shall be well." This popular quotation from Julian of Norwich appears on posters, bookmarks, and T-shirts. Julian was an English mystic and probably a Benedictine nun who became an "anchorite," living in simple quarters attached to a church. In 1373, Julian experienced heavenly revelations or visions that gave her a new understanding of God's love, the Incarnation, and redemption. "God loved us before he made us; and his love has never diminished and never shall," she wrote. And when we finally see his loving plan, she famously concluded, we'll understand that "all shall be well." [119]

Like the angels, Julian never tired of joyfully reflecting on God's goodness, patience, and mercy. Nothing else, she told the world, really mattered as much.

May 14

LIKE SHARDS OF LIGHT

 An Italian theologian and angelologist recommends that we think of angels as "shards of light." At a 2013 conference on angelic art in Rome, Father Renzo Lavatori said that angels "are a bit like sunlight that refracts on you through a crystal vase." A member of the Pontifical Theological Academy, Lavatori also admitted, though, that he doesn't really mind the beautiful winged angel images that are seen everywhere at Christmas. Angels, he believes, are more needed in our world than ever. Our increasingly secular and materialistic society, the priest explained, makes it easier for the devil to gain footholds and undermine faith. [120]

"Every breath of air and ray of light and heat, every beautiful prospect, is, as it were, the skirts of the (angel's) garments, the waving robes of those whose faces see God."

— Blessed John Henry Newman [121]

Saint Isidore the Farmer (1070–1130)

Angels Aid Us

Isidore seemed to be an ordinary farmworker near Madrid, Spain, but he was already considered a saint when he died. He and his wife, Maria, though poor themselves, were known for their generosity to others. As testament to Isidore's holiness, stories of miracles circulated. One time his fellow workers complained that Isidore was always late for work in the morning. When the owner of the farm went to investigate, he saw an angel plowing the field while Isidore was attending Mass. Another time, the master saw two angels working beside Isidore so that he accomplished three times as much as his fellow workers.

"Man has a longer road to travel than the angel, for man was set at a greater distance from God and must go in search of knowledge. But the angel, through his divinely shaped understanding, could attain directly to the divine without any seeking."

— Saint Thomas Aquinas, *Commentary on the Sentences of Peter Lombard*

May 16

The Angel's Announcement

 In the 1960s, Pope Saint John XXIII began the papal custom of praying the Angelus each Sunday at noon with the crowd assembled in St. Peter's Square. The ritual begins with a short address, the prayer, and a papal blessing, a tradition that subsequent popes, including Pope Francis, have honored. Pope John said that the angel's announcement to Mary "begins Christian history — and deserves to be honored by bells throughout the world three times a day." The Angelus is traditionally recited at dawn (6 a.m.), midday (noon) and night (6 p.m.) with bells ringing to signal the times. The prayer evolved from the monastic schedule of prayer that structured each day. By the sixteenth century, the current prayer had developed. The name of the prayer is the first words in the first verse: "The Angel" (in Latin, *Angelus*).[122] (See the appendix, page 377, for the complete prayer.)

> *The Angel of the Lord declared to Mary*
> *And she conceived by the Holy Spirit.*
> *Hail Mary....*

THE SERAPH OF THE EUCHARIST

Paschal, a Franciscan brother, was tending sheep on a rocky Spanish mountainside when he heard the consecration bell ring out from the monastery chapel. As he genuflected in prayer, an angel suddenly stood before him holding a chalice and Sacred Host, offering the Blessed Sacrament for his adoration. In 1897, Pope Leo XIII proclaimed Saint Paschal Baylon the "seraph of the Eucharist" because of his great devotion to the Eucharist. *Seraph* is the singular form of *seraphim*. Saint Gregory the Great's beautiful description of the seraphim (below) illustrates Saint Paschal's intense love of the Eucharist.

These choirs of holy spirits who because of their special closeness to the Creator burn with an incomparable love are called Seraphim. For since they are so close to God that no other spirits stand between them and God, the more closely they behold him the more ardently they love him. Their love is a flame: for the more vivid their perception of the glory of the Divinity, the more ardently they burn with his love. [123]

May 18

Angels in Perfect Harmony

 Musical angels first appeared in illuminated manuscripts in Italy and France around 1380. These richly illustrated parchments feature vivid ink drawings of singing angels. The concept of an angel singing developed from the Renaissance belief that divine messages would necessarily be conveyed in perfect harmony. By the early 1400s, angels were depicted not only singing but playing harps, lutes, and even pipe organs. Artists portrayed the harmony of angel voices and instruments as a symbol of God's creative harmony in the cosmos.

Praise the LORD from the heavens;
give praise in the heights.
Praise him, all you angels;
give praise, all you hosts....
Praise him with harp and lyre.
Praise him with flutes and strings.
Let everything that has breath
give praise to the Lord.
Hallelujah!
(Psalms 148:1–2, 150:3–4, 6)

PERSONALITY — ANGELS HAVE IT!

 It isn't as though some angels are extroverts while others are shy and reluctant to be caught in crowds — in heaven or on earth. Nonetheless, theologians assure us that angels have the necessary ingredients of personality. Angels can think. They exercise their wills. They can feel emotions like love and grief. Personality is an expression of individuality and doesn't really depend upon — or need — a physical body. Contemporary Catholic apologist and philosopher Peter Kreeft insists that angels are "more individually different than we are, for each angel is a distinct *species*." That means that because angels are nonmaterial in nature, the range of variation between individual angels is virtually unlimited. [124]

"Distinction and variety in the world is intended by the First Cause [God]. God brings things into existence in order that His goodness may be communicated and manifested. One solitary creature would not suffice. Therefore He makes creatures many and diverse, that what is wanting in one may be supplied by another."

— Saint Thomas Aquinas, *Summa Theologica*

May 20

THE WORK OF THE ANGELS

Meister Eckhart (1260–1329), a Dominican philosopher, theologian, and mystic, addressed a question about the status of our guardian angels in relation to heavenly angels. "A question arises regarding the angels who dwell with us, serve us, and protect us, whether their joys are equal to those of the angels in heaven, or whether they are diminished by the fact that they protect and serve us. No, they are certainly not; for the work of the angels is the will of God, and the will of God is the work of the angels; their service to us does not hinder their joy nor their working. If God told an angel to go to a tree and pluck caterpillars off it, the angel would be quite ready to do so, and it would be his happiness, if it were the will of God." [125]

Be firm, steadfast, always fully devoted to the work of the Lord, knowing that in the Lord your labor is not in vain. (1 Corinthians 15:58)

Your Angel Arrived Just in Time

 Saint Pio of Pietrelcina (1887–1968) referred to his guardian angel as the "companion of my childhood." From the age of five, he saw and talked to his angel and assumed that everyone else did the same. At times, he sent his angel to deliver messages for him. Sometimes, people who needed his help sent their guardian angels to Padre Pio. A humorous example is Father Eusebio, who was traveling to London by plane against Padre Pio's counsel. When they were flying over the Channel a violent storm put the airplane in danger. Amid the general terror, Father Eusebio prayed. Finally, in desperation, he sent his Guardian Angel to Padre Pio. When he returned to Pietrelcina, Padre Pio asked him, "Are you well? Everything ok?" Father Eusebio answered, "I thought I would die. But I sent my guardian angel to you." To which Padre Pio replied, "Fortunately, he arrived just in time." [126]

"Invoke your guardian angel that he illuminate you and will guide you. God has given him to you for this reason. Therefore use him!"

— Saint Pio of Pietrelcina

May 22
Saint Humility (1226–1310)

Powerful and Loving Angels

 Rosanna enjoyed a privileged childhood, married a nobleman at age fifteen, and had two sons who died in infancy. After her husband was nearly killed, they both entered a double monastery (one building for men and one for women) near Faenza, Italy. As a nun, Rosanna took the name Umiltà (in English, Humility). She founded a convent for nuns on Malta, where she served as abbess, and a second convent at Florence, Italy. Saint Humility loved to tell others about her two guardian angels. One was named Emmanuel, meaning "God in us." Humility described him as "a dazzling, fiery being with six wings." The other was Sapiel, meaning "Wisdom of God." "She" was "radiant, dressed in fine garments and precious jewels." Saint Humility said that Sapiel filled her heart with great joy. [127]

"In everyone you have some very powerful yet very loving friends because you have in them (or at least with them or against them) their own good guardian angels. Let your thoughts, then, be all sweetness, tenderness, and peace."

— Blessed Charles de Foucauld (1858–1916) [128]

ANGELS TO LIGHT THE WAY

 One of the Desert Fathers, Abba John the Dwarf, told the story of a holy man. Everyone in the city held him in high esteem, though he lived a secluded life. One time an old man in the city was dying and his final request was to embrace and pay respect to the holy man. When he was summoned, the holy man was reluctant to go because he did not want people to notice and run after him. So he decided to go in the evening to escape attention. But God sent two angels with lamps to give him light. Then the whole city came out to see his glory. In this we see what the Gospel teaches: "He who humbles himself will be exalted" (Luke 14:11). [129]

Your word, O LORD, is a lamp for my feet, a light for my path. (Psalm 119:105)

Show me your way, and I will see clearly; lead me and I will follow.

May 24

Saint David I of Scotland (1080–1153)

ON THE SIDE OF THE ANGELS

 As seventy-three-year-old King David of Scotland prepared to meet God, he recited the Psalms, gratefully received the Eucharist, and was anointed. He had been king for almost thirty years and had some regrets about the way he had used his power. He was sorry for the brutal invasion of England he ordered to try to win the crown for his niece Matilda. Largely, however, David's reign was a blessing for his people and the Church. He was charitable to the poor and treated his subjects with respect. David established new dioceses for the Church and built many monasteries. Like his Old Testament namesake, King David wanted to live "on the side of the angels." [130]

And he will send out his angels with a trumpet blast, and they will gather his elect from the four winds, from one end of the heavens to the other. (Matthew 24:31)

Built by an Angel?

In 1873, the Sisters of Loretto in Santa Fe, New Mexico, were happy with their new church until they discovered something missing. There was no stairway to the choir loft — and no way to put one in. The sisters began praying to Saint Joseph the Carpenter to send help. Then, a mysterious gray-haired man with a donkey and tool chest arrived looking for work. Within several months, he had designed and built an ingenious spiral staircase that makes two complete 360-degree turns. It is constructed with pegs and made with wood not native to New Mexico. The carpenter disappeared without notice and without being paid. Nobody could ask him how the staircase stood without a supporting center pole. [131]

"If we could perceive our angels for just a single day, this world would never be the same again, nor would it ever wish to be."

— Anonymous

May 26
Saint Philip Neri (1515–1595)

A Comedian's Angels

 If guardian angels laugh, Philip Neri's must have chuckled often during his eighty years. Even as a boy in Florence, Italy, "Pippo" loved outrageous pranks and jokes. Once, when he jumped onto a loaded donkey, it stumbled and rolled over on him. Philip wasn't injured but stopped trying to be so funny for a while. Someone might get hurt, and he was already overworking his poor angel! Later, he matured, developed a deep prayer life, and became a priest. In Rome, Father Philip was devoted to the poor and to spiritual direction for young people. He particularly promoted humility but always did it with humor. He'd appear in ridiculous clothing with his beard half-shaved off to make his point: Don't take yourselves too seriously! Philip founded the Congregation of the Oratory to sponsor centers for prayer and study of the faith.

On Saint Philip Neri's door hung a sign: "The House of Christian Mirth." Do laughter and humor draw you further into God's kingdom?

"Angles" and Angels

Known as the "Apostle to the English," Saint Augustine of Canterbury had never thought of going to England as a missionary. Born in Rome, Augustine was happy as a Benedictine monk and abbot. But years earlier, as a popular legend goes, Pope Gregory saw some tall, blonde men from Britain being sold as slaves in Rome. Something in their eyes touched Gregory. Learning that these pagans were "Angles," Gregory said their name, sounding like the word "Angels," was fitting. "They have angel faces," he explained. With faith in Christ, he believed, they would become "co-heirs with the angels in heaven." When the time was right, Pope Gregory ordained Augustine a bishop and sent him with forty monks to evangelize England. [132]

"All who live justly are 'angels' of God and hence are called confessors or martyrs; for one who bears witness to, and confesses, the truth of God is his messenger, i.e., his 'angel.'"

— Saint Anselm of Canterbury

May 28

Visions of an Angel Army

 One of the more interesting Old Testament accounts of angel visions is in 2 Kings 6. About eight centuries before Christ, a massive Aramean army had surrounded Dothan and the prophet Elisha. The king of Aram wanted to kill Elisha, who had succeeded Elijah as Israel's prophet. When Elisha's servant saw the soldiers and chariots surrounding Dothan, he was terrified. "What shall we do, my lord?" he moaned. "Do not be afraid," Elisha reassured him. "Our side outnumbers theirs." Suddenly, the servant's eyes were opened. Now he saw that fiery chariots with angelic warriors covered the whole mountainside. God planned to rescue Israel and his prophet.

Do you ever feel outnumbered, defeated before you begin? Remember, God's rescuing angels aren't just for prophets. They can gather to defend you, as well.

May 29

A PHILOSOPHER HOOKED ON ANGELS

 Although Mortimer Adler (1902–2001), an American philosopher and educator, didn't become a Christian until very late in life, nothing had ever interested him more than theology. Born to nonpracticing Jews, Adler discovered Saint Thomas Aquinas and Thomistic philosophy as a student. Adler also identified with Saint Thomas's fascination with angels. Over the years, he gave several lectures about the angels. They were so well attended that he decided to write a book about angels. *The Angels and Us* was published by a secular publisher in 1982. According to Adler, angels are "minds without bodies.... They are not merely forms of extraterrestrial intelligence. They are forms of extra-cosmic intelligence." [133]

Realizing that angels are "minds without bodies" transfixed a brilliant philosopher. What fascinates you most about the angels?

May 30

Saint Joan of Arc (1412–1431)

GUIDED BY SAINT MICHAEL

 A prayerful French peasant girl was experiencing heavenly visions and hearing the voices of saints at the age of twelve. Saint Michael the Archangel began instructing Joan about God's plans for her and France, which was under siege by England. In 1428, Joan took up arms and swiftly led French soldiers to victories and helped the royal heir gain his crown. Charles VII became king, but soon betrayed her. When Joan was captured, she was tried by the Church for heresy and witchcraft. She admitted that heavenly voices guided her and that she had seen angels. Politics blinded her judges. Whispering the name of Jesus, the nineteen-year-old was burned at the stake but later was exonerated and honored as the patron saint of France.

"I saw them with my bodily eyes as clearly as I see you. And when they departed, I used to weep and wish they would take me with them."

— Saint Joan of Arc, when asked about her visions of saints and Saint Michael the Archangel [134]

The Blessing of an Angel

Only Luke's Gospel shares the touching story of Mary's visit to her elder cousin, Elizabeth, who was also with child. Luke says that "when Elizabeth heard Mary's greeting, the infant leaped in her womb" (Luke 2:41). Then, filled with the Holy Spirit, Elizabeth joyfully greeted Mary as the mother of the Savior. Two holy women with unborn children whose births had been announced by an archangel! One child was the Son of God. The other would become the Messiah's prophet. In his mother's womb, John was blessed with the recognition of Jesus when Mary approached: "Rejoice! The Lord is near!"

The Hail Mary begins with the greeting of the Archangel Gabriel and continues with the words of Mary's cousin, Elizabeth. "Hail Mary, full of grace, the Lord is with you. Blessed are you among women and blessed is the fruit of your womb, Jesus." Pray the Hail Mary today to honor Mary as Gabriel and Elizabeth did.

June 1

Saint Justin, Martyr (c. 100–165)

ANGELS RESEMBLE CHRIST

 As a very young man, Saint Justin searched widely for the truth. When he found it in the Scriptures and the Christian faith, he defended it to the death. On trial for his life, Justin told the judge that he would not give up truth for falsehood. "We believe in the true God," he said. "We venerate, we adore, we honor in spirit and truth His Son who came forth from Him … and the host of other good Angels who escort him and who resemble him." [135] Justin's statement confirms that angels were honored very early in Christian tradition.

Saint Augustine expressed the proper Christian attitude toward the angels: "We honor them out of charity, not out of servitude." That is, we serve God and we honor and venerate his angels. [136]

ANGELS IN ART

 The Saint Peter we honor today was a Roman imprisoned because of his Christian faith. While there, he taught the jailer about Jesus and asked Marcellinus, a priest, to baptize the jailer and his family. When the governor found out what happened, he had both Peter and Marcellinus beheaded. The catacomb where they were buried is now named after them. One of the earliest pictures of the Annunciation is a fresco on the wall of the Roman Catacomb of Saints Peter and Marcellinus. Painted shortly after A.D. 100, the Archangel Gabriel appears as a young man dressed in white, but he has no wings. Artists generally began to depict angels with wings in the fourth century.

Whatever art does to depict the angel it does to convey some truth about him. It takes metaphorical liberties in order to do him justice. It shows him in human form ... because we cannot otherwise understand him; a human body reminds us of our likeness to him. [137]

June 3

A Favorite Feast of the Angels

 The Feast of the Most Holy Body and Blood of Christ (*Corpus Christi*) has ancient roots. In the United States, it falls on the Sunday after Trinity Sunday — typically in June. Corpus Christi celebrates Christ's institution of the Eucharist at the Last Supper. Followers of Jesus have always celebrated the Eucharistic meal because he commanded it: "Do this in memory of me." For centuries, long Corpus Christi processions made their way through cities and towns, led by priests carrying the sacred host. Saint Mechtild, a medieval mystic, said that three thousand angels from the choir of thrones worship at every tabernacle where the Blessed Sacrament is reserved.

"The sanctuary and the space around the altar are filled with celestial powers who are there to honor the one present on the altar."

— Saint John Chrysostom

THE BREAD OF ANGELS

In 1264, Saint Thomas Aquinas composed a complete liturgy for the newly created Feast of Corpus Christi. Six hundred years later, Cesar Franck set a verse of one of his hymns to music for solo tenor, organ, cello, bass, and harp. It begins with the words *Panis Angelicus* (Latin for "Bread of Angels") from Psalm 78. The lyrics timelessly express Church teaching on the Eucharist and its central importance to the Body of Christ. The hymn reminds us that the Eucharist was made not for angels, but for men. Only we have the privilege of this close Communion with Jesus.

> "The Bread of Angels becomes the bread of men
> The Living Bread from Heaven ends all symbols
> Oh, wondrous gift!
> The body of the Lord will nourish
> The poor and humble servant."

Gracious God, you opened the heavens and rained down manna to feed your hungry people in the desert (see Psalm 78:23–25). Thank you for the Bread of Angels that nourishes and strengthens us, your pilgrim people, as we journey, with the guidance and protection of your holy angels, to your heavenly Kingdom.

June 5

ANGELS SING PRAISE

 When we come together to celebrate the Eucharist, unseen angels add their praise of God to our human voices. The "*Sanctus*" prayer sung at Mass is the first part of the hymn of the Seraphim, according to Isaiah 6:3 and Revelation 4:8. *"Holy, holy, holy Lord God of hosts (of angels). Heaven and earth are full of your glory."* In the Roman rite, the Preface to the Eucharistic Prayer joins our voices with the choirs of angels in their unending hymn of praise. Though the wording varies, each Preface expresses the same fundamental concept.

"And so, with Angels and Archangels,
with Thrones and Dominions,
with all the hosts and Powers of heaven,
we sing the hymn of your glory,
as without end we acclaim:
Holy, Holy, Holy Lord God of hosts…."

— Preface I for Sundays in Ordinary Time

THE PURITY OF THE ANGELS

Saint Norbert belonged to a noble German family and enjoyed a carefree youth. A serious brush with death, however, made Norbert question his choices, and he gave up his self-centered lifestyle to help others. He founded a religious community of priests, the Canons Regular of Prémontré, often simply called the Norbertines. Norbert gave them habits of white wool as a sign of the purity of the angels and a reminder to live in God's presence and do his will as the angels do. The white habits were also a pledge to be witnesses to the resurrection of Christ since the Easter angels had dressed in white. The Norbertines ministered to families living near their abbeys and provided shelter and care for the sick and travelers. [138]

Consider wearing white today as a reminder of the joy of the Resurrection and your share in Christ's new life through Baptism.

June 7

Angels in the Kitchen

 A huge, mid-seventeenth century painting titled *The Miracle of San Diego* by the Spanish painter Bartolomé Murillo depicts angels in a monastery kitchen. Two large angels dominate the scene, one carrying a water jug. A third angel tends a huge copper pot on the stove, while another sets the dining table. Meanwhile, San Diego floats in the air in a kneeling position, eyes closed, absorbed in prayer. Bystanders include courtiers and Franciscan brothers. The painting is based on a story about a monk who was so occupied with his prayer that the angels did his work. It may have been San Diego de Alcalá who was canonized in 1588, the same San Diego for whom the California mission and city were named. [139]

Here is something we can all relate to: too much work in the kitchen (or elsewhere!), not enough time to get everything done, wishing we had more time for prayer, needing more help. Barring a miracle, we may ask our guardian angels for guidance in scheduling our time and the wisdom to ask for help when we need it.

ANGELS IN THE OUTFIELD

 When their baseball teams are losing, some fans find summer "comfort" in baseball movies like *Angels in the Outfield*. The 1994 version offered a star-studded cast: Danny Glover, Tony Danza, Christopher Lloyd, Joseph Gordon-Levitt, and Matthew McConaughey. Though it certainly didn't pretend to share theological truths about angels, the movie's message was solid. God hears prayers. Angels help us — though not necessarily in the outfield. The film tells the story of a foster kid (Roger) and his stubborn love of the Anaheim Angels, the major league's worst team. Roger's real concern, however, is getting his broken family reunited. When his deadbeat father promises to help if the Angels make it to the World Series, Roger starts praying. An angel named Al appears in the outfield, and the Anaheim Angels start winning.

> *"God, if there is a God … if you're a man or a woman … if you're listening. I'd really, really like a family. My dad says that will only happen if the Angels win the pennant. The baseball team, I mean. So, maybe you can help them win a little. Amen."*

> — Roger Bomman's Prayer in *Angels in the Outfield*

June 9

Saint Ephrem (c. 303–373)

AN ANGEL'S ADMONITION

 A deacon in what is present-day Turkey, Ephrem began composing beautiful Christian hymns to combat heresies that were spreading through songs. Ephrem's music shared dogmas of the faith, including the teaching that Jesus really rose from the dead. Through Ephrem's work, the Church learned that music is a wonderful teacher! When Ephrem's city, Nisiblis, fell to pagan Persians, he fled to Edessa. He wanted to become a hermit and live a quiet life of prayer in the desert. But an angel appeared to Ephrem, reminding him of Christ's warning about hiding our lights under bushels. Ephrem relented. He became the director of a Christian school and continued writing treasured homilies, Scripture commentaries, and hymns.

What are your gifts that could be shared with the Church or for others? Don't ignore an angel who could soon come to guide you.

June 10

BRIAN'S ANGEL

 A fog of sadness can descend on those who grieve. No light or happiness penetrates it. That's how Zena felt when her eleven-year-old nephew Brian was killed. She had helped to raise Brian and missed him terribly. Zena's fog began lifting at Mass one Sunday. A boy about Brian's age politely let her move past him into the pew where she usually sat. He sang the Mass hymns and recited responses. When the Our Father was recited, he smiled warmly, and offered his hand. Great peace unexpectedly filled Zena. However, after Communion, he disappeared. Zena asked several parishioners if they saw him leave. "There was no boy in your pew," they told her. "You were alone." [140]

God, you do send your angels of consolation when we are grieving. Thank you for the consolation, the light, and the peace that these wonderful messengers bring.

June 11

Saint Barnabas, Apostle (died 61)

ANGEL FOR THE JOURNEY

 Though he wasn't one of the Twelve Apostles, Barnabas is often called an Apostle. He may have been one of the seventy-two disciples Jesus sent out to the villages he planned to visit (Luke 10:1–11). The Acts of the Apostles reports that Barnabas was a traveling companion of Saint Paul's until a disagreement sent them different ways. Some say that Barnabas was a wealthy man sent to Jerusalem as a youth to study with Gamaliel, Paul's teacher. If so, Barnabas knew Scripture well and could recite many Psalms by heart. Until the end of his life and journeys, this "apostle" shared the Good News, trusting the angels to protect and guide him.

The angel of the LORD encamps around those who fear him, and he saves them. (Psalm 34:8)

Recite this line from the Psalms when you are afraid or need protection. Say it aloud!

THE HEART OF GOD

 The feast of the Most Sacred Heart of Jesus is associated with the visions of Saint Margaret Mary Alacoque (1647–1690), a French Visitation nun. It falls on a Friday, nineteen days after Pentecost. When Jesus appeared to Saint Margaret Mary before the Blessed Sacrament, he said he wanted devotion to his sacred heart because sin and indifference wound him. But, the feast and images of the Sacred Heart of Jesus are popular because people see the heart's importance. The heart is the core or center of a person. As the angels know, the bottomless heart of God is full of love. The world works best when our hearts are like God's.

"You have made us for yourself, O Lord, and our hearts are restless until they find their rest in you."

— Saint Augustine of Hippo, *Confessions*

Reflect today on Saint Augustine's great prayer. Finding God is a homecoming for the heart.

June 13

Saint Anthony of Padua (1195–1231)

THE ANGEL EXPRESS

 Anthony was in Padua, Italy, when he received the news that his father, who lived in his native Portugal, was accused of murder and was to be executed the following day. Anthony set off for Portugal immediately but was hardly underway when an angel transported him through the air to Lisbon. There, Anthony petitioned the judge, who refused to change the sentence. Anthony went to the grave of the murdered man, commanded him to rise, presented him in court, and asked him if it was his father who had killed him. The risen man replied, "No, it was not he." The judge ordered Anthony to ask the man who killed him. But Anthony protested. "I have come here to rescue the innocent, not to bring death to a guilty man," he said. His father released, Anthony was carried back to Padua by the angel. [141]

Saint Anthony's life story is studded with miracles and wonders, but that is not what made him a saint. Anthony was a man of great sanctity and wisdom, and a zealous preacher who brought sinners, heretics, and lukewarm Catholics back to God and the Church. He used the numerous gifts God gave him for the good of others. What gift could you share today?

June 14

Praying in the Presence of Angels

 Saint Jane Frances de Chantal was a wife, mother, widow, and founder of a religious community of women. Throughout her life she depended on God, and along the way she learned how to pray like the angels. We can all learn from her.

With God there is no need for long speeches. In heaven the angels utter no other word than this: "holy." This is their entire prayer, and in paradise they are occupied with this single word as an act of homage to the single Word of God who lives eternally. [142]

Let us be sure that we understand what an honor it is to spend time in prayer, as much time as we wish, as intimately as we wish. The man who wins an hour-long audience from his prince considers himself lucky. Our God, before whom the kings of the earth are less than a spark in the full blaze of the sun and less than a little worm in the presence of the highest angels, is eager to hear us no matter what hour of the day or night. [143]

> *"Angels are speaking to all of us … some of us are only listening better."*

— Anonymous

June 15

An Angel at the Door

 One day Abba Isaac of Thebes went to visit a monastery. He saw a brother committing a sin and judged him harshly. When Isaac returned to his home in the desert, an angel of the Lord was blocking the door and refused to let him go in. Abba Isaac was perplexed. "What is the matter?" he demanded. The angel replied, "God has sent me to ask you how you want to punish the guilty brother whom you have condemned." Abba Isaac understood and immediately repented. "I have sinned. Forgive me." Then the angel said, "You may go in; God has forgiven you. But from now on, be careful not to judge someone before God has done so." [144]

For we must all appear before the judgment seat of Christ, so that each one may receive recompense, according to what he did in the body, whether good or evil. Therefore, aspire to please him. (2 Corinthians 5:10, 9)

LIFTED UP BY ANGELS

 Through the Internet, BarbE shared her incredible rescue by God's powerful angels. "One afternoon I had just dropped a passenger off in front of her house. All of a sudden my car was going backwards down this hilly street with great speed. My brakes didn't work and slamming the car into park didn't stop it either! Through the panic I thought about picking a crash site at the foot of the hill. Then I remembered that I had seen a group of kids playing in the street on my way up earlier! My only choice was to try to steer the car toward a small shed on the opposite side of the street. Now traveling at almost 50 miles an hour, I cranked the wheel, closed my eyes, and braced for impact. Instead, my car and I were LIFTED UP and set back down safely in the correct lane. It must have been a literal BAND OF ANGELS! Many neighbors rushed over in disbelief at what they had seen."

Like many of us, BarbE said that she wanted to believe in angels (guardian or otherwise), but had remained skeptical. "It seemed completely fathomable that other people may be blessed by some supernatural power," she said, "but when it came to ME personally; that was another story! What, after all, had I ever done to deserve such a thing?" [145]

June 17

DON'T WORSHIP ANGELS

 Angels are such shining and glorious creatures that people have sometimes tried to worship them. Though angels are from heaven and have astounding power, they are still created by God — like us. In Revelation, the Bible's last book, the author says that he too felt compelled to adore a magnificent angel. "I fell at his feet to worship him," John wrote. "But he said to me, 'Don't! I am a fellow servant of yours and of your brothers who bear witness to Jesus. Worship God'" (Revelation 19:10). In the first Christian centuries, polytheistic religions vied for the souls of Christians. Church Fathers reminded them to revere angels but to worship only God. [146]

In a world where there are many false gods, reflect on a lesson taught by the mighty angels of the Lord: only the Creator is worthy of our worship. Are you worshipping anything or anyone that angels would not?

June 18

Banishing Fallen Angels

 In 2014, Pope Francis welcomed the International Association of Exorcists to Rome. Exorcists, the pope told the media, are specially trained priests who help free people from the control of devils — fallen angels. Around the world, every Catholic diocese is required to have its own exorcist. A spokesman for the International Association of Exorcists said that increased involvement in Satanic worship and the occult is expanding the need for exorcists. In the Rite of Exorcism, the exorcist blesses everyone with holy water, recites prayers, including the Litany of Saints and the Lord's Prayer. Then, he prays to cast out any evil spirits in the name of Jesus Christ. The afflicted person senses new spiritual freedom and joy. [147]

Saint Michael the Archangel, support and strengthen all those who work to free people from the control of evil and the fallen angels. Bless all priests and all those who pray for healing from many kinds of evil.

June 19

ANGELS IN THE TREE

 In 1767 in London, when he was ten, English artist, poet, and engraver William Blake saw angels in a tree near his home. Their bright wings "bespangled every bough like stars," he wrote. A lifetime of encounters with angels and other heavenly visitors followed. Once, he saw angels moving through a hayfield while men, oblivious to the angels, gathered the hay. He talked with the Archangel Gabriel and the Virgin Mary as well. A vision of his dead brother inspired Blake to invent a technique that revolutionized engraving. Blake's profoundly beautiful engravings of angels and Biblical subjects continue to interest and inspire the world. [148]

"When the sun rises, do you not see a round disc of fire somewhat like a guinea! Oh! no, no! I see an innumerable company of the heavenly host crying 'Holy, holy, holy is the Lord God Almighty!'" [149]

— William Blake

Few people have the angelic encounters that inspired William Blake. But, could it be that angels inspire us more than we know or can imagine?

ANGELS ON DIPLOMATIC MISSION

 In Europe, during the 1930s, Pope Pius XI (1857–1939) confronted Europe's dictators — Stalin, Hitler, and Mussolini. They were pushing the world into World War II, but dealing with such ruthless men was dangerous for the Church and Catholics in their countries. Pope Pius said that he never made a statement or decision without praying for specific guidance from his guardian angel. He began that practice as a young man. The pope shared another spiritual strategy with Vatican diplomats. Whenever he had a conflict with someone, he asked his guardian angel to consult with his counterpart's angel. "Once the two angels establish an understanding," Pope Pius explained, "the Pope's conversation with his visitor is much easier." [150]

"The angels take great pleasure in helping us with our enterprises, when they are in accordance with God's will."

— Saint John Vianney

Try it! Enlist your guardian angel to collaborate with the angels of others when conflicts or problems emerge.

June 21

THE ANGELIC ORDER OF PRINCIPALITIES

 Scripture scholars have concluded that there is a division or hierarchy of labor among angels. Since the sixth century, Church teachers have maintained that this angel ordering is part of God's perfect plan of creation. There are three angel hierarchies with three orders within each hierarchy. While angels of the first hierarchy (seraphim, cherubim, and thrones) are closest to God, the angels of the third hierarchy intersect with the created world and with us. Principalities are the highest order of angels in this third hierarchy. Archangels are special messengers, and angels are our individual guardians. Principalities are assigned to watch over and guide nations, kingdoms, cities, and perhaps larger communities, such as parishes or religious communities. [151]

God, your plan for Creation is loving and perfect. Help us to hear and follow the brilliant spirits you send to guide us, as individuals and as members of many communities.

RECEIVE CHRIST AND HIS ANGELS

Paulinus, a successful lawyer and governor, gave away his considerable wealth and possessions, and became a monk and bishop. Paulinus offered advice on the use of wealth and secular power to Pammachius, a Roman senator. It was based on faith and his personal experience. "Let us also, then, open our homes to our brothers, whether … we fear the danger of rejecting an angel when we repulse men, or whether we hope to deserve to have angels as our guests as we assist the passage of every stranger with ready kindness. For when our father Abraham entertained strangers, he received Christ the Lord and His angels; in his hospitable tent he saw that day … the Savior revealed in his presence." [152]

"Sell your belongings and give alms. Provide money bags for yourselves that do not wear out, an inexhaustible treasure in heaven that no thief can reach or moth destroy. For where you treasure is, there also your heart will be." (Luke 12:33–34)

June 23

A Guardian Angel's Job

 Pictures of guardian angels guiding children across a bridge or away from a cliff were once found in many Catholic homes and classrooms. These pictures illustrated Catholic teaching — but only part of it. "From infancy to death human life is surrounded by their watchful care and intercession," *the Catechism of the Catholic Church* says of angels (CCC, 336). But, it would be a mistake to think that angels are sent by God to protect us only from physical harm. The larger concern of these spirits is to protect us from spiritual harm. That is their true assignment. Day by day, throughout our lives, they guide us toward life — eternal life with God.

"Angel of God, my Guardian dear, to whom God's love commits me here, ever this day, be at my side, to light to guard, to rule, and guide. Amen."

— The Guardian Angel Prayer

May Angels Bring You into Paradise

In Paradisum is the final antiphon of the traditional Latin funeral Mass, sung as the procession leaves the church for the burial. The English translation of this beautiful prayer asks:

May angels guide you and bring you into paradise
and may all the martyrs come forth to welcome you home
and may they lead you into the holy city, Jerusalem.
May the angel chorus sing to welcome you,
and like Lazarus, forgotten and poor,
you shall have everlasting rest.

The reference in the hymn comes from the Parable of the Rich Man and Lazarus, a beggar at his gate. "When the poor man died, he was carried away by angels to the bosom of Abraham. The rich man also died and was buried, and from the netherworld, he raised his eyes and saw Abraham far off and Lazarus at his side." Take a minute to read the parable in Luke 16:19–31.

June 25

TALKING WITH ANGELS

 A true story about young people consoled by angels dates from World War II. The first angelic conversation took place on this date, June 25, 1943. Throughout the next seventeen months, four Hungarian friends engaged in a series of conversations with their angels. Once they received instructions to save one hundred Jews from Nazi arrest and execution. As young professionals, they faced uncertainty and peril with courage and hope as their country was drawn into war. Their angels led them to be as God created them. One of the women, Gitta, heard her angel say, "God created you after my image." Gitta was touched deeply by that idea, thinking, "I exist in the image of an angel!" It helped her to persevere even as her three Jewish friends were arrested. Two friends, Hanna and Lili, died in a Nazi concentration camp. Many years later, Gitta wrote a book, *Talking with Angels*, about their incredible experiences. [153]

"Your holy Angel is tender, gentle and mild," the Shepherd Hermas wrote in the second century. "When he takes possession of your heart, he speaks of justice, modesty, and benignity, of true love and piety. When such things make themselves felt in your heart, know that your holy Angel is with you." [154]

AN ANGEL'S DONKEY JOKE

During the Spanish Civil War (1936–1939), a ruthless persecution of the Church resulted in the murder of more than 6,800 priests and the destruction of many churches in Spain. Though many priests he knew had been assassinated, Father Josemaría Escrivá, Spanish founder of Opus Dei, trusted in God. One day in Madrid, an armed man preparing to shoot him boldly confronted Escrivá. As Escrivá began to pray, another man appeared and jumped between him and his would-be assassin. The attacker then ran! The mysterious protector approached the shaken priest, smiled, and whispered, "Mangy donkey, mangy donkey!" Then, he vanished. Escrivá laughed. His angel had rescued him! "Mangy donkey!" That's what he called himself — but only in private conversations with his confessor! [155]

"You are amazed that your guardian angel has done you such obvious favors. And you should not be amazed. That's why Our Lord has placed him beside you."

— Saint Josemaría Escrivá, *The Way*, 565

June 27
Saint Cyril of Alexandria (378–444)

Banquet of the Angels

 Cyril, bishop of Alexandria, prescribed the Eucharist as a remedy for sin. "If the poison of pride is swelling up in you, turn to the Eucharist; and that Bread, Which is your God humbling and disguising Himself, will teach you humility. If the fever of selfish greed rages in you, feed on this Bread; and you will learn generosity. If the cold wind of coveting withers you, hasten to the Bread of Angels; and charity will come to blossom in your heart. If you feel the itch of intemperance, nourish yourself with the Flesh and Blood of Christ, Who practiced heroic self-control during His earthly life; and you will become temperate. If you are lazy and sluggish about spiritual things, strengthen yourself with this heavenly Food; and you will grow fervent. Lastly, if you feel scorched by the fever of impurity, go to the banquet of the Angels; and the spotless Flesh of Christ will make you pure and chaste." [156]

Grain from heaven he gave them. Man ate the bread of the angels; food he sent in abundance…. They ate and were well filled; he gave them what they had craved. (Psalm 78:24–25, 29)

ANGELS WERE MADE BY GOD

Saint Irenaeus explained and defended Christian beliefs that were challenged by the popular teachings of Gnosticism. Gnostics, for example, held that an evil god accidentally created the material world. Irenaeus disagreed, saying that the one God alone formed all things in the world by his own goodness. "It was not angels who made us, neither had angels power to make an image of God, nor anyone else, except the Word of the Lord, nor any Power remotely distant from the Father of all things. For God did not stand in need of these [beings], in order to accomplish what He had Himself determined beforehand ... as if he did not possess his own hands. Taking from Himself the substance [he formed] the creatures, and the pattern of things made, and all the adornments in the world." [157]

"The glory of God is man fully alive" is a popular and appealing quote of Saint Irenaeus. Pope Saint John Paul II said that Irenaeus upheld the true value of man, which was denied by the Gnostics. The intrinsic dignity of man allows him to freely orient himself to God. Thus, we understand Irenaeus's meaning better if we say: The glory of God is man fully alive and turned toward God. [158]

June 29

Saints Peter and Paul, Apostles (First Century)

PILLARS OF THE CHURCH

 Saint Peter was crucified in Rome in 64, while Saint Paul, a Roman citizen, was beheaded there in 67. The joint celebration of these great apostles dates from the third century. In some ways, it's surprising that the Church honors them together. There were plenty of differences between the two men. Peter was one of the twelve Apostles. Jesus clearly selected this rough, impetuous but loyal fisherman to lead his Church. Paul was brilliant and well educated, but sometimes difficult to deal with. He persecuted Christians and never knew Jesus during his lifetime. But God saw how much alike Peter and Paul were. They loved Jesus completely. According to the Acts of the Apostles, God often sent his angels to rescue and support Peter and Paul.

"And so we celebrate this day made holy for us by the apostles' blood. Let us embrace what they believed, their life, their labors, their sufferings, their preaching and their confession of faith."

— From a sermon given by Saint Augustine of Hippo, Feast of Saints Peter and Paul, A.D. 395 [159]

ANGELS FOR THOSE FACING DEATH

When Jesus prayed in the Garden of Gethsemane after the Last Supper, overwhelmed with fear at his approaching death, Luke's Gospel says that an angel appeared to strengthen him (Luke 22:43). None of us dies alone. The angels who accompany us throughout our lives are with us at the moment of death, to help and guide us, no matter what the circumstances. In A.D. 64, Emperor Nero ordered the widespread execution of Christians. According to the Roman historian Tacitus, some Christians were burned alive as human torches. Others were torn apart and killed by wild animals. Others were crucified. In 1969, the Church calendar was revised and incorporated today's feast to honor the courageous Christian martyrs of Rome.

God, please send your angels to comfort and strengthen people of faith who are facing persecution, torture, and martyrdom around the world. Let me remember them in my prayers.

July 1

LOS ANGELES

 Los Angeles is the very short name for a huge city with a long history. In July 1769, Father Juan Crespi, a Franciscan priest accompanying the first European land expedition through California, described in his journal a beautiful river that he named *Nuestra Señora de los Angeles de la Porciúncula.* The name honored a fresco of the Virgin Mary surrounded by angels that decorated a little chapel near Assisi. This chapel, where Saint Francis often prayed, was known as Our Lady of the Angels at the Little Portion. In September 1781, Spanish Governor de Neve recorded a new settlement along that river, *El Pueblo de la Reina de Los Angeles,* The Town of the Queen of the Angels. There are many versions of this story, and variations of the official name of the city. The one constant is Los Angeles — the Angels. [160]

Your guardian angel is a constant in your life, always ready to come to your aid. It is the will of God, both infinite in scope and focused precisely on his love for you. The angels simply know and obey God's will.

July 2

Our Lady of the Angels

 Today, the tiny chapel of Our Lady of the Angels at the Little Portion is enclosed within the Basilica of Santa Maria degli Angeli in Italy. It is called the Porciuncula because it was situated on a very small portion of land, in Italian, a "porciuncula." This little chapel is where Francis gathered his first followers and where he chose to die. It is one of the churches he repaired. While praying for direction at the Church at San Damiano nearby, Jesus spoke to him from the large Byzantine cross above the altar. "Francis, rebuild my house, which you can see has fallen into ruins." Francis sold the fine fabric that his father, a cloth merchant, had stored and used the money to begin repairs. In time, Francis understood that Jesus wanted him to repair the spiritual wounds and divisions of the Church. [161]

"The little portion" is a perfect image for Saint Francis himself. It speaks of humility and poverty, both values that Francis honored and embraced. He sold his possessions to care for the sick. He begged for food and slept on a stony ledge in the mountainside. When he was dying, he told his brothers to place him naked on the bare earth. Extreme, yes, but aren't we sometimes extreme in accumulating material possessions? Today, let go of a little portion and give a larger portion to Christ.

July 3

Saint Thomas the Apostle (First Century)

A FLIGHT OF ANGELS

 Tradition says that Saint Thomas sailed to India in A.D. 52 to spread the Christian faith and landed in modern day Kerala where there was an established Jewish community. But Thomas is best known for his need to see and touch the wounds of Jesus before he believed in the Resurrection. A story in the apocryphal literature of the early Church counterbalances the Gospel account of doubting Thomas. It says that the apostles were transported by angels to Jerusalem to witness the death of Mary, Mother of God — all except Thomas, who was left in India. After Mary's burial, however, Thomas was carried by angels to her tomb where he alone witnessed her bodily assumption into heaven and received the sash she dropped to him. The other apostles did not believe Thomas until they saw for themselves the empty tomb and Mary's sash. [162]

Jesus said to Thomas, "Put your finger here and see my hands, and bring your hand and put it into my side, and do not be unbelieving, but believe" (John 20:27). Thomas professed his faith: "My Lord and my God!" (John 20:28). Then Jesus said something that should give us hope. "Blessed are those who have not seen and have believed" (John 20:29). "I do believe. Help my unbelief!" (Mark 9:24).

ANGELIC PEACEMAKER

It seems Elizabeth was always a peacemaker. It's said that her father, the king of Portugal, and her grandfather reconciled over the joy of her birth. As a young wife, Elizabeth resolved a serious dispute over estate properties between her husband and his brother. When her son led a rebellion against his father, the king, and they were about to engage in battle, Elizabeth charged on horseback onto the battlefield between the two armies. She implored them to declare a truce. No wonder she was called an Angel of Peace! When the king was near death, he made peace with Elizabeth, who then facilitated a reunion between him and their son. One of her last acts was to calm threats of war between her son, the king of Portugal, and his son-in-law, the king of Castile.

On the Fourth of July we celebrate our nation's peace and freedom. Consider the observation of James Madison, one of America's Founding Fathers and the Father of the Constitution: "If men were angels, no government would be necessary. If angels were to govern men, neither external nor internal controls on government would be necessary." [163]

July 5
Saint Anthony Zaccaria (1502–1539)

ANGELS ADORE THE EUCHARIST

 As a young man in Italy, Anthony studied medicine and became a doctor. But he soon realized that his true calling was healing souls, so he became a priest. His usual prescription for himself and others was to receive Holy Communion often. At Saint Anthony's first Mass, his great love of the Eucharist was apparent. Anthony was absorbed in prayer when the people present at the Mass witnessed a miraculous occurrence. During the consecration of the Eucharist, they saw an extraordinary light surrounding Anthony and a multitude of angels encircling him and adoring the Eucharist. Anthony Zaccaria went on to preach the Gospel with such love, clarity, and courage that hearts and lives were transformed.

"O Lord, my God, you ask me to open the door of my soul, which you alone have created, so that you may enter into it with your loving kindness and dispel the darkness of my mind. I believe that you will do this for … you numbered as your friends all who came to you with repentant hearts. O God, you alone are blessed always, now, and forever."

— St. John Chrysostom

Saint Maria Goretti (1890–1902)

My Good Angel

As Maria Goretti tried to fend off Alessandro Serenelli's sexual advances, he stabbed her fourteen times. Before she died the following day, Maria forgave him; he spent thirty years in prison. Nine years before his death in 1970, Alessandro wrote: "When I was 20 years old, I committed a crime of passion. That memory represents something horrible for me. Maria Goretti, now a Saint, was my good Angel, sent to me through Providence to guide and save me. I still have impressed upon my heart her words of rebuke and of pardon. She prayed for me, she interceded for her murderer.… I accepted to be condemned because it was my own fault. Little Maria was really my light, my protectress; with her help I have tried to live honestly when I was again accepted among the members of society." [164]

Holy Spirit, source of all virtue, bless our young people with the gifts of courage and wisdom. Help them to know and choose truth over deception. Help them to honor purity and avoid immorality and the exploitation of others. Show them how to choose to respect others and to value their own integrity. Strengthen our efforts to guide them and to be good examples of love and fidelity. Amen.

July 7

GIDEON AND THE ANGEL

 An angel of the Lord came one hot, dusty day to visit Gideon who was trying to thresh wheat in an inconspicuous way (Judges 6:11–24). Gideon didn't want the Midianites to steal his food as they often did. "The Lord is with you, you mighty warrior," said the angel. Not recognizing his visitor as an angel, Gideon asked why Israel was oppressed if God was with him. The angel promised that Gideon would soon help to free Israel. Remaining doubtful, Gideon asked for a sign — the burning of a sacrificial meal. When the angel touched the food Gideon prepared, it burst into flames. The angel instantly disappeared, but Gideon was terrified because he had doubted God's messenger. Soon, however, Gideon began freeing Israel as the angel predicted.

When angels in disguise come to tell us how wonderful we are in God's eyes, we often find it hard to believe. Somehow, like Gideon, we need to grow into the wonderful roles God prepares us for.

California's Mission San Rafael

 The twentieth of California's twenty-one missions was founded in 1817 as a satellite mission for the one in San Francisco. It began as a hospital for Native Americans and was named for Saint Raphael the Archangel, patron saint of hospitals and all health care workers. Because San Rafael was much warmer and drier than San Francisco, the sick got well more quickly. San Rafael was given independent mission status in 1822. In 1848, however, U.S. Army General John C. Fremont made the mission his headquarters in a campaign to make California a state. He stabled horses in the chapel, and the property deteriorated. In 1949, restoration of the original mission began. The mission San Rafael continues to draw visitors today.

"God sent me to heal you and your daughter-in-law Sarah. I am Raphael, one of the seven angels who stand and serve before the Glory of the Lord" (Tobit 12: 14–15). Don't hesitate to appeal to Saint Raphael the Archangel for healing that you or others need. Scripture makes it clear that healing is his mission.

July 9

BE ANGELS OF PEACE

 When meeting with heads of state and politicians from around the world, Pope Francis would give each one a medallion of the "angel of peace." The angel of peace, he explained, could help destroy the "spirit of war" afflicting many nations. In May 2015, however, the pope's gift and comments to Palestinian President Mahmoud Abbas set off a firestorm of controversy. Speaking in Italian, the pope told Abbas, "May you be an angel of peace." Mistranslating his comment, several media outlets reported the Holy Father's comment as: "You are an angel of peace." Angry reactions erupted in Israel and among Israel's supporters. Many see Palestinians as terrorists and enemies of peace. [165]

"Let us not be justices of the peace, but angels of peace."

— Saint Thérèse of Lisieux

Can you be an angel of peace in your world in a way that doesn't allow anyone to doubt your intentions?

Who Are the Seven Archangels?

 Although Catholic editions of the Bible mention only three archangels by name, there's a long tradition for seven archangels. In addition to the well-known Michael, Gabriel, and Raphael, some sources add the archangels Uriel, Jehudiel, Sealtiel, and Barachiel. Still other sources include Uriel but call the others Raguel, Remiel, Saragael. There are many Scripture references to seven angels serving God in a special way. In the Book of Tobit, Raphael finally identifies himself, saying, "I am Raphael, one of the seven angels who stand and serve before the Glory of the Lord" (Tobit 12:15). In the sixteenth century, Michelangelo was commissioned to paint a fresco in a church in Rome dedicated to Mary and the Seven Archangels.

In Revelation, among many references to seven angels, the author says, "And I saw that the seven angels who stood before God were given seven trumpets" (Revelation 8:2).

July 11
Saint Benedict (480–547)

SAVED FROM POISON — BY AN ANGEL

At age twenty, Benedict rejected the worldliness of Rome and became a hermit. He lived and prayed in a cave near Subiaco. When Benedict's reputation for holiness spread, he was asked to become abbot for a community of monks at Vicovaro. These monks lived easy lives of self-indulgence. When they saw that Benedict was determined to bring them closer to God through a life of silence and prayer, they rebelled. Since abbots were appointed for life, some monks quietly plotted to kill him. One night at dinner, when a cup of wine was set before him, Benedict knew it was poisoned. He calmly stood up and silently thanked his angel. Without a word, he left and returned to Subiaco and to peace.

No evil shall befall you, no affliction come near your tent. For he commands his angels with regard to you, to guard you wherever you go. (Psalm 91:10–11)

July 12

ANGEL IMPERSONATOR

 While Catholic healing ministers Judith and Francis MacNutt were in California at a conference on healing, the husband of a friend was in a Florida hospital, fighting for his life. Jim had suffered a massive heart attack, and the MacNutts were praying for him. Through the night in Florida, Jim woke several times to see a glowing light and Francis MacNutt praying over him. Not knowing the MacNutts were gone, Jim thanked Francis and slept peacefully. On the morning after his heart attack, Jim was sitting up in bed. His puzzled doctors ordered new medical tests but found no evidence of a heart attack. When the MacNutts heard Jim's story, they assumed an angel impersonating Francis came to heal Jim.

These angels rarely call attention to their angelic identity; they tend to remain anonymous. Often they disappear abruptly when their task is complete, and yet somehow leave behind the footprint of heaven. [166]

July 13

THE COSMONAUTS WHO SAW ANGELS

 In 2011, *Pravda,* the leading Russian newspaper, reported on an event that took place twenty-seven years earlier. In 1984, aboard the Soviet space station, six Russian cosmonauts (astronauts) reported seeing angels in space. They were busy with routine assignments when an orange cloud and then a blinding light filled the station. The five men and one woman saw seven figures with massive wings and halos moving outside the space station. The crew noted a sense of peace in the space station while the angels were nearby. Angel sightings were also reported by other cosmonauts several months later. Back in the Soviet Union medical and psychological tests found nothing wrong with the cosmonauts who were ordered to maintain silence about the angels. [167]

Praise the LORD from the heavens;
praise him in the heights.
Praise him, all you his angels;
give praise, all you his hosts.
Praise him, sun and moon;
praise him, all shining stars.
(Psalm 148:1–3)

ATTENDED BY ANGELS

 Camillus looked like a bad bet. As a young soldier he recklessly risked his life, both in battle and in rowdy gambling parlors. A serious leg wound finally slowed him long enough to notice the distressing conditions and suffering of the other patients in the hospital. After his own recovery Camillus returned to the hospital and devoted himself to nursing the sick. Other men were drawn by his passion, and they formed a religious order dedicated entirely to serving the sick and poor. Camillus was still reckless, caring for victims of a plague without concern of infection or death. His companions frequently saw angels attending Camillus as he worked — making him a sure thing.

"But let the angel of thy light come and restore to me the light which the darkness of my cell has taken from me; and let the right hand of thy majesty scatter the phantom hosts of thy ancient enemy. For we know, O Lord, that thy mercy will aid us in all temptations."

— Saint Margaret of Antioch [168]

July 15
Saint Bonaventure (1218–1274)

Angels as Steps to God

At a General Audience in March 2010, Pope Benedict XVI spoke about Saint Bonaventure, who said that the Church identifies nine orders of angels found in Scripture. The angels are ranked from simple "angels" to the seraphim. "Saint Bonaventure," Pope Benedict said, "interprets these orders of angels as steps on the human creature's way to God. Thus, they can represent the human journey, the ascent toward communion with God." Bonaventure, however, "knew well that the final step in the approach to God is always a special gift of God.… In the ascent toward God, love goes beyond reason, it sees further, it enters more profoundly into God's mystery." [169]

"Let us therefore say to the Lord our God: Lead me forth, Lord, in thy way, and let me step in thy truth, let my heart be glad, that it fears thy name."

— Saint Bonaventure, *The Journey of the Mind into God* I, 1

July 16

Her Angel Wept

 A little story told in Fyodor Dostoyevsky's novel *The Brothers Karamazov* reminds us that our guardian angels help us, but cannot save us. A woman died without a single good deed to her credit and was thrown into a lake of fire as punishment. Her angel recalled, "She once pulled up an onion from her garden and gave it to a beggar." God told the angel to give the woman one end of that onion and, holding on to the other, to pull the woman out of the fire. As the angel carefully pulled the woman through the lake of fire, other souls grabbed hold of her, hoping to be pulled out with her. She began to kick them away, protesting, "I'm to be pulled up, not you. It's my onion, not yours." With that, the onion ripped apart, and the woman fell into that fiery lake, where she is today. And her angel wept. [170]

Angels are "ministering spirits sent to serve, for the sake of those who are to inherit salvation" (Hebrews 1:14). Ask your guardian angel for help, especially when you are in need of repentance and conversion.

July 17

An Angel at My Side

 Jean Guitton (1901–1999), French philosopher and theologian, was a personal friend of Pope Paul VI and the first layperson to participate in the Second Vatican Council. He shared his thoughts on the role of a guardian angel: "Sometimes I have sensed — above and most of all at my side — a being barely perceptible, who removes obstacles, inspires me, protects me, and guides me. Who at times, with his fingers to his lips, brings me a message with which I have to agree. I find that the scene of the Annunciation, in which Gabriel communicates with the Virgin only to ask her to say, 'Yes,' is repeated often in human lives." It would be wrong to assume that Guitton was implying that the questions your guardian angel asks you are anywhere near the magnitude of Archangel Gabriel's question to the Blessed Virgin. However, the expected response is the same: "Let it be done to me according to your word" (Luke 1:38).

"Recall those persons you may have met by chance, on a train or in the air, who spoke a meaningful word to you and then disappeared. Persons whom you never saw again but who, with a simple word, profoundly changed your life. An angel is above all that visitor."

— Jean Guitton [171]

ANGELS AND GOD'S PROVIDENCE

Jesuit Karl Rahner (1904–1984) was one of the most influential theologians of the twentieth century. He taught that while angels may seem self-sufficient, they actually receive everything by the infinite grace of Christ. It is only within the context of Christology that the role of guardian angels derives significance. Rahner writes that "both the liturgy and Tradition have made concrete the union existing between men and angels in the one history of salvation, placing specific angels in relationship with specific human beings." He goes on to say that "the guardian angel is a real spiritual being so entirely at God's service that the Lord has involved him in the great adventure of our salvation, who are assigned to him out of God's own goodness and Providence." [172]

When a person makes his way through life in this way then two are always moving along the same street: the guardian angel and the human person, and both look on their own toward God, toward the one who is the content of eternal life for both. [173]

July 19

Pain Is a Holy Angel

 During World War II, German theologian Dietrich Bonhoeffer, a Lutheran, warned Christians about looking for "cheap grace." He meant that there is no salvation without the hard work of following Jesus. Bonhoeffer was young and engaged to be married when Nazis arrested him in 1943. A well-known critic of persecution of the Jews, Bonhoeffer knew his own cross — and death — were coming. But, he didn't despair. "Pain is a holy angel," he wrote, "who shows us treasures that would otherwise remain forever hidden." Like angels who bring God's messages, his pain and suffering were teaching him about God's enduring love. Shortly before Allied forces arrived, Bonhoeffer was hanged for allegedly plotting to kill Hitler. [174]

Has pain ever been a holy angel for you? Did you find that gracefully accepting suffering brought you a message from God?

WHAT'S THE ANGEL POPULATION?

 How many angels are there? Some angel authorities say they can't even be counted. Many Scripture passages seem to agree. "I looked again and heard the voices of many angels who surrounded the throne and the living creatures and the elders. They were countless in number." (Revelation 5:11). The Letter to the Hebrews reassures followers of Jesus that heaven is "the city of the living God, the heavenly Jerusalem, and countless angels in festal gathering" (Hebrews 12:22). When warning against causing scandal or tempting others to sin, Jesus confirmed that even little children have guardian angels. His statement implied that God assigns an angel to each person (Matthew 18:10).

Today the world's population numbers more than 7.3 billion. All over the world, on every continent and in every nation, angels of the Lord are busy protecting and guiding God's children.

July 21

Saint Lawrence of Brindisi (1559–1619)

FINDING THE ANGEL IN OTHERS

 When Lawrence was preaching to Jews in Italy about Christ, they assumed he had been raised as a Jew. His Hebrew was remarkable! In fact, his parents were Christians who had expected great things from him. But they didn't live to see him enter the Capuchin order, become a priest, scholar, and the master of eight languages. However, it wasn't really his ability to speak several languages that made him so successful in sharing the Gospel. His "secret" was that he could find the angel in everyone. He said that we have much in common with the angels "for like them we have been formed in the image and likeness of God."

Every day, remind yourself that God made human beings only "a little lower than the angels." Can you see that reality in others? Can you see it in yourself?

SENT BY THE ANGELS

In all four Gospels, Saint Mary Magdalene encounters an angel — or two — at Christ's tomb. Mary was the one recruited by angels to share the Resurrection news. In John's Gospel Mary initially failed to recognize that the two young men in the empty tomb were angels. She cried when she found Christ's body gone. Blinded by tears, she told the young men, "They have taken my Lord, and I don't know where they laid him." Outside the tomb, Mary then questioned a man she assumed to be a gardener. Mary asked where he had placed the body. When Jesus said her name in reply, she recognized his voice, and quickly went to embrace him.

The angels sent Mary Magdalene to tell others that Jesus had risen from the dead. Thank God for this Good News. Pray that you'll be ready to follow in Mary's footsteps, spreading the Resurrection news.

July 23
Saint Bridget of Sweden (1303–1373)

ANGELS LIKE BEAMS OF THE SUN

 Saint Bridget was a wife, mother of eight, founder of an order of nuns, and a visionary. Once she described a vision of a cosmic Mass. She said that everything on the earth and in the water was lifted up to Heaven and bowed in reverence. The sun, moon, stars, and planets moved in their spheres. She heard melodies and harmonious voices impossible to imagine. After the priest pronounced the words of Jesus over the bread, it seemed to become three figures, although it remained in the hands of the priest. "That Bread became a living Lamb, in the Lamb was the face of a man and on the inside and on the outside of the Lamb and on that face there was an ardent flame … and the Angels attending were as great a multitude as the beams of the sun." [175]

In another vision, Christ called Bridget a "Messenger of the Great Lord." Like an angelic messenger, Bridget humbly received God's communications and delivered them, even to rulers and Church leaders, as God directed her. What message, insight, or revelation do you have for me today, Lord? [176]

JEWISH PRAYER TO THE ANGELS

 There are many references to angels in the Jewish Scriptures (the Old Testament). But, many Christians assumed that Jewish prayer never referred to angels — even as God's intermediaries. The reason is Judaism's strong monotheistic identity. Prayer was directed to God alone. Yet, scholars have found Jewish prayers from the Middle Ages that appeal for angelic help. One prayer, "Usherers of Mercy," is still recited before and after Rosh Hashana, the Jewish New Year celebrated in early fall. It describes angels as couriers or messengers of mercy and asks them to intercede with God for us. The prayer asks the "ushers of mercy" to carry our prayers, needs, and even our tears to the throne of God. [177]

"Usherers of Mercy, usher in our [plea for] mercy, before the Master of mercy. You who cause prayer to be heard, may you cause our prayer to be heard before the Hearer of prayer, You who cause our outcry to be heard, may you cause our outcry to be heard, before the Hearer of outcry."

— Usherers of Mercy (see complete prayer
in the appendix, page 387)

July 25
Saint James, Apostle (First Century)

ANGELS ALONG "THE WAY"

 For centuries, angels have been protecting pilgrims traveling El Camino de Santiago (The Way of Saint James). One of Christianity's most famous pilgrimages, it ends at Santiago de Compostelo (Saint James of Compostelo) in Spain. James, the Apostle, reportedly preached the Gospel in Spain but was beheaded in A.D. 44 by King Herod in Jerusalem. According to tradition, the saint's remains returned to Compostelo in a boat piloted by an angel. Today, pilgrims prayerfully walk or bike to Compostelo, staying in pilgrim hostels and stopping at churches along the route. In 2010, Martin Sheen and Emilio Estevez starred in *The Way*, a film about an American father who completes his son's pilgrimage after his son's death. In 2010, over 272,000 pilgrims traveled "the Way."

Angels are invisible companions on our lifelong pilgrimage. Ask them to keep you safe and joyful along the way. Pilgrims understand that there's a wonderful destination ahead.

The Angel's Joyful Sign

We have no factual information about the parents of the Virgin Mary, but Tradition names them Joachim and Ann and says that for many years they longed for a child. Then the happy day arrived when an angel appeared to Joachim to tell him that he and Ann would have a daughter. The angel said, "Go now to the Golden Gate, where you will receive a sign." Meanwhile, Ann was watching two sparrows in a laurel tree. "Why was I born, O Lord?" she cried, "The birds build nests for their young, yet I have no infant to hold in my arms." At that moment, the angel visited her. "The Lord has heard your prayer. Go to the Golden Gate now and your sorrow will turn to joy." Joachim and Ann both hurried to the Golden Gate. When they saw one another there, they knew it was true. Their hearts overflowed with joy as they shared the news they had received from the angel. [178]

Like a fruitful vine, your wife within your home.
Like olive plants, your children round your table.
May the Lord bless you all the days of your life.
That you may share Jerusalem's joy
    and live to see your children's children.
(Based on Psalm 128)

July 27

An Angel in Disguise

 Abba Agathon, one of the desert fathers, came upon a man on the roadside whose legs were paralyzed. The paralyzed man asked Agathon to carry him into town. When they arrived, he said, "Put me down while you sell your wares." Agathon did so. When Agathon sold something, the poor man asked him to buy him some bread. Agathon bought him bread. Each time he made a sale, the man asked for something else. When Agathon had sold everything, he carried the man back to the place where he found him. The paralyzed man said, "Agathon, you are filled with divine blessings, in heaven and on earth." Then Agathon saw that it was not a man, but an angel of the Lord, come to test him. [179]

"All God's angels come to us disguised;
Sorrow and sickness, poverty and death.
One after another lift their frowning masks,
And we behold the Seraph's face beneath,
All radiant with the glory and the calm
Of having looked upon the front of God."

— James Russell Lowell [180]

ANGEL FOOD, ANYONE?

Do you prefer Angel Food cake or Devil's Food cake? Angel Food cake has a light, airy texture, a subtle vanilla flavor, and is a relatively healthy dessert. It's low in calories and cholesterol and is often served with fresh fruit instead of frosting. Devil's Food Cake, on the other hand, is chocolate — fudgy, rich, decadent, sinfully delicious. It begs for frosting and ice cream. Why is Angel Food good, while Devil's Food is delicious? Why does choosing what's good seem so blah, while decadence can be so enticing? F. Forrester Church suggests that "if angels came in packages we'd almost always pick the wrong one. Even as the devil is evil disguised as good, angels are goodness disguised." [181]

A Recipe for True Goodness: Let love be sincere; hate what is evil; hold on to what is good; love one another with mutual affection; anticipate one another in showing honor … be fervent in spirit, rejoice in hope, endure in affliction, persevere in prayer…. Rejoice with those who rejoice, weep with those who weep. Be concerned for what is noble in the sight of all. If possible, on your part, live at peace with all. (Romans 12:9–12, 15, 17–18)

July 29

THE NATURE OF ANGELS

 Many people believe in the possibility of discovering other intelligent life in the universe. In truth, non-human intelligent life already exists in our universe — angels! Angels have a purely spiritual nature of powerful intellect and will. Angels, by nature, are superior to man, and much closer to God. When angels communicate with humans, it is always by the will of God, and they are able to appear in a bodily form in order to communicate with us. They can never become human, and humans can never become angels. However, both the angelic nature and the human nature were made for eternal union with God.

"A fish cannot drown in water,
A bird does not fall in air....
Each creature God made
Must live in its true nature;
How could I resist my nature,
That lives for oneness with God?"

— Mechthild of Magdeburg [182]

An Angel's Message of Life

This Greek Doctor of the Church was nicknamed Chrysologus, "golden speaker," for his eloquent and masterful teaching. Preaching on the Annunciation, he said that the Angel Gabriel and the Virgin Mary spoke of the "regeneration of mankind." Humanity would return to life by the same means through which it had fallen into death. Gabriel spoke with the Virgin Mary concerning salvation because an angel had spoken with Eve concerning destruction. "By a mystery beyond understanding," Chrysologus said, "God assumed a place on earth and man a place in heaven. God and man are joined together in one Body; at the message of an angel the weak human nature we share became strong to bear the whole glory of God." [183]

"It was when Lucifer first congratulated himself upon his angelic behavior that he became the tool of evil."

— Dag Hammarskjöld [184]

July 31
Saint Ignatius Loyola (1491–1556)

ANGELS ENTER IN SILENCE

 Saint Ignatius Loyola described how the angels react when a person grows closer to God. "In the case of those who are making progress from good to better, the good angel touches such a soul sweetly, lightly, and gently, as a drop of water enters a sponge; and the evil angel touches it sharply and with noise and disturbance as when a drop of water falls upon a rock. If the soul is contrary, the angels enter with noise and commotion and disruption, but if the disposition of the soul is similar to the angels, they enter in silence, as into their own house, by an open door." [185]

Behold, I stand at the door and knock. If anyone hears my voice and opens the door, I will enter his house and dine with him, and he with me. (Revelation 3:20)

ANGEL IN THE REARVIEW MIRROR

"It was a nice warm summer night. I decided to take the top off of my Jeep and drive downtown. On my way, however, I had to pass through a high crime area. About two blocks before I actually reached that area, I glanced at my rearview mirror and saw my mother! Suddenly I felt very exposed with the top down. I knew it had to be a warning. I immediately made a U-turn in the middle of the street and headed home. I realized right then that an angel in my mother's image had appeared in my rearview mirror. I feel certain that my life was saved, or some great harm avoided because my angel warned me about the danger ahead."

— Virginia Smith [186]

"Jesus Christ my God, I adore you and thank you for all the graces you have given me this day. I offer you my sleep and all the moments of this night, and I ask you to keep me from sin. I put myself within your sacred side and under the mantle of Our Lady. Let your holy angels stand about me and keep me in peace. And let your blessing be upon me. Amen."

— Night Prayer of Saint Alphonsus Liguori

August 2

ENLISTING THE ANGELS' HELP

 Saint Peter Faber was just one man, but he had an army of guardian angels on his side. Peter travelled on foot through Germany, Spain, and Portugal to preach and teach. Whenever he entered a new town or region to speak, Faber asked for help from his guardian angel and the guardian angels of all the people who would hear him speak. Their combined spiritual power was very effective. Saint Peter Faber liked to call himself "God's broom." He felt that God was using him to sweep away sin, indifference, and errors of faith. [187]

Follow the example of Saint Peter Faber. When you are preparing for a meeting at work, a family discussion, even coffee with a friend, take a moment to seek the counsel and aid of your guardian angel and the angels of those to whom you are speaking.

August 3

ANGELS IN EVERY MOMENT

When God came to dwell among us, only a few people were aware of it. The message was given by the Archangel Gabriel to Mary, and to Joseph in a dream. Angels sang in Bethlehem — to a few poor shepherds. "Why, when the door of heaven opened, and the brilliant light of eternity became visible from dark earth, were there not more people to see it, and why was the glimpse so brief?" author Judith Lang wonders. Perhaps that one moment is enough, she concludes. "Angels appear at particular moments to particular people; when this happens, that place and time share in eternity. In Christ, God came to earth at a particular moment, in order to show that he is with us at every moment. Angels become visible at particular moments and show that they are at work in every moment. Their function is first to bring heaven to us so that they may bring us to heaven." [188]

Reflect on this: Angels are little epiphanies of the divine amid the ordinary. They come in moments of time selected by God. But, the significance of their visits and message is eternally important. [189]

August 4

Saint John Vianney (1786–1859)

Your Angel's Notebook

 Saint John Vianney, pastor of the tiny French village of Ars, was a very humble and holy priest. He struggled with the devil and was devoted to the angels. He understood the desires of the human soul. So many people came to him that he spent hours each day in the confessional. His spiritual guidance was always down to earth. Which words of advice could help you today?

• Take great care never to do anything before having said Morning Prayers. The devil once declared that if he could have the first moment of the day, he was sure of all the rest.

• If you find it impossible to pray, hide behind your good angel and charge him to pray in your stead.

• The devil writes down our sins — our guardian angel all our merits. Labor that the guardian angel's book may be full, and the devil's empty.

• Offer your temptations for the conversion of sinners. When the devil sees you doing this, he is beside himself with rage and makes off, because then the temptation is turned against himself.

• When you awake in the night, transport yourself quickly in spirit before the Tabernacle, saying: "Behold me, my God, I come to adore You, to praise, thank, and love You, and to keep You company with all the angels." [190]

August 5

A Multitude of Angels

 An angel of the Lord announced the birth of Jesus to the shepherds and suddenly "a multitude of the heavenly host" appeared (Luke 2:13). Only one angel was needed to deliver the message. Why did so many appear? Saint Thomas Aquinas reasoned that number belongs exclusively to the material world and that sheer number allows the weakest species to survive extinction. In the spiritual world, multitude means something else. Each angel reflects God's glory in a unique way. So, a multitude of angels perfectly reflects and praises God's glory. In the physical world, the grains of sands on a beach and the stars in the sky are said to be innumerable, yet sand blows and washes away; stars flare and burn out. God cannot be diminished in any way and an innumerable multitude — thousands of thousands and myriads upon myriads (Daniel 7:10) — of angels reflects the inexhaustible perfection of God. [191]

Oh, the depth of the riches and wisdom and knowledge of God! How inscrutable are his judgments and how unsearchable his ways! For who has known the mind of the Lord or who has been his counselor? Or who has given him anything that he may be repaid? For from him and through him and for him are all things. To him be glory forever. Amen. (Romans 11:33–36)

August 6
Feast of the Transfiguration of Christ

ANGELS IN BORROWED GARB

 Jesus granted three apostles — Peter, James, and John — a glimpse of his glory. His appearance was changed, transfigured. His face became brighter than the sun and his garments were dazzling white. Then Jesus was joined by Moses and Elijah, and they talked together. The apostles recognized them. It is quite different when angels appear. Jesus, Moses, and Elijah all had physical human bodies. The apostles saw their glorified human bodies. But humans can never really see angels because angels are wholly spirit — they do not and never had a body of any kind. As mortals, we just cannot picture that. We cannot think in purely spiritual terms. We use words when there are no words. We imagine images where there are no bodies. If they look and sound like us, it is only because angels always appear "in borrowed garb." [192]

Have you ever wondered what a saint might say to express a sudden, strong emotion, such as surprise? When she was excited, Katharine Drexel would exclaim, "Holy Angels!" [193]

August 7

THE MIGHTY SERAPHIM

 Designated as the highest in the celestial hierarchy, the Seraphim represent the essence of angelic holiness. The prophet Isaiah described them: "Each of them had six wings: with two they veiled their faces, with two they veiled their feet, and with two they hovered aloft." They are the picture of profound adoration. The Seraphim cover their faces and feet in a gesture of deep reverence and submission. It is as if they cannot humble themselves enough before the Lord. Two wings quiver as a sign of their constant readiness to serve the Lord without hesitation. Their mighty voices ring out in praise of God, a cry so loud that "the frame of the door shook" (Isaiah 6:1–4).

"Holy, holy, holy is the LORD of hosts!" they cried one to the other. "All the earth is filled with his glory!" (see Isaiah 6:3). The worship of the seraphim is communal, one crying out to the other, building to a crescendo. The next time you are at Mass, try to be more conscious of the responsorial psalm and the dialogues between priest and assembly as cries "one to the other" in praise of God.

August 8
Saint Dominic (1170–1221)

BREAD DELIVERY FROM THE ANGELS

 Was it angels who brought bread for dinner that night in 1218? Forty hungry Dominican friars always thought so. They were seated at the table but knew there was very little to eat. The Dominicans, a newly founded order, were mendicants. They begged for their needs but were still largely unknown in Rome. Brother Dominic was at the head of the table, thanking God for the meager meal they were about to share. Just then, two handsome young men bustled into the room with heavy sacks of fresh bread. Without a word, they put down the sacks and left. Dominic smiled and blessed the bread that was quickly passed around the table. And Dominic added a silent prayer of thanks to the angels. [194]

"So do not worry and say, 'What are we to eat?' or 'What are we to drink?' or 'What are we to wear?' All these things the pagans seek. Your heavenly Father knows that you need them all." (Matthew 6:31–32)

AN ANGEL IN PRISON

On this date in 1942, Saint Teresa Benedicta of the Cross (Edith Stein) and her sister Rosa died in a gas chamber at the Nazi Auschwitz Concentration Camp. At another prison, a few months earlier, Teresa had cared for little Jewish children whose mothers were immobilized with fear. The guards reported that she "moved like an angel" bringing calm among the terrorized people facing death. Teresa and Rosa were Jewish converts to Catholicism. Teresa was a brilliant philosopher and university professor until Germany's anti-Jewish policies banned her from teaching. Then, she became a Carmelite nun, expecting that she would one day be arrested and executed by the Nazis.

Saint Teresa Benedicta of the Cross, a victim of discrimination and persecution, saw that the only answer to hatred is love. She wrote, "On the question of relating to our fellowman — our neighbor's spiritual need transcends every commandment. Everything else we do is a means to an end. But love is an end already, since God is love." [195]

August 10
Saint Lawrence (225–258)

ANGELS OF THE POOR

 Food for the Poor, Inc., an ecumenical, Christian nonprofit calls its monthly donors "Angels of the Poor." Donors support the organization's outreach to the poor in Latin America and the Caribbean. Christian commitment to the poor is as old as the Church. It is especially celebrated on this feast of Saint Lawrence, a deacon in Rome charged with care for Rome's needy. Soon after Pope (Saint) Sixtus II was martyred, Roman officials ordered Lawrence to surrender all Church treasure. Lawrence quickly gave all the money and gold he could to the poor. Then, he gathered a group of blind, leprous, orphaned, homeless, and destitute people. "These are the Church's treasure," he announced with conviction. Lawrence was burned to death over a slow fire.

Angels carry God's message and help. Lord, show me how I can share in the ministry of your angels to the poor and to those in need.

August 11

PRAYER LIKE AN ANGEL'S

The prayers of Saint Clare were like an angel's. Unimpeded by selfish concerns and blazing with faith, they flew straight to God. Once, a woman from Pisa said that Clare, who was in Assisi, had freed her from five demons through her prayers. As the demons left her, they shrieked that Clare's prayers were "burning" them. Pope Gregory IX also had great confidence in her prayerful intercession. He often wrote to Clare, humbly asking for her prayers when he was faced with difficult problems and decisions. Always he felt support. Clare was only ten when she saw her friend Francis return his expensive clothes to his father in order to give himself completely to God. At eighteen, Clare also left home to begin a life of voluntary poverty and prayer.

> *"Give me a person of prayer, and such a one will be capable of accomplishing anything."*
>
> — Saint Vincent de Paul [196]

Today, consider Saint Vincent's statement about the power of prayer and Saint Clare's example of selfless prayer.

August 12

Saint Jane Frances de Chantal (1572–1641)

HUMILITY AND TRUST

 Jane Frances de Chantal was a young wife and mother when her world turned upside down. In 1600, her beloved husband Christophe was accidentally shot and died in her arms. After months of depression, Jane emerged from her darkness. Her children and her husband's sizable estate needed her. While grieving, her prayer life deepened, and she gave generously to the poor. But, she also wondered what God wanted of her. In 1604, she met Saint Francis de Sales, the bishop of Geneva. A lifelong friendship began. Francis helped Jane learn to pray for guidance with humility and trust. She told others that this was how the angels must pray — with complete dependence on God. Once her children were grown, Jane founded the Order of the Visitation of Mary for older women and those with fragile health.

"We should go to prayer with deep humility and an awareness of our nothingness. We must invoke the help of the Holy Spirit and that of our good angel, and then remain still in God's presence, full of faith that he is more in us than we are in ourselves."

— Saint Jane Frances de Chantal [197]

August 13

VATICAN CONSECRATED TO SAINT MICHAEL

 In the summer of 2013, two living popes consecrated the Vatican to Saint Michael the Archangel. In the Vatican Gardens, Pope Emeritus Benedict XVI assisted Pope Francis in dedicating a new statue of the archangel. Pope Francis said the addition of Michael's statue to the gardens was particularly fitting during the Year of Faith. He also noted that Saint Michael defends the people of God against our primary enemy, the devil. Clearly, both popes believe that the Church needs Saint Michael's protection more than ever.

"We are not alone on the journey or in the trials of life, we are accompanied and supported by the Angels of God.... In consecrating Vatican City State to St. Michael the Archangel, I ask him to defend us from the evil one and banish him."

— Pope Francis, Vatican Gardens, July 4, 2013

Today, ask for the special protection of Saint Michael the Archangel. [198]

August 14

Saint Maximilian Kolbe (1894–1941)

GOD'S WILL AND THE ANGELS

 From a very early age, Raymond Kolbe had something in common with the angels. He lived to do God's will. When he was twelve, the Blessed Mother appeared to Kolbe and offered him a choice between two mystical crowns — one for purity or one for martyrdom. Raymond chose both. As a Franciscan priest, Father Maximilian Kolbe founded the Immaculata Movement to promote Marian devotion, and started a Catholic radio station and publishing company. In 1941, he was arrested for publishing anti-Nazi material and sent to the Auschwitz concentration camp. When ten men were condemned to starve in a bunker, Kolbe volunteered to die in the place of a family man. Because he was the last alive, he was given a lethal injection on August 14, 1941.

In contrast to the fallen angels, who rose in revolt against God because they could not be like him, the holy angels are completely one with God and His will. They accept the place assigned to them in God's creative order. [199]

THE ANGELS DANCE WITH JOY

Saint John Damascene had a deep devotion to the Blessed Mother. In his second homily on the Assumption of Mary, given in Jerusalem around 740, he envisioned the angels celebrating her arrival in heaven. "This day the Holy and Singular Virgin is presented in the sublime and heavenly Temple;... and the angels dance with joy, and the Archangels applaud, and the Heavenly Powers give praise, and with them the Principalities rejoice, and the Dominions exult, and the Powers are filled with gladness, and Thrones share in this glorious feast of praise; the Cherubim celebrate with song, and the Seraphim proclaim her glory. Nor are they less honored, adding glory to the Mother of glory." [200]

Mary proclaimed: Behold, from now on will all ages call me blessed. The Mighty One has done great things for me, and holy is his name. (Luke 1:48–49)

August 16

Saint Stephen of Hungary (c. 969–1038)

THE ANGEL'S PROMISE

 The story spread about an angel appearing in a dream. How else to explain the extraordinary transformation of Geza, the fierce leader of the Huns, into a ruler whose fervent desire was that his people accept Christ? The angel had told Geza that his son was chosen by God to accomplish this plan. The angel also said that a man of God would come to him, whom he should receive graciously. The very next day, Saint Adalbert, bishop of Prague, arrived and instructed Geza and his wife in the truths of the faith. They were baptized, along with their young son, who was named Stephen, after the first Christian martyr. Stephen became the first king of Hungary. He united the people, shared his wealth with the poor, and spread the faith as the angel had once promised.

"Since God often sends us inspirations by means of His angels, we should frequently return our aspirations to him by means of the same messengers."

— Saint Francis de Sales

August 17

THE FACE OF AN ANGEL

 Seraphim of Sarov (1759–1833) was a holy monk and a saint of the Russian Orthodox Church. He received his angelic name when he made his vows at the monastery of Sarov where his holiness was apparent to all. During prayer, he often saw angels singing and praying with the monks. Once he saw Christ surrounded by angels during Liturgy. When he was about thirty years old, Seraphim sought permission to live as a hermit in the forest outside the monastery, praying, growing his own vegetables, chopping wood, and doing penance. After fifteen years of solitude, people began coming to Seraphim in search of spiritual counseling and healing. Many said that "his face was joyous and bright, as that of an angel." His reputation as a healer of both body and spirit spread. He embraced this challenging ministry for the rest of his life, and called each visitor "my joy."

"Every good deed done for Christ's sake gives us the grace of the Holy Spirit, but prayer gives us it most of all, for it is always at hand. Prayer is always possible for everyone, rich and poor, noble and humble, strong and weak, healthy and sick, righteous and sinful."

— Seraphim of Sarov [201]

August 18

Draw Near, All Holy Angels

 Confined in a prison camp in Northern Siberia from 1946 to 1955, four Lithuanian girls secretly wrote down the prayers that formed deep in their souls. With no hope of release, their only source of consolation was Christ Crucified and Mary, Mother of Sorrows. Eventually, they collected the pieces of scrap paper with the prayers and bound them together creating a small booklet, two by three inches. This little booklet was smuggled out of the prison, out of Russia to Lithuania and out into the world. The prayers reveal the tremendous faith, resignation, forgiveness, and hope of four faith-filled girls.

Draw near, all holy Angels;
draw near, all saints of heaven,
Immaculate Mother, Saint Joseph,
Saint Thérèse, come to praise
the Lord of Mercy, the God of Love.
Teach me how to be humble, how to love,
that everywhere and always I may live in gratitude
and with my entire life I may proclaim
God's love and goodness. [202]

August 19

ANGELS AND QUANTUM PHYSICS

 The idea that angels move instantaneously from one place to another without passing through any space or time dates back to Saint Thomas Aquinas in the thirteenth century. Mortimer Adler, an American philosopher, said that when he explained Saint Thomas's theory of how angels move to Niels Bohr, the great twentieth-century quantum physicist, he was amazed. Bohr said, "That's exactly the point of modern quantum theory. So a thirteenth-century theologian discovered one of the basic principles of modern nuclear physics seven hundred years ago!" Aquinas had deduced from philosophical principles a kind of movement that modern science induced from observation and experiment. [203]

"Most of our life is unimportant, filled with trivial things from morning till night. But when it is transformed by love it is of interest even to the angels."

— Dorothy Day [204]

August 20

Saint Bernard of Clairvaux (1090–1153)

ANGELS OBEY WITH LOVE

 Saint Bernard was a Benedictine abbot and founder of the Cistercian order of monks. Bernard fostered a deep devotion to the guardian angels. "The angels," Bernard said, "are not only with you, but for you. They are with you to protect you; they are with you to help you. Although it is God who gives angels charge over us, it is they who with such love obey his bidding, and assist us in all our necessities. Let us therefore cultivate a pious and grateful spirit toward our noble guardians; let us love and honor them as much as we can and as is fitting."

"How happy you would be if you could see how they hasten to join in singing the Psalms.... With great solicitude they go back and forth between God and us, bearing our sighs to the throne of God. Let us therefore strive earnestly to make their joy complete."

— Saint Bernard of Clairvaux [205]

Definitely Not an Angel

 One day, Abba John said to his older brother, "I want to be free, like the angels, who have no cares except to praise God ceaselessly." Then he went off into the desert. A week later, Abba John returned. When he knocked on the door, his brother did not open it, but called out, "Who are you?" He replied, "I am John, your brother." The older brother declared, "John has become an angel, and he is no longer living among men." At that, John began to beg, but his brother refused to let him in, and left him in distress until morning. Then he opened the door and said to John, "You are a man, not an angel, and you must once again work in order to eat." Abba John bowed deeply before his brother, saying, "Forgive me." [206]

May the favor of the Lord our God be ours.
Prosper the work of our hands, O Lord!
Prosper the work of our hands.
(Psalm 90:17)

August 22
The Queenship of Mary

The Angels' Temptation — and Victory

 Revelation 12:1–6 describes a great sign in the sky: a woman clothed with the sun, with the moon under her feet. On her head, rests a crown of twelve stars. The woman gives birth to a son who is caught up to God and his throne, while the woman flees to a place prepared for her by God. Then war breaks out in heaven (verse 7). The faithful angels "accept the kingship of a nature lower than their own. They have not rebelled against the exaltation of the human nature in Christ Jesus.... This observance of the order established by God is the true angelic virtue, the one thing in which they might fail; it might even be called their temptation, and the temptation overcome, it is their victory." Today, the Church honors Mary, the Mother of God, as the Queen of the Angels. [207]

Regina Coeli
Queen of Heaven, rejoice, alleluia.
For He whom you did merit to bear, alleluia.
Has risen, as he said, alleluia.
Rejoice and be glad, O Virgin Mary, alleluia.
For the Lord has truly risen, alleluia.

August 23

One Angel Lost in Translation

 The Book of Judith tells the story of a virtuous widow who saves the people of Israel from destruction by the mighty Assyrian army. Begging God's protection, Judith uses her beauty to gain entry into the Assyrian camp. When Holofernes, the general of the army, is asleep, Judith sneaks into his tent. Using his own sword, she beheads him. She slips out of the camp, and carries his head back to her own city where the watchmen are waiting for her. "As the Lord lives," Judith tells the people, "his angel has been my keeper both in my going and coming: and the Lord has not allowed his handmaid to be defiled, but has brought me back to you sinless, rejoicing for his victory, for my escape, and for your deliverance" (Judith 13:20). [208] Later versions of the Bible renumbered the verses in chapter 13 in the Book of Judith — and the angel was lost in translation.

In the New American Bible, and other modern translations, Judith says, "Yet I swear by the Lord, who has protected me in the way I have walked, that it was my face that seduced Holofernes to his ruin, and that he did not defile me with sin or shame" (Judith 13:16).

August 24

Saint Bartholomew (First Century)

PURE AS AN ANGEL

 There was something about Bartholomew that immediately caught the eye of Jesus. "Here is a true Israelite," Jesus said. "There is no duplicity in him." Bartholomew loved the truth and avoided easy answers and excuses. In John's Gospel, Bartholomew was called Nathaniel. In that Gospel, Jesus told Nathaniel that he saw him sitting under a fig tree. Awed, Nathaniel instantly confessed his faith. "Rabbi, you are the Son of God; you are the King of Israel." Jesus must have smiled. One of his Beatitudes promised that the "pure of heart" would see God. Few people boldly spoke the truth about him as Nathaniel did.

Jesus promised Bartholomew (Nathaniel), "You will see the sky opened and the angels of God ascending and descending on the Son of Man" (John 1:51). Jesus loved Bartholomew's great honesty. Commit yourself to living in the light, to speaking the truth at all times.

August 25
Saint Louis (King Louis IX of France) (1214–1270)

SAINTE-CHAPELLE — PROTECTED BY THE ANGELS

 For centuries, Christian tourists have visited Sainte-Chapelle, a magnificent Gothic church in Paris built between 1241–1248 by Louis IX, the only French king to be named a saint. After the fall of Constantinople, Louis acquired relics from the Holy Land and designed the chapel to resemble a reliquary. More than one thousand exquisite windows sparkle like jewels, and tell Bible stories so vividly that they are called "the Bible of the poor." Innumerable angels appear in glass and stone and atop steeples. On the western façade, beneath the great rose window, two kneeling angels appear on a balustrade of *fleurs de lis*. The French credit the angels for protecting Sainte-Chapelle — twice from fires that destroyed every building nearby, from the flooding of the Seine River, and from angry mobs who threatened to tear it down during the French Revolution. [209]

Holy places already have the protection of the angels. Because God lives in you, ask these same angels to protect your home and place of work.

August 26

GOD'S SECRET AGENTS

 In *Angels: God's Secret Agents*, Billy Graham explained that he had never planned to write a book on angels. But that changed. "When I decided to preach a sermon on angels, I found practically nothing in my library," he wrote. "Upon investigation I soon discovered that little had been written on the subject in this century." So, the man known as "America's pastor" wrote to address what he saw as "a strange and ominous omission. Bookstores and libraries had plenty of books on demons," he said. Why were God's messengers ignored? "Angels," he pointed out, "have a much more important place in the Bible than the devil and his demons." Graham's book brought attention to angels, selling more than three million copies. [210]

"I believe in angels because the Bible says there are angels; and I believe the Bible to be the true Word of God. I also believe in angels because I have sensed their presence in my life on special occasions."

— Billy Graham

An Angel's Reassurance

 As a fervent Christian, Monica was devastated when her son Augustine came home to Tagaste in present-day Algeria. Augustine was carousing and had converted to Manichaeism, a heresy that denied God. One day when Monica was praying, an angel appeared and asked why she was weeping. When she explained, the angel told her. "Your son is with you." When Monica told Augustine about the vision, he agreed. They would be together if she abandoned Christianity. Not to be outdone by her brilliant son, Monica countered, "He didn't say I was with you … he said that you were with me." Years later, the angel's promise was fulfilled. Augustine became one of Christianity's greatest saints and theologians. [211]

Are there prayers you long to offer for someone else? Begin or begin again to pray each day for this person. Be encouraged by Saint Monica who was encouraged by an angel.

August 28

Saint Augustine (354–430)

ANGEL AT THE SEASHORE

 According to legend, Augustine often walked along the seashore, reflecting on divine mysteries. One day, he encountered a young boy running back and forth from the sea, pouring seawater into a hole dug in the sand. Smiling, Augustine asked what he was doing. "Can't you see?" the boy said. "I'm emptying the sea into this pool." "You can't," Augustine said. "The sea's too big." Looking intensely at Augustine, the boy responded. "It's no more impossible than trying to fit the mystery of the Trinity into your small mind!" Stunned, Augustine looked to see if the boy's mother or father was nearby. When he turned back to address this amazing boy — or angel — he was gone. [212]

Augustine said, "Faith is to believe what you do not see; the reward of this faith is to see what you believe." Are you growing in your ability to believe in what you do not see? [213]

August 29

Father Rohr's Mother Sees His Angel

 In 1993, Franciscan friar Richard Rohr was home in Topeka, Kansas. Father Rohr's elderly mother was dying of cancer and slipping in and out of consciousness. "So, I quietly approached the foot of her bed to see if she was alert," he wrote. Suddenly, she opened her eyes and focused on something to his left. "What are you looking at, Mother?" Father Rohr asked. "Oh, it's your guardian angel," she said calmly. Stunned, her son, a nationally known speaker and writer, had nothing to say. "What does he look like?" he finally asked. "Well, he looks just like you," she said. "Oh, I thought he would be better looking," the son told his mother. Mrs. Rohr smiled, peacefully closed her eyes and died several days later. [214]

"All my theological training and years of ministry had not allowed me to see, fully understand, or even be prepared for what Mother saw — and what so many see — in those last luminal days and hours when the 'veil is thin' between this world and the next."

— Father Richard Rohr

August 30

Oak Angels

 On this date in 2005, Hurricane Katrina devastated much of the Gulf Coast, including historic New Orleans. Besides the 1,700 people killed, thousands of homes, and hundreds of schools, businesses, and cultural attractions were washed away. After the city's levees broke, forty-foot-high saltwater surges also spelled the ultimate death of many treasured oak trees. Once the waters receded, leaving behind rubble and broken dreams, some artists carved beautiful angels from the dead oaks. People of the Gulf Coast needed reminders that God and his angels hadn't left them. At Bay St. Louis in Mississippi, the "Angel Tree" stands today near the city's marina. In 2005, a woman, two men, and a small dog survived high above the ground in the huge oak's protective limbs. [215]

Even in the midst of the greatest and deadliest storms, there is always hope and there are angels to remind us that God cares for us.

August 31

A Pope Stands Up for the Angels

 In 1950, seventy-four-year-old Pope Pius XII published the encyclical *Humani Generis* ("On the Human Race"). He wanted to remind the world that theological opinions should be subject to the teaching authority of the Church. He didn't deny that theologians can and should engage in scholarly research. But some scholars were denying that God had created an "unseen world," a spiritual world. As a result, the pope said, the very existence of angels as "personal creatures" was being questioned. Angels were being dismissed as metaphors of God's care and love. This line of thought emerged especially from the "New Theology" movement in France. The pope and others felt that centuries of Catholic teaching — and the angels — should be defended. [216]

"We must be linked up with the Holy Angels: we must form with them one strong family."

— Pope Pius XII

September 1

PROTESTANTS AND THE ANGELS

 Although there are nearly three hundred angel references in the Protestant Bible, Protestant views about angels are often different than those of Catholics and Orthodox Christians. One of the complaints (or protests) of Martin Luther was that Catholics worshipped angels, along with the Virgin Mary and saints. As Protestantism spread in Europe, statues and pictures of angels were often destroyed. Today, most Protestants believe that God sends angels to protect human beings. There is also common belief among Protestants that angels can be agents of miracles and that often they guide dying people to God. [217]

> *"We Christians should have the sure knowledge that the princes of heaven are with us [and] not only one or two, but a large number of them as Luke records (Luke 2:13) that a multitude of heavenly host was with the shepherds. And if we were without this custody, and God did not in this way check the fury of Satan, we could not live for one moment."*

> — Martin Luther [218]

How Smart Are Angels?

"The angel has an intelligence second only to God's," wrote American Cardinal John Wright (1909–1979). Wright said that the Scriptures confirm that the intellect of angels has no earthly comparison. Angelic intelligence is fundamentally different than a person's. It is not burdened by the physical limitations of a human brain and what it needs to function well: adequate blood flow, nutrition, and the absence of disease. The angelic intellect is agile and can make instantaneous deductions. In a flash, an angel "learns" or "knows" what a human mind can grasp only after much mental work and time. [219]

Jesus once referred to the superior knowledge and wisdom of the angels by explaining that not even the angels knew the day or hour of judgment. Thank you, God, for the brilliant and loving creatures you have sent to guide us.

September 3

Saint Gregory the Great (540–604)

A POPE'S CHARITY

 On this date in 590, Gregory became a priest and then pope! He would have preferred to remain a Benedictine monk. A brilliant theologian and writer, he wrote extensively about angels. Calling himself "the servant of the servants of God," Gregory served dinner daily to twelve poor people. One day, he saw a thirteenth guest. When Gregory questioned the man, he discovered the guest was actually an angel who once came as a beggar. Gregory had given him money and his mother's silver dish. Because of this charity, the angel told him, "God has given you the Chair of Saint Peter and sent me to be your guardian as long as you remain in this world." [220]

"Nearly every page of Scripture testifies to the fact that there are angels and archangels."

— Saint Gregory the Great [221]

September 4

THE WORLD IS FILLED WITH ANGELS

 When early Christian writers wrote about the angels, they were also teaching about the "unseen world," a world created by God just as surely as the "seen world." Saint Hilary of Poitiers, who was raised as a pagan, tried to explain this spiritual reality wherever he went. Despite his reluctance, Hilary was named bishop of Poitiers in present-day France. "Man lives in the middle of a supernatural world," wrote the man who had studied Greek philosophy and even the Bible before his conversion. "Everything that seems empty is filled with the angels of God and there is no place that is not inhabited by them." [222]

Reflect today on Saint Hilary's spiritual insight: What we see as empty and meaningless is actually filled with angels — and the loving care of God. [223]

September 5

Saint Teresa of Calcutta (1910–1997)

TREATED LIKE AN ANGEL

 Mother Teresa was walking past an open drain in Calcutta, India, when she caught a glimpse of something moving in it. She investigated and found a dying man inside. She took him to a Home for the Dying she had opened where he could die with dignity. "I lived like an animal in the streets," the man told her as she personally cared for him. "Now I will die like an angel" — surrounded by love and heavenly peace. [224]

"Holy Angels, our advocates, our brothers, our counselors, our defenders, our enlighteners, our friends, our guides, our helpers, our intercessors, pray for us."

— Saint Teresa of Calcutta [225]

September 6

Saint Petersburg's Enduring Angel

 On September 6, 1991, the name "Saint Petersburg" was restored to the city of Leningrad, Russia's second largest city. Religious rights were also being restored. From 1917 until its collapse in 1989, the Soviet Union banned religion and confiscated religious property. Atheism was the state religion. Monuments like the Alexander Column in Saint Petersburg, however, were problematic. Erected in 1834 to celebrate Russia's victory over Napoleon, the six hundred ton, red granite column was topped with a magnificent angel holding a cross. In 1952, Soviets discussed replacing the column's angel with a statue of Soviet leader Joseph Stalin. But Saint Petersburg's angel wasn't to be displaced and still guards the city. [226]

"We shall find peace. We shall hear angels, we shall see the sky sparkling with diamonds."

— From the last scene of the play *Uncle Vanya*, by Anton Chekhov (1860–1904)

September 7

In the Hands of Angels

 At age forty-four, Blessed John Henry Newman (1801–1890) left the Anglican Church to become Catholic. Soon after, he was ordained a Catholic priest. Throughout his ministry, Newman tried to help people see Creation's hidden truths. According to Newman, we should recognize that God's hand — through his angels — has set everything in motion. Changing seasons, flowers blooming, animals migrating. All these and more are in the hands of the angels, insisted one of England's most brilliant scholars. Newman believed that man would be astounded to discover the existence and power of angels in the visible world.

"Surely we are not told in Scripture about the Angels for nothing, but for practical purposes; nor can I conceive a use of our knowledge more practical than to make it connect the sight of this world with the thought of another."

— Blessed John Henry Newman,
The Powers of Nature, Sermon 29

An Angel Is an Idea of God

Today we celebrate a birthday — a day to rejoice in the life God gives us. Celebrating a birth is so human — and so divine. When Mary was born in Nazareth, her family praised and thanked God. But they couldn't know what God had in mind for her. Meister Eckhart (1260–1329) wrote that "an angel is an idea of God. For this reason the angel was sent to the soul, so that the soul might be re-formed by it." Everything created began as an idea of God. Eckhart was speaking of God's desire for each of us to become, in fact, what God first conceived us to be. At her birth, God sent an angel to guard and guide Mary, to prepare her, heart and soul, to be the mother of his Son. So human, so divine. [227]

"The Glorious Virgin did not have a stain in her birth because she was sanctified in her mother's womb and safeguarded there by angels."

— Saint Anthony of Padua

September 9

THE ANGELS' CREDENTIALS

What would we think of an astronomer who admitted the existence of the firmament but excluded the stars? With just such relevancy, the angels belong to Scripture. "Angels owe their credibility to divine revelation. Once we admit the Bible to be God's word and his vehicle of communication with man, admitting to the existence of angels should quickly follow." [228]

"It might be noted further that the greatest among the saints and men of God, from Augustine to John Henry Newman, have always lived on familiar terms with them [the angels]. And the tradition of the Church has always accorded them a very large place in her theology."

— Jean Danielou, S.J. [229]

September 10

Can Your Guardian Angel Read Your Mind?

 Yes and no — it's up to you. Your guardian angel, or any angel, can know your thoughts if you freely choose to reveal them, or if God chooses to reveal them. God, of course, always knows your thoughts and may, for reasons of grace or blessing, dispatch your angel with necessary information. If you don't intend to share your secret thoughts, your mind will be closed to your angel. It's amazing, though, that you can communicate without using words — if you let your angel read your mind. [230]

Saint Rose of Lima (1586–1617) would sometimes return home just in time to see her angel appear and open the gate for her as she approached. [231]

September 11

 We can be pretty sure that angels don't chat about what they did all day or, heaven forbid, gossip. But angels do share among themselves their thoughts, knowledge, affections, desire, joy, gratitude, and happiness. Angels reveal whatever they wish to convey to other angels by a simple act of will, without the help of spoken word — think telepathic communication. It is much more beautiful than that, however. The language of angels is so clear, compelling, and perfect that it is called *illumination*. Theologians say that God enlightens the angels of the highest orders with supernatural understanding and they in turn enlighten, or illuminate, the angels of lower ranks. When the angels "speak" to God they express their openness to God's grace and they adore and praise the Holy Trinity.

"Consider how august a privilege it is, when angels are present, and archangels throng around, when cherubim and seraphim encircle with their blaze the throne, that a mortal may approach with unrestrained confidence, and converse with heaven's Sovereign!"

— Saint John Chrysostom [232]

September 12

A Voice from Heaven

 Saint Augustine described the heavenly voice that led him to conversion. One afternoon, he sought solitude in a neighbor's garden. "Suddenly I heard a voice from a house nearby — singing over and over again, 'Pick it up and read, pick it up and read.' ... I began to think hard whether children ordinarily repeated a ditty like this in any sort of game, but I could not recall ever having heard it anywhere else. I rose to my feet, believing that this could be nothing other than a divine command to open the Book and read the first passage I chanced upon.... I opened it and read in silence the passage on which my eyes first lighted ... I had no wish to read further, nor was there need. No sooner had I reached the end of the verse than the light of certainty flooded my heart and all dark shades of doubt fled away." 233

The verse Saint Augustine read: "Not in dissipation and drunkenness, nor in debauchery and lewdness, nor in arguing and jealously; but put on the Lord Jesus Christ, and make no provision for the flesh or the gratification of your desires" (Romans 13:13–14).

September 13

Saint John Chrysostom (c. 347–407)

WE REPRESENT THE CHERUBIM

 The Divine Liturgy of Saint John Chrysostom is the primary worship service of the Eastern Orthodox Church. It was so named because the anphora (Eucharistic Prayer) is attributed to him. As archbishop of Constantinople, this great Doctor of the Church had a strong influence on the development of the liturgy. He taught that through the liturgy, the people are not only joining in with the angels, but actually representing them, as they approach the solemn moment of consecration. This vision is expressed in their hymn: "We who mystically represent the Cherubim, sing the thrice-holy hymn to the life-giving Trinity. Let us put away all worldly care, so that we may receive the King of All, invisibly escorted by the angelic hosts."

"When you are before the altar where Christ reposes, you ought no longer to think that you are amongst men; but believe that there are troops of angels and archangels standing by you, and trembling with respect before the sovereign Master of Heaven and earth."

— Saint John Chrysostom [234]

THE SERAPHIC VISION

On the Feast of the Holy Cross, 1224, Saint Francis of Assisi received the stigmata of Jesus. He had gone up to his retreat high on a rocky Tuscan mountain called La Verna. There Francis was contemplating the Passion of Christ when he saw, coming swiftly from heaven, a resplendent seraph with six wings. As it came closer, Francis saw upon the wings the crucified figure of Jesus. Francis was filled with joy in the presence of Jesus but also deep sorrow at the marks of his suffering. While Jesus spoke to Francis the whole of La Verna was ablaze with a brightness that was seen for miles around. When the seraphic vision vanished, Francis's hands, feet, and side were pierced with the wounds of Christ. Francis bore the bloody and painful wounds for two years before his own death. [235]

Through his life Francis conformed himself to Christ; now he took on the suffering of Christ in his own person. We too are all called to conform ourselves to the life of Christ through the sacraments and to participate in his saving death by uniting our suffering to his.

September 15
Our Lady of Sorrows

ALWAYS TURNED TOWARD GOD

 Much like the angels, Mary was always turned toward God. Angels are sent as God's messengers but are simultaneously present before his throne. Free of Original Sin, there were no barriers to Mary's orientation toward her Creator. "Behold, I am the handmaid of the Lord," she told the Archangel Gabriel. Today, the Church celebrates Mary's turning toward God — even in sorrow. Since 1814, the whole Latin Church has remembered the sorrows Mary accepted as the mother of the Savior: Simeon's prophecy, the flight into Egypt, the loss of Jesus in the Temple, meeting Jesus on his way to the cross, his Crucifixion, receiving Jesus' body, the burial of Jesus. [236]

What would it mean in your life if you could turn toward God in every situation, in every time of need and sorrow, as well as during times of rejoicing?

September 16

Saints Cornelius (died 253) and Cyprian (c. 200–258)

ANGELS AND REPENTANCE

 Perhaps those words of Jesus in Luke's Gospel about angels rejoicing over repentant sinners (Luke 15:10) were written on the heart of Saint Cornelius, the twenty-first pope. Although his papacy was only two years long, Pope Cornelius and his good friend Bishop Cyprian agreed that the Church should forgive repentant Christians who took part in pagan sacrifices in order to save their lives. During this era of violent persecution and martyrdom of Christians, some Christians weakened. Within the Church, there was disagreement about how remorseful Christians should be treated. Pope Cornelius, like Pope Francis many centuries later, believed that the Church should offer mercy. The return of sinners should be cause for our rejoicing, just as Jesus said it is for the angels.

Though Saints Cornelius and Cyprian were both martyred during Roman persecutions, their example of offering the Lord's forgiveness and mercy to those who were afraid of martyrdom is a lesson in mercy for our times.

September 17

Saint Hildegard of Bingen (1098–1179)

O GLORIOUS ANGELS

 Hildegard was a renaissance woman long before the period of history that we call the Renaissance began. She was a Benedictine nun, abbess, mystic, musician, composer, poet, artist, and author of texts on theology, science, and medicinal plants. Her music and poetry is sublimely beautiful and often described as "angelic." Hildegard's major work was *Scivias (Know the Ways of the Lord)*. It describes her visions concerning the relationship between God, humanity, and the cosmos. Though she was long considered and called a saint, Hildegard was officially canonized on May 7, 2012. On October 7, 2012, Pope Benedict XVI also declared her a Doctor of the Church, an "authentic teacher of theology and a profound scholar of natural science and music."

O Gloriosissimi lux
Angels, living light most glorious!
Beneath the Godhead in burning desire
in the darkness and mystery of creation
you look on the eye of your God
never taking your fill:
What glorious pleasures take shape within you! [237]

Monastery Life and the Angels

 According to Cistercian monk Mark Scott, there are many ways that monastic life imitates the angels. For instance, monks are to practice obedience without hesitation. Similarly, the obedience of angels to God is instantaneous. "Angels are spirit, they are light," Scott said, "and not a hair's breadth exists between God's willing something and their doing it." Like angels, monks are also willing to go where they're sent and serve with single-hearted dedication. What's more, added the author, monks don't say more than what's necessary. "They know when to be quiet and they know when to be invisible." Just like the angels! [238]

Most of us don't live in a monastery, but there are ways that what we choose to do and say can come closer to the example of the angels and the daily practice of monks.

September 19

Was It God or an Angel?

 Scripture scholars say that in some Old Testament narratives, the identity of heavenly visitors isn't always clear. Was the visitor an angel? Or, was it Yahweh, God himself? In some cases, explained theologian Lawrence Cunningham, "the angel is a kind of mask for God actually speaking." God was presented as an angel because Jewish writers wanted to protect the transcendence, the incomparable magnificence of God. God could not be presented as one among many characters in a narrative. As a result, said Cunningham, the use of the word "angel" was occasionally just a literary device. An angel was to be understood as God himself directly interacting with and speaking to his people. [239]

"It is not because angels are holier than men or devils that makes them angels, but because they do not expect holiness from one another, but from God alone."

— William Blake [240]

September 20

An Angel to Clean the Blackboard

 In the 1950s, millions of television viewers chuckled when an auxiliary bishop from the Archdiocese of New York joked each week about the angel who cleaned his chalkboard. Archbishop Fulton J. Sheen (1895–1979) used the chalkboard during his Emmy-winning television show *Life Is Worth Living*. Blessed with a sonorous voice, Irish good looks, and a flair for the dramatic, Sheen used humor, stories, and Scripture to address topics of family and social interest. America's favorite bishop wouldn't have denied that it was the studio stage crew — not his angel — who cleaned his chalkboard. Angels and their role as messengers of God's love were frequent topics. [241]

Archbishop Sheen knew how to tell a joke even as he taught about the faith. "I pray every day to Saint Raphael [the Archangel] to guard me when I fly. When I travel, it's TWA … Travel With Angels," joked Archbishop Fulton J. Sheen.

September 21

Saint Matthew (First Century)

ANGEL AND EVANGELIST

 Since the days of Saint Jerome, the symbol for Saint Matthew, an Apostle and evangelist, has been a winged man — an angel. The word "angel" means "messenger" and is the root of the word "evangelist." Matthew was the messenger who showed how Jesus fulfilled all of the Messianic prophecies that God gave to his Chosen People, the Jews. Initially, Jesus' call to Matthew — a tax collector — shocked and offended the Jewish community because tax collectors were seen as traitors. But Jesus saw something else in Matthew — something that his kingdom needed — "a winged man."

Matthew's life changed completely when Jesus called him to share God's Word. Would you let your life change to share God's Word in your world?

September 22

Angels at the Airport

 On the way home to Salt Lake City, Utah, Margo Fallis's flight was fogged in at Atlanta. Broke and hungry, Margo was feeling down. When Andrew, a friendly and strangely reassuring man bought her a sandwich and asked her about her family, she relaxed. When the fog cleared, Margo's flight resumed. She looked forward to introducing Andrew to her husband. When the plane landed, Andrew had vanished. A few weeks later, Margo was looking at old family photos just sent from England. Suddenly, she gasped. One dated "1897" was of a man with a very familiar face and smile. It was her great-grandfather, Andrew Donaldson. [242]

Angels can appear as anyone when they come. But their thoughtful inclination seems to be visiting in ways that comfort and encourage us as we journey.

September 23

Saint Pio of Pieltrelcina (1887–1968)

SEEING ANGELS

 Padre Pio was a Capuchin priest who interacted with angels so naturally that many people who knew him also developed a love for the angels. In 1947, Father Dominic Meyer was summoned from Saint Felix Friary in Huntington, Indiana, to San Giovanni Rotondo in Italy to assist Padre Pio by translating for German and English-speaking visitors. One day he opened a letter from an American woman who wanted to know if Padre Pio saw her guardian angel when she sent him with a message, or if he could only hear the angel's voice. Father Dominic thought this was ridiculous. His tone was quite sarcastic when he posed the question to Padre Pio. The latter was not pleased and firmly replied, "Father Dominico, when that woman sends her guardian angel to me, I see the angel just as I see you!" [243]

"Have great devotion to your good angel; how consoling it is to know that near us is a spirit who, from the cradle to the tomb, does not leave us even for an instant, not even when we dare to sin. He guides us and protects us like a friend, a brother."

— Saint Pio of Pietrelcina [244]

JESUS IS OUR GUARDIAN ANGEL

 Jesus Christ is the Lord of all creation, Lord of the Angels and all Powers. Even the guardian angels who are our personal protectors serve him and help us because it is God's will. The angels help us to understand Jesus' love and saving grace in our lives and in the world. Ladislaus Boros (1927–1981), a Jesuit priest and theologian at the University of Munich, wrote, "To survive the great mysteries of life, man needs a higher form of aid: assistance that we simply can't count on in the human realm. Jesus shows himself to be our guardian angel. Jesus brought everything to unity and gave us the grace to experience God's closeness in human form, to be holy, to live things in their original holiness, and to love with all the effort of all his life." [245]

"Jesus stands in a direct relationship to every single man, helping him and accompanying him. In that way our Lord Jesus is our only guardian angel."

— Ladislaus Boros

September 25

ANGELS SHELTER THE HOMELESS

 Saint Hilary of Poitiers described the ministry of the guardian angels: "It is not God who has need of their intercession, but rather our weakness. They are, in fact, sent for the benefit of those who are to inherit salvation, since nothing of what we do is hidden from God, and our infirmity is in need of their ministry." The angels are as God created them to be. Humans are not yet there; we are on the way. Now we are homeless, sometimes lost, and always longing for our true home. At the end of our journey, our spiritual inheritance awaits. In the meantime, angels shelter us and try to keep us on the right track. [246]

See, I am sending an angel before you, to guard you on the way and bring you to the place I have prepared. Be attentive to him and obey him. (Exodus 23:20–21)

September 26

HEALED BY AN ANGEL

 Fourteen-year-old Chelsea had a history of serious health issues and lay dying of pneumonia in a hospital room in Charlotte, North Carolina, in 2008. Her mother had just given doctors permission to take Chelsea off life support. As Colleen Banton waited for her daughter to take her last breath, an image of bright light appeared on a security monitor. Within an hour, the dying girl began a recovery that doctors were at a loss to explain. But Colleen Banton has an explanation. "This was an image of an angel," she told NBC News in a story reported on the *Today* show. She credited the apparition with saving Chelsea's life. "It's a blessing, a miracle," she said. Others — including nurses who were on duty — agreed that the three vertical shafts of light were "undisputedly" an angel.

In an interview on Today, *a minister told Ann Curry that she believes that angels are messengers from God. "They bring the message of hope" she said. A rabbi told Curry, "The real question is: Can we be open to wonder? Even at the very last moment, the very darkest moment, can we actually be open to the new possibilities that are always there?"* [247]

September 27

Angels of Lower Wacker

 Dr. Patrick Angelo, a Chicago dentist, had been helping the homeless on the city's Lower Wacker Drive for fourteen years. He bought them food and clothing and delivered the items at least once a week. His efforts made such an impact that the homeless began to know him by name. After a WGN-television feature about Angelo aired, other people started to reach out. Curlene West-Hastings was one who felt moved to help. She became the "second angel on Lower Wacker." Concerning her ongoing commitment to Chicago's homeless, Curlene said, "I think it's something that God has put inside of me. I would rather be with the people that need me." The two "angels" have partnered up with other organizations and are now covering Lower Wacker and other locations every night of the week. Their long-term plan is to expand the program and offer job training and educational opportunities to the homeless. [248]

God and Father of the homeless, help me to see and then act like the angels when I encounter those without homes, without food, without hope.

The Example of the Angels

It is important to remember that Church doctrine was not handed down to us all wrapped up and tied with a bow. Throughout the earliest centuries of the Church, false teachings and philosophies caused Church Fathers to clarify the proper place of the angels. Saint Paul warned the Colossians (2:18) against the worship of angels. Christian theologian, Origen, refuted various philosophies that distorted the intermediary role of angels. He explained that "every prayer and supplication and intercession is to be sent up to the Supreme God through the High Priest [Jesus Christ] who is above all the angels.... It is enough to secure that the holy angels be propitious to us, and that they do all things on our behalf, that our disposition of mind towards God should imitate, as far as possible for human nature, the example of these holy angels, who themselves imitate the example of God." [249]

An angel is "the most excellent of creatures because he bears the strongest resemblance to God," stated Saint Thomas Aquinas. Take comfort in that today. That splendid creature who accompanies you resembles the loving God who made you — and everything else.

September 29

Saints Michael, Gabriel, and Raphael, archangels

SAINT MICHAEL, DEFEND US

This is the feast of three archangels: Saints Michael, Gabriel, and Raphael. Michael is the best known. For thousands of years, Saint Michael the Archangel has been regarded as the strong defender of God's people. Michael was the guardian of the Israelites in the Old Testament. In 1886, Pope Leo XIII revived the idea of seeking Saint Michael's special protection. He wrote a prayer asking Saint Michael to protect God's people. The pope ordered the *Prayer to Saint Michael* to be recited after all daily Masses around the world. The practice continued until 1964. Some say Pope Leo wrote the prayer after he had a terrifying vision about evils that would take place in the twentieth century.

Saint Michael the Archangel, defend us in battle. Be our protection against the wickedness and snares of the devil. (See the complete Prayer to St. Michael in the appendix, page 381.)

September 30
Saint Jerome (c. 340–420)

Saint Jerome and the Angel

 Saint Jerome was a popular subject of medieval and Renaissance art. A large oil on canvas painting titled "Saint Jerome and the Angel" hangs in the National Gallery in Washington, D.C. Painted by French artist Simon Vouet around 1622–1625, it shows Jerome seated at a desk with scrolls and a pen in hand. He and the angel are deep in conversation, or, perhaps in consultation. Jerome devoted his life to the study of Scripture and translating the Bible into Latin. He established monasteries for men and women, but he himself chose to live as a hermit. We should all remember that we have an angel looking over our shoulder. [250]

"So valuable to heaven is the dignity of the human soul that every member of the human race has a guardian angel from the moment the person begins to be."

— Saint Jerome

October 1

Saint Thérèse of Lisieux (1873–1897)

THE COMPANION OF MY EXILE

 Even as a young child, Thérèse spoke often to her guardian angel as to a best friend, and she developed a deep devotion to all the angels. She noted in her autobiography, *Story of a Soul*, "Almost immediately after my entrance at the Abbey, I was received into the Association of the Holy Angels. I loved the pious practices it imposed, as I had a very special attraction to pray to the blessed spirits of heaven, particularly to the one whom God gave as 'the companion of my exile.'" Thérèse was keenly aware that heaven was her true home. Once there, she would pray and help others more effectively. She promised, "If God answers my desires … I want to spend my heaven in doing good on earth. This isn't impossible, since from the bosom of the beatific vision, the Angels watch over us." [251]

"My holy Guardian Angel, cover me with your wing. With your fire, light the road that I'm taking. Come, direct my steps … help me. I call upon you, just for today."

— Saint Thérèse of Lisieux [252]

October 2

Feast of the Holy Guardian Angels

WISE AS AN ANGEL

 "Guardian angels are not the stuff of fantasy," Pope Francis said. "They are really present as wise travel companions. Nobody walks alone and none of us can believe we are alone. All of us have an angel who watches over us and lets us hear, deep inside, wise words meant to help us make the right choices. Don't ignore the inner voice that says, 'Well, you should do this.' 'That's not right.' 'Watch out!' It's the voice of your travel companion helping you to navigate life's journey. To turn one's back on a guardian angel is dangerous because no man, no woman can advise themselves. I can give advice to someone else, but I can't give advice to myself, if it's going to be objective and wise advice — like an angel's." [253]

"An angel of Paradise, no less, is always beside me, rapt in everlasting loving ecstasy with his God. So I am ever under the gaze of an angel who protects and prays for me. What a thought!"

— Pope Saint John XXIII [254]

October 3

Saint Mother Theodore Guerin (1798–1856)

GUARDIAN ANGELS OF INDIANA

 Mother Theodore Guerin founded the Sisters of Providence at Saint Mary-of-the-Woods near present-day Terre Haute, Indiana. When Mother Theodore first arrived in 1840, the area was a dense forest wilderness. Despite daunting hardships and extreme privation, her community endured and thrived. Upon her return from a journey to her native France, Mother Theodore was filled with "inexpressible joy.... This land was no longer for me the land of exile; it was the portion of my inheritance, and in it I hope to dwell all the days of my life. I saluted the Guardian Angels of Indiana and prayed them to take the souls of these poor people under their protection, especially those who we are called upon to benefit." [255]

> LORD, my allotted portion and my cup, you have made my destiny secure. Pleasant places were measured out for me; fair to me indeed is my inheritance.... With him at my right hand, I shall never be shaken. Therefore my heart is glad, my soul rejoices;... You will show me the path to life, abounding joy in your presence, the delight at your right hand forever. (Psalm 16:5–6, 8–9, 11)

AN ANGEL NAMED WONDERFUL

While one of Saint Francis's first followers, Friar Bernard, was returning to Assisi from a long journey, he stopped at a great river. A young man greeted him in his own language. Surprised, Bernard asked where he was from. The young man replied that he'd just come from visiting the monastery of Friar Francis. When he asked Friar Bernard why he wasn't crossing the river, Bernard admitted that he was afraid of deep water. The youth took his hand and instantly transported him to the other side. Only then did Bernard know that the young man was an angel. With reverence and joy, Bernard exclaimed, "O blessed angel of God, tell me your name." The angel answered, "Why do you ask my name, which is Wonderful?" Then, he vanished. Back home, when Bernard described the angel, he learned that it was the same angel who visited them. [256]

Do not fear, for I have redeemed you; I have called you by name: you are mine. When you pass through waters, I will be with you; through rivers, you shall not be swept away.... For I, the LORD, am your God, your savior.... Because you are precious in my eyes and honored, and I love you. (Isaiah 43:1–4)

October 5

Saint Faustina Kowalska (1905–1938)

THE APOSTLE OF DIVINE MERCY AND HER ANGEL

 Sister Faustina Kowalska knew that telling the world about God's mercy would make her Satan's target. Once when the young Polish Sister of Our Lady of Mercy was walking home from church, demons suddenly blocked her path. Because her prayers were snatching souls from their grasp, she wrote, "they threatened me with terrible tortures." Frightened, Faustina prayed for help. "Immediately, the evil spirits vanished and the faithful Guardian Angel accompanied me, in a visible manner, right to the very house." Saint Faustina's Divine Mercy message spread rapidly after World War II. Many people had seen God as a strict and unforgiving judge. Learning of his "unfathomable mercy" was Good News indeed. [257]

Some spiritual writers say that of all the traits of God, mercy is his supreme trait. God is love, and love put into action is mercy. Today, be alert for opportunities to show mercy, putting love into action.

October 6

THE CATHEDRAL OF THE ARCHANGEL

 In the heart of Moscow, the Cathedral of the Archangel merges into the skyline near the Kremlin. Dedicated to the Archangel Michael, the Russian Orthodox Church was built between 1505 and 1508 by order of Ivan the Great. It was the place of prayer before battle, and the site of the solemn ceremonial coronation and burial of tsars. In the eighteenth century, the central dome, which had previously been round, was replaced with a traditional golden onion-shaped dome. The iconostasis of the cathedral was replaced in 1813 after Napoleon's troops used the former one for firewood. In 1995, the cathedral was turned into a museum. Through it all, the cathedral has retained possession of its oldest and most precious icon of the Archangel Michael in full armor defeating the forces of Satan. [258]

Then war broke out in heaven; Michael and his angels battled against the dragon. The dragon and its angels fought back, but they did not prevail.... The huge dragon, the ancient serpent, who is called the Devil and Satan, who deceived the whole world, was thrown down to earth, and its angels were thrown down with it. (Revelation 12:7–9)

October 7

Our Lady of the Rosary

 In the encyclical "Most August Virgin Mary," Pope Leo XIII reflected on the role of the angels in the mysteries of the Rosary. "The Angels revealed each of these mysteries in its due time; they played a great part in them; they were constantly present at them.... Gabriel was sent to announce the Incarnation of the Eternal Word to the Virgin. In the cave of Bethlehem, Angels sang the glory of the newborn Savior. The Angel gave Joseph command to fly with the Child into Egypt. An Angel consoled, with his loving words, Jesus in His bloody sweat in the garden. Angels announced His resurrection, after He had triumphed over death, to the women. Angels carried Him up into Heaven; and foretold His second coming, surrounded by Angelic hosts." [259]

Saint Alphonsus Liguori once said that each time we pray a Hail Mary we attract the angels and repel the devils. Each Rosary involves praying the Hail Mary fifty-three times. That's a lot of angel power. [260]

THE ANGEL OF THE NORTH

 The world's largest angel sculpture stands in an unexpected place, just as angels often do. This is where it belongs, however, at Gateshead in the north of England. Created with two hundred tons of steel and standing higher than a five-story building, the angel has industrial strength and an eerie beauty. It has outstretched wings almost the width of a jumbo jet. Antony Gormley, the sculptor of the "Angel of the North," said that beneath the site, coal miners worked for two centuries in the dark. His work aims to celebrate light and visibility. We have moved from the industrial to the information age, Gormley explains, but our fears and hopes are the same. Poised between earth and sky, the angel embraces everything and everyone in its purview with a slight forward angle of its wings.

The towering angel is a reminder that things that are invisible are real. The artist concurs: "You make things because they cannot be said. You need to imagine them." [261]

October 9

WHO HAS A GUARDIAN ANGEL?

While early Christian theologians agreed on the existence of guardian angels, there was no consensus on who has a guardian angel. Some held that *every person* has a guardian angel.

- "Great, therefore, is the dignity of the human soul, since each has an angel assigned to it as its attendant." (Saint Jerome)
- "Each soul is in the custody of an angel." (Saint Anselm)

Others seemed to take the position that *only baptized people* have guardian angels.

- "Beside each believer stands an angel as protector and shepherd." (Saint Basil)

Saint Thomas Aquinas acknowledged both views, but concluded that "each man has an angel guardian appointed to him" through "the execution of Divine providence." He said that man is "on a road by which he should journey toward heaven ... threatened by many dangers both from within and from without ... so an angel guardian is assigned to each man as long as he is a wayfarer."

The fact that we cannot see our guardian angel does not mean that the angel is not with us at all times and in every circumstance.

October 10

THE BEAUTIFUL ANGELS

 "I am a nurse who works in a large hospital. One time I assisted another nurse with putting a patient to bed. The patient, a soft-spoken woman, suddenly became very agitated and excited. She began crying out, and grabbing at us, and pulling at sheets we had just straightened out. We finally got the patient somewhat settled and went to pull up the blankets, when she started saying, "Oh, how beautiful, look how beautiful the angels are!" The other nurse and I looked at the ceiling and rolled our eyes in disbelief. Later, when the other nurse returned to check on this patient, she found that the woman had died. I do believe to this day that the angels came for her."

— Marilyn K. [262]

"When someone dies, an angel is there to meet them at the gates of Heaven to let them know that their life has just begun."

— Anonymous

October 11

Saint John XXIII (1881–1963)

Angels Never Leave Us

 Today, the Church celebrates Pope Saint John XXIII, who was canonized in 2014 along with John Paul II. Typically, a saint's feast is the date of death. That was June 3 for Saint John XXIII. But, since the Second Vatican Council, called by this pope, opened on October 11, 1962, John's feast was transferred. Saint John XXIII had a lifelong devotion to angels. Born Angelo (Angel) Roncalli, he often counseled parents to remind their children that angels were assigned to guide and protect them. "Tell them they are never alone," he advised. The pope also privately told a Canadian bishop that the idea to call the Second Vatican Council (1962–1965) came to him in prayer — through his guardian angel. [263]

Guidance, protection, and peace are there for me — through the ministry of the angels. God, help me to be open. Help me to remember how the angels have inspired such wonderful things in those with open hearts and minds.

DO ANGELS LOVE?

It would be easy to assume that angels can't really love. Emotions are strong feelings that develop in response to our physical and spiritual experiences in the world. So, we could conclude that angels don't have emotions because they don't have bodies. But the highest form of love is a matter of the will — not of the emotions. Philosopher Peter Kreeft says that charity or agape means "willing the good of the other. Since this love comes from the will rather than the feelings, and since angels have wills, angels have this love. Angels do will the good of other angels and those whom they guard." [264]

In his first epistle, Saint John wrote, "Everyone who loves is begotten by God and knows God. Whoever is without love does not know God, for God is love" (1 John 4:7–8). Like us, angels are "begotten" by God. So, love must be part of their nature. Today, ask for your angel's help to grow in love — in your ability to give and receive it.

October 13

ARCHANGEL OF MERCY

 Although the Catholic Church has occasionally discouraged devotion to archangels not named in the Bible, interest in them has never died. They are honored in other religious traditions. Zadakiel is one of those archangels whose name never appears in Scripture. "Zadakiel" is Hebrew for the "righteousness of God." He is the archangel of freedom, generosity, and mercy. Zadakiel is the patron saint of all those who forgive. Jewish scholars maintain that Zadakiel was the unnamed angel who prevented Abraham from sacrificing his son Isaac. But in 2002, concern over unbalanced New Age angel devotions led the Vatican to ban veneration of Zadakiel and several other nonbiblical archangels.

How much the world needs angels — heaven's messengers — to whisper to us: "Go ahead; show mercy. Forgive those who have wounded or wronged you. Mercy is from God's heart."

Saint Callistus I (c. 222)

ANGEL OF GOD'S MERCY

 As pope, Callistus seems to have been an angel (messenger) of God's mercy. His early life as a Christian slave likely sensitized him to the need for mercy. When the bank he was managing failed, Callistus was so afraid that he ran away. Finally captured, he was sentenced to grueling work in the mines in Sardinia, Italy. Callistus barely survived. When he returned to Rome, he became a deacon and was later elected pope. After much prayer and study, he permitted absolution for all sins of repentant sinners — even for adultery or murder. Opposition to this "leniency" was so great within the Church that the first antipope, Hippolytus, was elected to oppose him. But Callistus believed that a Church offering mercy was God's plan.

> *The Lord remembered us in our low estate,*
> > *for his mercy endures forever;*
> *Freed us from our foes,*
> > *for his mercy endures forever;*
> *And gives bread to all flesh,*
> > *for his mercy endures forever.*
> *(Psalm 136:23–25)*

October 15
Saint Teresa of Ávila (1515–1582)

AN ANGEL'S GOLDEN SPEAR

 For years, Saint Teresa was thoroughly bored by prayer. This Carmelite nun preferred any penance over prayer. In her forties, things changed as she began to put her heart into prayer. Often, God's presence overwhelmed her. She grew to love God deeply. Once, an angel appeared very close to her. "He was not large, but small of stature, and most beautiful — his face burning, as if he were one of the highest angels, who seem to be all of fire." With a golden spear, the angel pierced her heart — but not physically. The piercing filled her with even deeper love of God. The "pain," she said, was so indescribably sweet that she hoped it would never end. [265]

"Prayer is an act of love; words are not needed. Even if sickness distracts us from thoughts of God, all that is needed is the will to love."

— Saint Teresa of Ávila

October 16
Saint Hedwig (1174–1243)

ANGELS FOR THE POLISH POPE

 On this date in 1978, the first Polish pope was elected on the feast of Saint Hedwig. Hedwig was a thirteenth-century Polish princess whose love for the Church and poor was legendary. Pope Saint John Paul II (Karol Wojtyla) was a brilliant scholar, writer, and teacher who spoke ten languages. When he saw that he would be elected, the cardinal from Krakow wept. So much responsibility! But, angels were ready to guard this pope. During his twenty-seven-year papacy, he made 104 foreign trips and was personally seen by more people than anyone else in history. In Saint Peter's Square in 1981, Pope Saint John Paul was shot and almost killed. He believed he'd been saved by Our Lady of Fatima, and perhaps by the angels.

"Therefore the Church confesses her faith in the guardian angels, venerating them in the liturgy with an appropriate feast and recommending recourse to their protection by frequent prayer, as in the invocation 'Angel of God.' This prayer seems to draw on the treasure of the beautiful words of St. Basil: 'Every one of the faithful has beside him an angel as tutor and pastor, to lead him to life.'"

— Pope Saint John Paul II

October 17

Saint Ignatius of Antioch (35–107)

EARLY TEACHINGS ABOUT ANGELS

 When Ignatius was born in Syria, people were still talking about angels seen in Christ's empty tomb in Jerusalem a few years earlier. Ignatius converted to Christianity as a young man and became a student of Saint John the Evangelist. Later, Ignatius was the third bishop of Antioch. An Apostolic Father, Ignatius is especially remembered for six letters he wrote to console and instruct Christians while he was being led to Rome for execution. His letters provide an early look at theological teaching. Ignatius promoted devotion to the Eucharist and warned Christians to leave behind Jewish practices. In his letters, he also taught about angels and "heavenly things."

Heading toward death, Ignatius wrote that he had studied "the angelic orders, and the different sorts of angels and hosts … and above all the incomparable majesty of the Almighty God." [266] *All this knowledge was good and important, he said, but faith was more important than anything else.*

October 18

ANGELS AND FARMING

 Many organic farms, farm markets, and food co-ops are named after angels. Fresh produce and local wines were featured weekly at an open market at Angels Camp, in Calaveras County, California. At Angel Acres Farm in Wisconsin, livestock is humanely raised for market. Gourmet mushrooms were organically grown at 2 Angels Mushroom Farm in Tennessee. St. Michael's Farm Market, an outreach of an Episcopal Church in Dallas, Texas, helped provide healthy food for the needy. Associating a business with angels might be nothing more than savvy marketing, but surely, angels are "assigned" to help us cultivate the earth. Farming was, after all, the first task God gave mankind — even before the Fall.

In the Our Father, we routinely ask God to "Give us this day, our daily bread." God, through your angels, guide us in raising and sharing healthy food.

October 19

A Dog ... or an Angel?

 In times of peril, a large, gentle gray dog often came to the assistance of Saint John Bosco (1815–1888). The dog would suddenly appear when John was passing through dangerous neighborhoods, traveling on foot through the dark countryside, or, most famously, when he was attacked by thugs. As suddenly as he turned up, the dog would trot away after his service to the priest. John called his companion Il Grigio, Italian for "The Gray One." John admitted that it seemed unbelievable to say that Il Grigio was an angel, yet he was no ordinary dog. He firmly believed that his mysterious guardian saved him and his ministry on more than one occasion. [267]

A salutation among French peasants as late as the nineteenth century was "Bonjour à vous et votre compagnon" ("Good day to you and your companion") — acknowledging the presence of one's guardian angel. [268]

October 20

TARGETED BY DEMONS

 Saint Paul of the Cross had many visions and close encounters with angels — both angels of the Lord and their evil counterparts. As a young man in Genoa, Italy, he founded a religious order to honor Christ's Passion — the Passionists. Stories about demons tormenting him circulated, and there were witnesses to validate the reports. Once, Father Paul and Father Marcellinus were staying with a family while giving a mission. During the night, the family heard loud noises — like furniture being thrown around the priests' room. In the morning, a pale Father Marcellinus had to explain. Devils had attacked Paul and beaten him because his ministry was bringing many people to God.

"Paul of the Cross didn't dwell on the evil spirits who frequently persecuted him. He focused on God's love. God, he wrote, 'is a father and a most loving father who would rather let Heaven and Earth collapse than abandon anyone who trusted in Him.'"

— Saint Paul of the Cross [269]

October 21

ANTIPHON FOR THE ANGELS

 Antiphons are short verses that are sung or recited during liturgical celebrations. Some antiphons, like those written by Saint Hildegard of Bingen (see September 17) may be sung as separate chants. Her Antiphon for the Angels offers a glimpse into the mystery of God and our redemption.

Spirited light! on the edge
of the Presence your yearning
burns in the secret darkness,
O angels, insatiably
into God's gaze.

Perversity
could not touch your beauty;
you are essential joy.
But your lost companion,
angel of the crooked
wings — he sought the summit,
shot down the depths of God
and plummeted past Adam —
that a mud-bound spirit might soar.

— Saint Hildegard of Bingen [270]

October 22

Saint John Paul II (1920–2005)

Angels of Light

 At a general audience on August 20, 1986, Pope Saint John Paul II spoke about a "mystery of our salvation which must be profoundly important for every Christian: that there are pure spirits, creatures of God, initially all good and then, through a choice of sin, irreducibly separated into angels of light and angels of darkness. And while the existence of the wicked angels requires of us that we be watchful so as not to yield to their empty promises, we are certain that the victorious power of Christ the Redeemer enfolds our lives, so that we ourselves may overcome these spirits. In this, we are powerfully helped by the good angels, messengers of God's love."

"Angel of God, who are my guardian, enlighten, guard, govern, and guide me, who have been entrusted to you by the heavenly goodness. Amen."

— Prayer of Pope Saint John Paul II

October 23

THREE HEAVENLY VISITORS

 Around 1411 Andrei Rublev, a Russian monk, painted an extraordinary icon depicting the three travelers who visit Abraham and Sarah (Genesis 18) as the Holy Trinity. The entire icon shimmers with a golden light. The three angels are of equal size and dignity; all are clothed in heavenly blue to signify divinity. Their faces are identical, representing their oneness. Symbols and other colors differentiate the Three Persons. They are seated at a table to show both the hospitality of Abraham and how we are to welcome the Lord into our lives. Though their heads are inclined toward one another, the three angels face outward, inviting the viewer to join the circle of love. [271]

"As we place ourselves in front of the icon in prayer, we come to experience a gentle invitation to participate in the intimate conversation that is taking place among the three divine angels and to join them around the table. The movement from the Father toward the Son and the movement of both Son and Spirit toward the Father become a movement in which the one who prays is lifted up and held secure."

— Henri Nouwen [272]

October 24

An Angel in Solitude

 The spirit of Blessed Genoveva Torres Morales (1870–1956) soared above and beyond her physical limitations. Born into a Spanish working-class family, Genoveva experienced personal loss early. At thirteen, she had a leg amputated. Instead of feeling bitter, she recognized the pain that others endured. After learning to support herself by sewing, Genoveva founded a religious congregation, the Sisters of the Sacred Heart and the Holy Angels, commonly called the "Angelicas." At her beatification in 1995, Pope Saint John Paul II said, "A woman of humble origin and background, she possessed the knowledge of divine love. This love led her to devote her life to caring for retired women, to remedy the loneliness and deprivation in which many of them lived, looking after them materially and spiritually in a true home, beside them like an 'Angel in solitude.'" [273]

"Loneliness and neglect ... are among the most distressing evils of every age," Pope Saint John Paul II said. How can I, even in a small way, imitate Blessed Genoveva Torres Morales? How can I be an angel in solitude, bringing care, consolation, and compassion to someone in need?

October 25

When the "Sons of God" Shouted for Joy

 There was a "time" when angels did not exist, when time did not exist. Within the timeless and eternal existence of God, everything else had a beginning. Scripture affirms that the angels were created. "In [Christ] were created all things in heaven and on earth, the visible and the invisible, whether thrones or dominations or principalities or powers: all things were created through him and for him" (Colossians 1:16). Augustine taught that angels, being creatures of light, were created as part of the heavens. Other Church Fathers, including Ambrose and Jerome, held that the angels were created long before the material world and were present when the earth was made. To illustrate, they cited Scripture: "Where were you when I founded the earth?... While the morning stars sang together and all the sons of God (angels) shouted for joy?" (Job 38:4, 7).

> *"The first creative act produced (angels) to the image and similitude of God, creatures able to understand, love, thank and praise God. When the whole material world had been created, the Lord formed another similar creature 'a little less than the angels,' consisting of body and spirit, able to know, love and serve God on earth as the Angels do in heaven"* [274]

October 26

An Angel Saved My Daughter

 "When my daughter was 15 and just learning to drive, I had her drive home on a country road. The day was hot and the sun was shining directly in her eyes. I became nervous and asked her to pull over at a small country store to switch drivers. At the moment she stepped out of the car a truck zoomed around the curve. It was obvious the driver of the truck had also been blinded by the sun. The truck was speeding straight for my daughter who was still standing by our vehicle. Though I did not see an angel, I sensed one. In a flash, the truck whooshed by her. The space between the truck and my daughter was about the width (not length) of a pencil, yet it did not touch her. If there is anything I believe, it is that an angel of God saved my daughter that day."

— Irma Vela [275]

"It is not possible for me to explain how I sensed the presence of this angel," said Irma Vela, "but I knew it was coming to save her." Abide in this profound state of confidence when you pray for your own safety or the safety and welfare of those you love.

October 27

ANGELS SCREENING BLOOD PRESSURE

 One day in the mid-1990s, Kay and Johnny Wood-house welcomed two women into their summer cottage near Marion, Iowa. The women were gathering local feedback about the 1993 Mississippi River flood. They were also taking blood pressures. The Woodhouses soon learned that Johnny's blood pressure was too high. The visitors suggested that Johnny and Kay go to the hospital immediately! But Johnny balked. He wanted to play golf. Abruptly, the women rose and left. "Wait," Kay called, suddenly anxious. When she followed to ask more questions, the women had disappeared into thin air. Within an hour, Johnny was having chest pains. In the emergency room, he had a heart attack. The next day, Johnny underwent a quadruple bypass but suffered no permanent heart damage.

"I checked with my neighbors to see if any of them had been visited at noon on Monday by two women conducting a very odd survey about the Flood of '93 — and taking blood pressures at the same time," Kay says. "No one knew what I was talking about."

— Kay Woodhouse [276]

October 28

Saints Simon and Jude (First Century)

OUT OF THE SPOTLIGHT

 Simon and Jude were among the Twelve Apostles called by Jesus. Their names appear in the Synoptic Gospels although Matthew and Mark identify Jude as "Thaddeus." Simon, called "the Zealot" belonged to a nationalistic Jewish sect that saw Roman control of Israel as blasphemous. However, little else is really known about these two. They have the same feast day because they may have preached the Gospel together in Persia and Mesopotamia. Unlike Peter, James, and John, Simon and Jude weren't called to serve in the spotlight. That brings the angels to mind. Angels also sidestep the spotlight. They find their reason for existence, their unending happiness, and their source of light in God alone.

Lord, help me see where I belong today. Let me see the place you have planned for me and the work you want me to do —
in or out of the spotlight.

October 29

Why We Cherish Angels

 Some of the angels among us are made of plastic, ceramic, granite. Others show up on plaques or coffee mugs. Why do we have such an attraction to angels? "In terms of popular culture, I think that belief in angels is so widespread because we don't like the idea of being totally alone." That's the view of theologian Lawrence S. Cunningham. "If you have to do something that's really dangerous — cross a mountain pass or get through a jungle ... it's comforting to say 'Someone is watching over me.'" Cunningham, whose academic interests include Christianity and culture, says people see angels as protectors even if they forget to ask where angels come from. [277]

He will shelter you with his pinions,
and under his wings you may take refuge;
his faithfulness is a protecting shield.
(Psalm 91:4)

October 30

CHAGALL'S ANGELS

 Angels were central figures in many paintings by Russian artist Marc Chagall (1887–1985). Born in a Jewish ghetto in Belarus, Chagall went to Saint Petersburg as a young man to study art. Since it was illegal for Jews to live in the capital, Chagall lived in constant fear. Then one night, he woke to the sound of rustling wings. When he opened his eyes, he felt as if many pins were piercing his forehead. A blue light flooded the room and an angel hovered above him. Slowly, the angel floated up through the ceiling followed by the unforgettable blue light. From then on — for almost eight decades — Chagall labored to share the beauty, peace, and color first brought to him by an angel.

"When I am finishing a picture, I hold some God-made object up to it — a rock, a flower, the branch of a tree, or my hand — as a final test. If the painting stands up beside a thing man cannot make, the painting is authentic." Because of an angel, Marc Chagall understood that when our work reflects our Creator, it is authentic and beautiful. Apply this understanding to your own work today. [278]

October 31

ANGELS ARE NOT GHOSTS!

 Today, people turn into witches, goblins, and ghosts — just for fun. But, it's important to know the differences between Halloween and the *real* world of the unseen. Ghosts, for instance, shouldn't be confused with angels or saints who have been sent by God to living human beings. Philosopher Peter Kreeft says a ghost is the soul of a dead person who appears to the living. Ghosts, he explained, may not realize they're dead, or may be attached to possessions or places. Ghosts could also be doing penance or consoling loved ones and will receive new resurrection bodies if they go to heaven. Angels never had human bodies or human lives. They appear only at God's command.

"Most of what I know about angels I learned from Saint Thomas Aquinas. Not all my answers are directly from him, but the principles from which I deduce my answers usually are. He was surely the greatest theologian of all time, and he happened to be also the one who wrote the most definitive treatise on angels, in the Summa Theologica.*"*

— Peter Kreeft [279]

Angelic Escorts

On this feast of All Saints, it's good to know that the primary duty of guardian angels is to help us become saints! Such is the trust that our heavenly Father has placed in them. They guard and guide us not only in our natural lives, but also, and most importantly, constantly direct us to the right spiritual path. "We are called to the kingdom of heaven; the angels see in us their fellow participants in the graces of the Holy Spirit, and they have the additional mission of leading us to heaven." According to Origen, "At the hour of death the celestial escort receives the soul." It is then that "the good angel shows the greatest zeal in protecting and defending the soul committed to its care." [280]

"If you go to heaven, your angel will be with you in glory as an eternal companion and friend."

— Saint Thomas Aquinas [281]

November 2

All Souls' Day

AN ANGEL'S JOY

 Saint Lidwina of Schiedam (1380–1433) was acquainted with a sinful man in Holland, and she prayed earnestly for his conversion. Eventually, the man repented and made a good confession. But, he died soon after. Some time later, Lidwina asked her guardian angel if the man was still in purgatory. "He is there," said her angel, "and he suffers much." Then, Lidwina saw in a vision the guardian angel of the sinner grieving for the man's soul. Lidwina continued to pray for the man and offered the merits of her sufferings. One day, the angel who had been so dejected appeared to Lidwina with a joyful countenance. The man's soul had been freed and the gates of Heaven opened to him. [282]

> "Should the departed soul be not quite ready to enter Heaven because it has not fully satisfied Divine Justice for its faults, and must therefore remain for some time in Purgatory, the Guardian Angel ... will often visit ... and comfort it." [283] The guardian angel also prompts and inspires people on earth to continue to pray for him until the angel can escort the soul into Paradise.

November 3

Saint Martin de Porres (1579–1639)

The Flying Brother

 Martin de Porres was a humble Dominican lay brother in Lima, Peru. When word spread of his healing abilities, the monastery garden became a haven for the city's sick and homeless. He begged for food, clothing, and medicine for the poor. Martin was called "the flying brother" because people saw him doing charitable work in Asia, Mexico, Algeria, and France, even though he never left Lima. God exists outside of time and space, and sometimes allows humans to do the same. Like an angel, Martin moved faster than light.

> *"Let us think of the whole host of angels, how they stand by and serve his will, for Scriptures say: 'Ten thousand times ten thousand were doing service to him.'... Then let us gather together in awareness of our concord, as with one mouth we shout earnestly to him that we may become sharers in his great and glorious promises."*

> — Saint Clement of Rome [284]

November 4

May the Angels Come to Meet You

 November, the last month in the Church year, begins with the remembrance of All Saints and All Souls. The liturgy turns our attention to the end of the world and to our own final days on earth. But the tone is not melancholy or mournful. When the Church prays for the dying, "she speaks with gentle assurance. The Christian who unites his own death to that of Jesus views it as a step towards him and an entrance into everlasting life" (*Catechism of the Catholic Church* 1020). A traditional prayer as death approaches is the Prayer of Commendation.

> Go forth, faithful Christian!…
> May you return to [your Creator]
> who formed you from the dust of the earth.
> May holy Mary, the angels, and all the saints
> come to meet you as you go forth from this life….
> May you see your Redeemer face to face.

Toward your soul as it goes forth from the body, there hastens the glorious company of angels.

My Angel Will Serve Mass

Each day, numerous visiting and local priests in Rome line up at the side altars in the large churches to offer Mass. In 1950, Brazilian Archbishop Dom Hélder Câmara (1909–1999) waited patiently for his turn, but he was a small and humble man, and another priest always managed to step forward first. A Franciscan friar was on hand at the altar to serve Mass for each of the priests, and thinking they were finished, began to clear the altar. When he noticed Dom Hélder he was instantly annoyed, but quickly recovered and prepared the altar for Mass. He told Dom Hélder, however, that he would not be able to stay to serve Mass. "Don't worry," Dom Hélder replied. "My angel will serve the Mass." At that moment, a brilliant light filled the church, and the friar fell to his knees trembling and weeping until the end of the Mass. [285]

Dom Hélder Câmara named his guardian angel José, after the childhood nickname his mother had given him. He depended on Jose for protection in times of danger, assistance when he needed help, and courage to defend the oppressed. He said that he had never seen an angel — not even Jose — but he was convinced they are present for all of us. [286]

November 6

"Speedy" Angels

Since they are spiritual creatures and don't have bodies to "slow" or "weigh" them down, it's somewhat academic to consider the "speed of angels." Angels are not subject to the laws of gravity or space. They exist and "move" in an entirely different reality — in the unseen world. Nonetheless, reminding ourselves of certain physical laws guiding our cosmos helps us to better appreciate the amazing angels of the Lord. Light travels at 186,000 miles per second, and at 671 million miles per hour. Angels are "faster" than that. It takes light from the sun eight minutes and seventeen seconds to reach earth as each new day dawns. Angels, creatures of unearthly light, "arrive" as God messengers as soon as they are sent.

Then I saw another angel flying high overhead, with everlasting good news to announce to those who dwell on earth, to every nation, tribe, tongue, and people. (Revelation 14:6)

PÈRE LAMY AND THE ANGELS

 Père (Father) Jean Lamy (1855–1931) was a French parish priest, not a military chaplain, but during World War I, he often ministered to wounded soldiers. Many had lost limbs, were blinded by poison gas, or shell-shocked. Some were dying. Lamy, a mystic with a deep prayer life, also experienced heavenly visions, including visions of angels. One day at the Paris railway station, Lamy found two hundred wounded soldiers on stretchers. "When I arrived," Lamy said, "I always asked my guardian angel to cure some of them. I saw the angel and the archangel blessing them, and I passed on.... In the midst of so much sorrow and distress, I had the consolation of seeing that the archangel was very merciful to the soldiers."

> *"We do not pray enough to our guardian angels.... We give them just a bit of a prayer at the end of our night prayers; that's all. Their mercy in our regard is very great, and often we do not make sufficient use of them. They regard us as brothers in need, and they are very good to us."*

> — Père Jean Lamy [287]

November 8

YouTube Exposes Devil's Strategy

 Evidence of the devil's work has always been the same, explained Father Robert Barron in one of his more popular Word on Fire YouTube videos. "Look at the names that the Bible gives for the devil," he said. "The word *diabolos*, means 'liar' or 'accuser.'" Typical signs of the devil's involvement are division or scattering. "When families get scattered, when business organizations or communities or cultures get divided, that's a sign of the dark powers," Barron said. "But God is a great gathering force. Whenever things come together and a community forms, that's a sign of the Holy Spirit." A pioneer of Catholic evangelization through modern media, Father Barron was ordained as an auxiliary bishop for the Archdiocese of Los Angeles in 2015. [288]

"The devil loves darkness. He always operates in the dark because he knows that if he is discovered he is beaten."

— Saint John Bosco [289]

ANGELS ON HIGH

A feast day for a church? That might puzzle some people, but Rome's 1700-year-old Saint John Lateran Basilica is much more than an ancient building. It is the official see or home church of the pope. Once Christianity was legalized in the Roman Empire, everyone in Rome was baptized there. Despite its great age, remnants of many fourth-century mosaics from the original church have been preserved. Among them in the central apse or domed roof is a glorious mosaic of Christ surrounded by nine shining angels. As if they're appearing out of a brilliant blue sky, the Savior and his golden angels overlook the pope's *cathedra* — bishop's chair — far below.

Saint John Lateran Basilica is a beloved and historically significant church for the worldwide Catholic family. Reflect on the places that are sacred or significant in your life. Do they remind you of your beliefs, your story, and what you hold dear?

November 10

Saint Leo the Great (400–461)

THE POPE AND ATTILA THE HUN

 By 452, Pope Leo had strengthened the papacy and the Church, but, could he stop Attila the Hun from destroying Rome? As he traveled by horseback to Attila's camp, the pope prayed that God's angels would protect Rome. He also asked for help from Saint Peter, the first pope. Nobody knows why Attila changed his mind and left Rome alone. A fresco done one thousand years later by Raphael may suggest an answer. The fresco depicting the meeting of Leo and Attila shows two imposing figures in the air above the pope. Attila and his troops cringe in fear. Armed with swords, Saints Peter and Paul have come like angels of judgment to defend Rome.

Saint Leo the Great is most remembered for his remarkable encounter with Attila the Hun. Leo believed that his best strategy and his only hope was to trust completely in God. Don't forget this when terrible threats are at your doorstep.

November 11

Saint Martin of Tours (c. 316–397)

With Angels as Witnesses

 In the middle of an extremely cold winter, Martin, a twenty-year-old soldier, met a destitute man begging at the gate of Amiens, a fortified city in Gaul. The man's suffering moved Martin, but he had nothing to give except the military cloak he wore. So, taking his sword, he divided his cloak into two equal parts, and gave one part to the poor man. Then he wrapped the other half around himself. That night, Martin had a dream — a vision of Christ wearing the piece of cloak he gave to the beggar. Martin heard Jesus saying with a clear voice to the multitude of angels standing round: "Martin, who is still but a catechumen, clothed me with this robe." The very next day, Martin hurried to be baptized. [290]

At this time of year we are presented with many opportunities to share what we have with those who do not have enough. In recognition that all you have comes from God, and in an act of thanksgiving and love, could you give a portion of your sweaters or blankets to keep others warm?

November 12

THE SMILING ANGELS

 There are thousands of angel statues in the magnificent French cathedral of Rheims — all carved out of stone between 1236 and 1245. But two of the angels are not stony-faced — they are smiling! During World War I, the cathedral was bombed several times. On September 19, 1914, one of the smiling angels — the one usually known simply as "The Smile" — was decapitated during a German artillery attack. The pieces of the head that fell to the floor were recovered and stored. But, for the remainder of the war, the image of the damaged statue was widely used as a powerful example of French culture under attack. After the war, the pieces were recovered, and the statue was restored and reinstated on February 13, 1926. The angels are smiling again. [291]

"Angels are sweet and sour and salty, wet and dry, hard and soft, sharp and smooth. They fly, yes, but only so that we can visualize their movement. To awaken to their presence, we too must learn to fly. We must let our imaginations and our faith soar."

— F. Forrester Church [292]

November 13

Saint Frances Xavier Cabrini (1850–1917)

It Must Have Been Your Guardian Angel

 As a child in Italy, Francesca Cabrini dreamed of being a missionary so that others would love Jesus as much as she did. She made little paper boats and set them afloat on the river near her uncle's house, loaded with violets representing missionaries sailing to China. Once, she slipped and fell into the icy water and was quickly caught in a swift current. A boy who saw the accident ran to alert her uncle. He rushed to the scene to find Francesca lying on the riverbank. "Who rescued you?" he asked. When Francesca declared that she had seen no one, he concluded: "Then it must have been your guardian angel." Despite a lifelong fear of water due to this incident, Frances Xavier Cabrini crossed the Atlantic Ocean numerous times. She opened schools, orphanages, and hospitals in the United States and in Central and South America where poor Italian immigrants had settled in search of a better life.

Mother Cabrini prayed, "Give me a heart as large as the universe, so that I may love You, if not as much as You deserve, at least as much as I am capable of." Today, expand your heart to aid someone in need — for the love of Christ. [293]

November 14

BRINGING ANGELS INTO THE WORLD

 The eyes of faith can see angels. The earliest Christians were taught to participate in the Eucharist by imagining themselves among heaven's angels worshipping God. When they sang "Holy, Holy, Holy" in the liturgy, they weren't just repeating the Seraphim in Isaiah. They were singing with the angelic choir. In the fourth century, Christian worship was permitted by imperial decree. As the social position of Christians shifted in the wider Roman world, the place of angels also shifted. In his homilies on Ephesians, John Chrysostom told his listeners to "imagine that heaven is opened on high and the angels are descending.... You are standing at the time of the mysteries with the cherubim, with the seraphim!" Christians still saw angels in church, but instead of joining the community in heaven, they were bringing angels into the world. [294]

"Who among the faithful could have a doubt that the choir of angels is present at this mystery of Jesus Christ — where the highest and lowest are united, the earthly and heavenly joined, and the invisible and visible made one?"

— Saint Gregory the Great [295]

Two Majestic Angels for Two Great Saints

 Albert was a leading scientist of his time, and a gifted teacher. Albert's greatest student at the University of Paris was Thomas Aquinas. It has been said that Thomas could not have written the *Summa* without the superb intellectual training he received from Albert. As they were together in life, so they were seen in death. A mystical vision described by Saint Mecthild revealed the souls of Albert and Thomas entering heaven. Each was preceded by two majestic angels, one from the choir of the Seraphim, representing knowledge, and the other of the Cherubim, representing love. As they drew near to the throne of God, the words that the two saints had written seemed to be inscribed on their garments in letters of blazing gold, each word reflecting a wonderful glory on the Divinity itself. [296]

"Albert and Thomas entered heaven like two noble princes; great angels went before them, and their souls were filled with overwhelming joy. Thus, they came before the throne of God."

— Responsory of First Vespers for the Feast of Saint Albert in the Dominican Breviary [297]

November 16

Saint Gertrude the Great (1257–1302)

ANGELS CARRY OUR PRAYERS

 Saint Gertrude was a Benedictine nun at Helfta, Germany, during a period of great learning and growth for the Church. At the age of twenty-five, Gertrude experienced the first of numerous visions that continued throughout her life. These visions made her one the great mystics of the thirteenth century. One time when she was praying fervently at Mass, Gertrude saw her guardian angel bearing her prayers heavenward and presenting them to the three Divine Persons. Her prayers were accepted, and each person of the Trinity blessed Gertrude. In Eucharistic Prayer I, we too pray that our offering of the holy Bread of eternal life and the Chalice of everlasting salvation will be carried to God by the angels who are present with Mass. [298]

In humble prayer we ask you, Almighty God, command that these gifts be borne by the hands of your holy Angel to your altar on high in the sight of your divine majesty.

DRESSED BY THE ANGELS

At fourteen, Elizabeth married twenty-year-old Prince Ludwig, heir to the kingdoms of Thuringia and Hesse in present-day Germany. But, Ludwig's mother and sister despised Elizabeth. Her strong faith and ministry to the poor seemed unbecoming for a princess. While Ludwig disagreed, Elizabeth struggled to keep the peace. According to one legend, Elizabeth arrived home one evening, realizing she was late for a court dinner. She'd spent the day distributing alms, dressed in a simple gray dress. As she crossed the castle threshold, angels appeared with a crown and elegant gold gown. Instantly, Elizabeth was royally dressed and entered the dining room, drawing every eye and taking her place beside her proud, beaming Prince Ludwig.

If you lavish your food on the hungry and satisfy the afflicted, then your light shall rise in the darkness, and your gloom shall become like midday. (Isaiah 58:10)

November 18

Saint Rose Philippine Duchesne (1769–1852)

KINDRED SPIRITS

 While growing up in France, Rose Duchesne heard that Native peoples in America believed that everything — a fish, a rock, a wildflower — had a spirit. Rose was intrigued. Without the Bible or Church, these people had a sense of the unseen world. Rose later came to America as a sister of the Society of the Sacred Heart to help establish Catholic schools and missions in Saint Louis. In 1841, at seventy-one, Sister Rose moved to Kansas to serve the Potawatomi people. But learning the Potawatomi language proved too difficult for Rose, so she prayed. She prayed so much that the children gave her a Potawatomi name that meant "the woman who prays much." They recognized her loving spirit just as she had recognized theirs.

"We cultivate a very small field for Christ, but we love it, knowing that God does not require great achievements but a heart that holds back nothing for self."

— Saint Rose Philippine Duchesne

In a way that Saint Rose would appreciate, look for ways today to show your faith and love — despite all language barriers.

CLOISTERED ARCTIC ANGELS

Several decades ago, Carmelite nuns from Iceland established a new Carmelite foundation in Norway. Norwegians were stunned that contemplative Catholic nuns were settling in Tromso, two hundred miles north of the Arctic Circle. Norway, once a Lutheran nation, was admittedly very secular. It seemed an unlikely home for women devoted to prayer. But, as the Carmelites settled in, stories about their kindness circulated. Construction workers building their monastery told how surprised and grateful they were when the sisters pledged to pray for their safety and their families. Norwegians also heard that the sisters sang like angels; they were full of joy — no matter what. Norwegians were deeply touched. In 2009, a documentary about the Tromso Carmelites, *Angels of the Arctic Circle*, aired on Catholic television.

When someone gives joyfully and unconditionally, it does seem as if angels have arrived. Perhaps they have — quietly inspiring ordinary people to offer extraordinary love and kindness.

November 20

Prophecy — Satan Falls

 After seventy-two of Christ's disciples returned from sharing the Good News, Jesus had things to tell them. Luke's Gospel says Jesus wanted his followers to know that they had power to defeat "the enemy" — evil spirits. In the same breath, Jesus said, "I have observed Satan fall like lightning from the sky" (Luke 10:18). What did Jesus mean? Scripture scholars say that Christ's statement referred to future events. The kingdom of God was being established, but it wouldn't be complete until Satan's influence in the world ended. Christ's use of the past tense — "I have observed" — was a common literary device for introducing prophecy. Jesus wanted to encourage his disciples. He could see the coming victory.

In the Lord's Prayer, we pray, "your kingdom come, your will be done on earth as it is in heaven." Jesus promises that this prayer — the prayer he gave us — will be answered someday.

November 21

Presentation of the Blessed Virgin Mary

PERFECT LIFELONG PRAISE

 As beloved as Mary is, we know nothing from Scripture about Mary's parents, or early life. However, there might be some answers in the Apocrypha, ancient texts of doubtful authenticity. The apocryphal Gospel of James says that Mary's parents were Joachim and Ann (see July 26). They dedicated their only child to God in the Temple when Mary was just three. According to this tradition, Mary served and was educated in the Temple until adolescence. The Eastern Church celebrated Mary's Presentation long before the Church in the West. It was a celebration of Mary's lifelong devotion to God. Like the angels, Mary acknowledged and praised God from the beginning of her existence — and never stopped. [299]

Completely unburdened by sin, Mary could see the goodness of God more clearly than any human being before or since. Call on her to help you see your life and God's plans for you more clearly.

November 22

Saint Cecilia (c. 230)

AN ANGEL WITH FLAMING WINGS

 Saint Cecilia is one of the most popular early Roman martyrs. She is honored as the patron saint of musicians because it is said that at her wedding she sang to Christ in her heart. According to legend, Cecilia married a pagan, Valerian, to whom she revealed, "There is an angel who watches me, and wards off from me any who would touch me." He said, "Dearest, if this be true, show me the angel." Cecilia replied, "That can only be if you will believe in one God, and be baptized." After being baptized, Valerian returned to find Cecilia praying in her chamber, and an angel beside her with flaming wings, holding two crowns of roses and lilies, which he placed on their heads and vanished. [300]

> *Saint Thomas Aquinas once fell into a mystical sleep accompanied by a vision. Two angels came to him from heaven and bound a cord around his waist, saying, "On God's behalf, we gird you with the girdle of chastity, a girdle which no attack will ever destroy." Angels cherish and praise the virtue of chastity — faithfulness to one's vows and state in life.* [301]

As the Angel Directed

The remarkable biography of Saint Columban (c. 540–615), an Irish monk and missionary to France, Switzerland, and northern Italy, is based on stories told by the saint's companions shortly after his death. They remembered a time when Columban was unsure which direction to go. "Then the angel of the Lord appeared to him in a vision, and showed him in a little circle the structure of the world, just as the circle of the universe is usually drawn with a pen in a book. 'You perceive,' the angel said, 'how much remains set apart of the whole world. Go to the right or the left where you will, that you may enjoy the fruits of your labors.' Therefore Columban remained where he was, until the way to Italy opened before him." [302]

Like Columban, we are all called to bring the light of the Gospel to our little part of the world. Are you open to God's direction and guidance?

November 24

The Archangel and the End Times

 As the liturgical year draws to a close, the Church asks us to focus on "the end times." Theologian Alexander Schmemann wrote about the completion of God's plan. "While there is much we do not know about the completion of God's plan for our salvation, what we do know should give us joy and consolation. I do not know when and how the fulfillment will come. I do not know when all things will be consummated in Christ. I know nothing about the 'whens' and 'hows.' But I know that in Christ this great Passage of the world has begun.... I know that it is this faith and this certitude that fill ... the words of Saint Paul: 'For neither life nor death can separate us from the love of Christ.'" [303]

For the Lord himself, with a word of command, with the voice of an archangel and with the trumpet of God, will come down from heaven, and the dead in Christ will rise first. Then we who are alive, who are left, will be caught up together with them in the clouds to meet the Lord in the air. Thus we shall always be with the Lord. (1 Thessalonians 4:16–17)

The Angel of Confidence

Marie Luise Kaschnitz (1901–1974) a German poet and novelist, told a story about ship owner Giovanni di Mata, who gave all his gold to some Barbary pirates to buy freedom for their prisoners. As di Mata was about to put to sea with the freed prisoners, the pirates demanded more money. Because he could not meet their demands, they smashed his mast and helm and ripped his sails to shreds. Nevertheless, di Mata gave the signal to set out. To everyone's astonishment, even without mast, sails, and helm, the ship slowly began to move and reached the open sea.

The confident do not walk blindly through the world. They see when danger looms. But they know that an angel protects and shields them and frees them from all their fears. [304]

November 26

A Season for Thanksgiving

 In medieval times, Christians in Europe celebrated the harvest. Their thanksgiving festivities, like ours, took place in November — but on November 11, the feast of Saint Martin of Tours. Everyone went to Mass to thank God for good harvests and for their families, faith, and communities. The day was also set aside for games, dances, and a delicious feast with roast goose. Thanking God is essential to Christians of all times. During this Thanksgiving season, an "attitude of gratitude" to God can restore a deeper meaning to this holiday. Praising and thanking God is just. It's scriptural, and it puts us into the joyful company of the saints and angels.

During this Thanksgiving season, thank and praise God, first of all. Think, too, of those who should have your thanks. Offer it, and thank God for these people in your life.

AN ANGEL'S INSISTENT VOICE

 When a volunteer firefighter was called about a burning mobile home in his Ohio hometown, he came quickly. Outfitted with heat-resistant gear and air packs, Mark and another firefighter crawled along the trailer floor, dousing pockets of fire with the fire hose. But, Mark soon felt uneasy and heard a male voice say, "Mark, you need to go." Mark knew it wasn't his partner, who was too far away. A few minutes later, the warning came again, loud and clear! "You need to go *now!*" As the two firefighters backed out, they saw the flashover coming. An explosion and superhot flames engulfed the room they'd just left. Mark believed a guardian angel had warned him. [305]

"Wherever you go, whatever you do, may your guardian angel watch over you."

— Anonymous

What the Angels Can't Understand

 Advent directs our attention toward Christmas and the birth of Jesus: God becoming one of us. That's a mystery that the angels don't really understand, author C. S. Lewis maintained. Because "the angels have no senses," he said, "their experience is purely intellectual and spiritual." That's not how human beings are made. Our shared identity with Jesus as creatures with bodies and spirits is special. "That is why we know something about God which they don't," Lewis shared his view in a magazine article published at Christmas time in 1945. "There are particular aspects of His love and joy which can be communicated to a created being only by sensuous experience." [306]

"Something of God, which the seraphim can never quite understand, flows into us from the blue of the sky, the taste of honey, the delicious embrace of water whether cold or hot, and even from sleep itself."

— C. S. Lewis

November 29

Entertaining Angels

In 1996, the film *Entertaining Angels: The Dorothy Day Story*, was released to share Day's story as an American Catholic activist. During the darkest days of the Depression, she founded the Catholic Worker newspaper and movement with Peter Maurin, a French intellectual. Catholic Worker houses of hospitality for the poor and homeless followed. A convert, Dorothy Day was a devout Catholic who attended Mass daily. She was also deeply committed to the Gospels and a Scripture passage that advises, "Do not neglect to show hospitality to strangers for thereby some have entertained angels unawares" (Hebrews 13:2). Day died on this date in 1980 in New York City, where the archdiocese opened an investigation of her life that could lead to her canonization. [307]

Dorothy Day teaches us that even if the strangers we meet are ordinary and sometimes difficult people, we should treat them as if they were angels. As you go about your day, treat everyone like an angel.

November 30

Saint Andrew (First Century)

ANGELIC AURA

 A Galilean fisherman like his brother Simon (Peter), Andrew must have loved searching for the truth. Once Saint John the Baptist said that Jesus was the Messiah, Andrew's eyes were fixed on Jesus. Jesus invited Andrew to "come and see." According to legends, Andrew preached the Gospel in Greece and Turkey after Christ's Ascension. Like his brother Peter, Andrew was crucified, but on an X-shaped cross called a saltire. Andrew's Christian converts wept near his cross during his two-day agony. On the second day, when the first Apostle of Jesus began to pray, a strange angelic light surrounded him. After a half-hour, the light disappeared and Andrew offered his soul to the one he followed.

Like the other Apostles, Saint Andrew left everything behind to follow Jesus, but he found everything he was looking for. If you could leave some things behind to find what you're truly looking for, what would they be?

December 1

The "Angels" of Advent

 As Advent moves into the last month of the year, December itself testifies: "Nothing is impossible with God." In early December, cold days seem never-ending. Daylight is in short supply. The prospect of Spring looks "impossible." But, by the winter solstice, light and hope return. Isaiah's prophecies of "impossible" events strike a familiar and joyful note within us. "The people who walked in darkness have seen a great light. Upon those who lived in a land of gloom a light has shone" (Isaiah 9:1). Isaiah predicted another "impossible" event, one which the Archangel Gabriel would announce. "The Lord himself will give you a sign; the virgin shall be with child and bear a son" (Isaiah 7:14).

Hang on to hope during these dark days of winter. Advent reminds us to embrace Isaiah's joyful promises. God's plans make impossible events possible. New light and life is on the horizon.

December 2

Anything but an Angel

 Angelo Roncalli, the future Pope Saint John XXIII, wrote in his notebook during a retreat at the seminary he attended in Bergamo in 1898: "I ought to be like an angel in the sight of God. Divine Providence wanted to show me that this was my duty, and so had me baptized Angelo. But what a disgrace for me, always to be called Angelo, with the obligation of behaving like an angel, when on the contrary I am no angel at all. So, the name Angelo must inspire me to be indeed an angel seminarist. Moreover, when I hear my name spoken, I must desire the perfection which I must achieve, and leads me to make an act of humility, thinking of what my name is and what I am in fact, anything but an angel." [308]

It is easy to forget that saints are as human as we are, but that they strived for the perfection God wanted for them. May the humility of the future pope and saint inspire us to truthfully ask and eagerly try to achieve what God is calling us to do this very day.

December 3

Saint Francis Xavier (1506–1552)

ANGEL INTERPRETERS

 After ordination as a Jesuit in 1537, Francis Xavier sailed from Portugal to carry God's Word to new lands and peoples. Francis wasn't good at learning new languages, however, and knew that it would hinder his work as an evangelist. If the Gospel took root in India, the Philippines, Japan, or China, it would not be because of his preaching alone. So Francis depended on his guardian angel to help him say the right words, and he asked the angels of his listeners to open hearts. At the same time, Francis did his best to speak with love, and showed Christ's love as he served the poor and sick. By his death in 1552 near the Chinese mainland, Francis — and the angels — had brought thousands to Christ.

"When trying to evangelize, no tool is more effective than that of personal witness.... People can argue with points of doctrine, but no one can argue with a personal testimony."

— Saint Francis Xavier

December 4

Saint John Damascene (c. 675–749)

How Angels Pray

 Saint John Damascene was born into a Christian family in Muslim-controlled Damascus, where he received an excellent education. In his early thirties, he left Damascus to become a monk and devote himself to study and prayer. When Emperor Leo III banned the veneration of icons, John strongly objected, defending icons as tools for prayer — not objects of prayer. Many of his religious poems, hymns, and essays remain Church treasures. But John may be remembered most for his classic definition that introduces prayer in the *Catechism of the Catholic Church* (CCC 2559). "Prayer is the raising of one's mind and heart to God," he wrote. He prayed like an angel, totally open to God and desiring to be in communion with God.

How did Saint John Damascene know that prayer isn't just a matter of words? What a wonderful inspiration! When your heart and mind are turning toward God, that's prayer!

December 5

ANGELS AND UNITY

 Although they won't interfere with the way their human charges exercise free will, angels are certainly not indifferent to the choices we make and the lives we live. That was the teaching of Saint Bernard of Clairvaux, the twelfth-century founder of the Cistercian monks, who often wrote about the angels. Bernard said that there are many things that angels rejoice to see in us, which includes sobriety, chastity, voluntary poverty, a desire to be with God, and heart-felt prayer. Even more, angels are happy to find unity and peace in our hearts and in our communities "So let there not be divisions among us," advised the holy abbot. "Rather, let us all together form one body in Christ, being all members of one another." [309]

Unity is a wonderful theme for the Christmas season. The author of the Letter to the Hebrews offers us timeless advice: "Strive for peace with everyone, and for that holiness without which no one will see the Lord" (Hebrews 12:14).

December 6

Saint Nicholas of Myra (270–343)

UNHEARALDED ANGELS

 One of the most popular saints is cherished for his acts of kindness and gift giving, often done in secret. Nicholas was Greek and grew up in Myra in present-day Turkey. As a young priest, he lived in the Holy Land until he felt called back to Myra where he became a bishop. His selfless service to the people quickly won their hearts. Nicholas heard of a man with three daughters who'd lost his fortune. Because his girls had no marriage dowries, they expected to become prostitutes to support themselves. One night the bishop tossed three bags of gold through the family's open window. This famous Nicholas story contributed to the legend of Santa Claus delivering gifts at night. Like Nicholas, angels help people, unseen and unheralded.

Like Saint Nicholas, angels are unseen and unheralded as they joyfully help us. When we realize the gifts they give to us — in secret — it feels like Christmas.

ANGELS GUARDED THE BASILICA

 Ambrose was Milan's governor when a riot broke out over who would become Milan's new bishop. When Ambrose arrived, people chanted "Ambrose for bishop!" The young governor turned pale. Though Christian, he didn't want Church leadership. Eventually, however, Ambrose agreed and prepared to lead the Church. In 383, Empress Justina ordered him to give Milan's basilica to Arians, heretics who denied Christ's divinity. Ambrose refused, and hundreds of people joined him in the basilica. When imperial soldiers came to arrest him, an invisible contingent of angels intervened. As Ambrose later wrote, soldiers repeatedly circled the basilica, but couldn't find the entrance. They eventually withdrew in confusion and defeat. [310]

Saint Ambrose had great faith in the presence and protection of the angels. "Air and earth and ocean, everything is full of angels," he said. However, he believed that asking for their help was important. "But if these beings guard you, they do so because they have been summoned by your prayers."

December 8

Solemnity of the Immaculate Conception

Exalted above the Angels

 During Advent, we are keenly aware of the role of Mary, the Virgin Mother of God, in the story of salvation. Today's feast celebrates her sinlessness from the moment of her conception. Because she was without sin, she was full of grace. Her "virginity is not a negation, not a mere absence; it is the fullness and the wholeness of love itself. It is the totality of her self-giving to God.... She is the best and holiest of earthly creatures, exalted above the angels, the God-Bearer is the pride of this earth, a fitting gift from mankind to the Creator and Savior." [311]

Mary of Nazareth fulfilled the long and patient growth of love and expectation that fills the Old Testament — and our season of Advent. Pray for the growth of love and expectation in your heart as Christmas nears.

THE ANGELS SERVE CHRIST

 In a sermon on Christmas, Saint John Chrysostom reflected on the angels as servants of the Lord, and the Lord who became like a servant. "The angels call the shepherds, the stars summon the wise men. Even the angels are servants, having the Lord as Master. The Lord Himself appeared in the form of a servant, yet creation knew its Lord. The very voice of nature itself proclaims more loudly than any trumpet, that the King of heaven has come. For God's own Son became the Son of man that he might make the sons of men children of God." This is the true meaning of Christmas. [312]

"Angels are sent to bring us messages from God's heart."

— Charles Hunter

Today, open your heart to God's love. Ask yourself how you can bring a message of love from God's heart to someone else.

December 10

Touch the Angel's Hand

 On Christmas Eve, 1513, Fra Giovanni Giocondo wrote a letter to his friend Countess Allagia Aldobrandeschi about the gifts we receive from God. "Life is so generous a giver. But we, judging its gifts by their covering, cast them away as ugly or heavy or hard. Remove the covering, and you will find beneath it a living splendor, woven of love, with power. Welcome it, grasp it, and you touch the angel's hand that brings it to you. Everything we call a trial, a sorrow, or a duty, believe me, that angel's hand is there. The gift is there and the wonder of an overshadowing presence. Your joys, too, be not content with them as joys. They, too, conceal diviner gifts. Life is so full of meaning and purpose, so full of beauty beneath its covering, that you will find earth but cloaks your heaven." [313]

"The Angel that presided o'er my birth
Said, 'Little creature, formed of joy and mirth,
Go love without the help of anything on earth.'"

— William Blake

December 11

The Angel Portal

 To help support her family, Saint Zita (c. 1218–1278) served as a maid of the wealthy Fatinelli family, in the Tuscan city of Lucca. Zita's concern for the poor soon became known about town, and the needy began to seek her out. This did not suit the Fatinelli family, who believed that her charitable work detracted from her household duties. The story goes that one bitterly cold Christmas Eve, Zita gave a treasured family cloak to a shivering man in the doorway of the local church. Later, as Signor Fatinelli raged at Zita, an elderly man came to the door and returned the heirloom. When townspeople heard of the event, they decided that the man must have been an angel. From that point on, the doorway of St. Fredaino church in Lucca has been called the "Angel Portal." [314]

Have you ever thought, "It must have been an angel?" Believe it!

December 12
Our Lady of Guadalupe

THE ANGEL OF GUADALUPE

 The 450-year-old image of Our Lady of Guadalupe is more than a simple picture. Miraculously imprinted on the *tilma* of Juan Diego, the image reveals a message for the people of the Americas. The colors and designs are cultural symbols and keys to understanding her message. At the bottom of the picture an angel supports the Lady. By this, she is portrayed as a queen, because among the native peoples only royalty would be carried on the shoulders of someone. Moreover, the angel is transporting the Lady to the people as a sign that a new age is beginning. The angel looks like a young Eagle warrior belonging to the Aztec army known as Soldiers of the Sun. The back of his head, his shoulders and arms are illumined by light that emanates from her body, embracing him as a tender and loving mother. [315]

Our Lady's words of comfort for Juan Diego are for all her children: "Listen, put it into your heart … that the thing that disturbs you, the thing that afflicts you, is nothing. Do not let your countenance, your heart be disturbed…. Am I not here, I, who am your Mother? Are you not under my shadow and protection? Am I not the source of your joy? Are you not in the hollow of my mantle, in the crossing of my arms?" [316]

December 13
Saint Lucy (died 304)

CREATURES OF LIGHT

 The feast day of Saint Lucy, an early Christian martyr, was once designated as the Winter Solstice, the day with the fewest hours of daylight in the Northern Hemisphere. In many cultures, the short, dark days were countered with celebrations of light, particularly in Scandinavian countries, where girls dressed as Saint Lucy wore a crown or wreath of candles on their heads. In fact, the name "Lucy" is derived from the Latin for "light." Appropriately, her day always occurs during Advent, the season of hope and longing for Christ, the Light of the World. Today is also a perfect day to recall that angels, whom Saint Augustine called "creatures of light," reflect the glory of God — light from Light.

On March 13, 1958, Thomas Merton had an "epiphany of light." "I have the immense joy of being man, a member of a race in which God Himself became incarnate.... Now I realize what we all are," he wrote. "And if only everybody could realize this! But it cannot be explained. There is no way of telling people that they are all walking around shining like the sun." [317]

December 14

Saint John of the Cross (1542–1591)

THE ANGELS ARE MINE

 After John joined the Carmelite order in Spain, Saint Teresa of Ávila asked him to join her effort to reform the order. Like Teresa, John believed that the Carmelites had drifted from their commitment to a life of penance and prayer. When he worked for reform, members of his own order who felt threatened locked him in a dark, cold, solitary cell. The mystical poetry he wrote while imprisoned reveals the desolation and sense of abandonment that is known as "the dark night of the soul." As a result, his total dependence on God produced a love and faith that were like fire and light. After nine months, John escaped and shared his experience of God's love.

> *"Mine are the heavens and mine is the earth; mine are the people, the righteous are mine and mine are the sinners; the angels are mine and the Mother of God, and all things are mine; and God Himself is mine and for me, for Christ is mine and all for me. What then do you ask for and seek, my soul? Yours is all this, and it is all for you."*

> — Saint John of the Cross [318]

December 15

Angels in "The Bleak Midwinter"

 English poet Christina Rossetti (1830–1894) had a special place in her heart for angels, especially angels who announced the Savior's birth. Rossetti's poetry was simple, direct, and brimming with tender sentiments and truths. Several of her Christmas poems were later set to music and became favorite Christmas carols. In 1906, a dozen years after Rossetti's death, composer Gustav Holst wrote music to accompany "In the Bleak Midwinter." In the poem, Rossetti says that Jesus, though adored by angels and archangels, was born into a cold, dark world "in the bleak midwinter" when … "Earth stood hard as iron, Water like a stone." In a drafty stable, he nonetheless found love and warmth in "a breastful of milk and a mangerful of hay."

Angels and archangels / May have gathered there,/ Cherubim and seraphim / Thronged the air / — But only His mother / in her maiden bliss / Worshipped the Beloved / With a kiss.

What can I give Him, / Poor as I am?/ If I were a shepherd / I would bring a lamb; / If I were a wise man / I would do my part, / Yet what can I give Him / Give my heart.

— Christina Rossetti, "In the Bleak Midwinter" [319]

December 16

Angels and Machine Guns

 On this date in 1944, Germany launched its last western offensive, the Battle of the Bulge. It surprised Allied Forces and killed nineteen thousand American soldiers. American G.I. John Masterson never forgot that World War II battle or his guardian angel's help. Nervous, freezing American soldiers were in their foxholes when a counterattack order finally came. Masterson's company was to retake a nearby Belgian town. John was shot in both legs. As he lay bleeding, bullets flew all around him. German machine gunners knew he was alive and wanted to finish him. John wrote, "I remember closing my eyes and praying with all my heart: 'Please, dear God! Don't let me die now.'" After dark, American medics rescued John, but John said he survived because his guardian angel knew how to deflect machine-gun bullets. [320]

In Exodus, Yahweh told Moses: "See, I am sending an angel before you to guard you on the way and bring you to the place I have prepared" (Exodus 23:20). Give your thanks to God. Throughout our lives, on many different battlefields, he sends his angels before us to guard us.

December 17

ANGELS AND THE O ANTIPHONS

 For centuries, the Church has added short prayers — "antiphons" — to the liturgy during these last seven days of Advent. Each prayer begins with "O" and addresses the coming savior using a different Biblical image from Isaiah. The "O Antiphons" begin on December 17 and conclude on December 23. During this week, some Catholics recite the antiphons each night as a prayerful countdown to Christmas. Certainly, the angels join in since the antiphons praise Jesus as savior and ask him to come soon. When the first letters of each antiphon's second word are written down in reverse order, they form a two-word Latin acrostic: *Ero Cras*. In English, it means, "Tomorrow, I will be there." O Come, Emmanuel.

Today's O Antiphon reminds us that Jesus is Wisdom. Ask Jesus to bring his wisdom into your life, its challenges, and relationships. "O Wisdom, Who didst come out of the mouth of the Most High, reaching from end to end and ordering all things mightily and sweetly: come and teach us the way of prudence." Pray with the remaining O Antiphons during these last six days of Advent.

December 18

THE ANGELS OFFER THEIR SONG

 In this Christmas hymn, the Orthodox Church looks beyond the poverty of a cave, beyond the infant lying in a feed box for animals, beyond a mother's anxiety for her child, to events outside the world's natural order: The best and holiest of earthly creatures, exalted above the angels, the God-Bearer is a fitting gift from mankind to the Creator and Savior.

What shall we give you, O Christ,
For coming to earth for us?
Each of your creatures brings you thanksgiving:
The angels offer their song,
The heavens its star,
The earth a cave; the woods a manger,
The wise men their gifts,
The shepherds their wonder
And we — the Virgin Mother.[321]

"What God commands, an angel relates. His spirit fulfills it and his power brings it to perfection. The virgin believes it, and nature takes it up."

— Saint John Chrysostom [322]

December 19

BETHLEHEM'S CHAPEL OF THE ANGELS

 Since the first Christian centuries, believers have celebrated the visit of angels to humble shepherds at Bethlehem. One of Bethlehem's earliest churches was built on a field where shepherds were reportedly buried. A Byzantine church and monastery flourished near Shepherd's Field from the fourth to the seventh centuries. Even after Muslims destroyed it, Christian pilgrims continued to pray near the church ruins. The modern Chapel of the Angels, designed by twentieth-century Italian architect Antonio Barluzzi, resembles a sloping shepherd's field tent. When brilliant light floods the interior, visitors remember that night when the angel of the Lord appeared to shepherds and "the glory of the Lord shone around them" (Luke 2:9). [323]

Bethlehem is holy ground. Hosts of angels came to the lowliest, most scorned residents of that region. Angels bring that same exciting message today! "Jesus, your Redeemer is born!"

December 20

Angels Steering the Car

 "We were headed to my parents' house one Christmas Eve before we had kids, when my husband and I encountered at least a dozen deer on the highway. We saw oncoming cars flashing their lights and wondered what was going on so we slowed down a bit. I looked up seconds later and we were surrounded by deer in the road. I mean they were everywhere! I had an image flash in my brain of angels steering our car — we didn't hit a single deer. I still get goosebumps just thinking about it. Other than divine intervention, I have no idea how we managed to miss all those deer." [324]

"All the faithful are helped in a very considerable way by these divine messengers in accordance with what has been written, namely, that the angel of the Lord stays near to those who fear the Lord."

— Saint Hilary of Poitiers [325]

December 21

Angels Appear to the Sincere of Heart

 In a sermon for the Mass of Midnight on Christmas, Saint John Chrysostom said that the angel appeared only to the sincere of heart, because they were able to hear and act upon the angelic message. "An angel appeared in his sleep to Joseph, as to a man who was readily disposed to believe; to the shepherds he appears visibly, as to men unaware. But an angel did not go to Jerusalem nor seek out the Scribes and Pharisees; for they were corrupted, and tormented with envy. But the shepherds were sincere of heart, observing the ancient teachings of the patriarchs and of Moses. For blamelessness is one of the paths that lead to wisdom." [326]

"Behold this wondrous progress: He first sends angels to men, then leads men to heavenly things. A heaven is made on earth, since heaven must take to itself the things of earth."

— Saint John Chrysostom [327]

December 22

The World Is Filled with Angels

 Origen of Alexandria (185–254) offered this insight on the angels who inhabit our world. "When the angels saw the Prince of the heavenly host come down to earth to dwell, they too took the route which the Lord had opened up, acting in obedience to him, the Master who assigned them their various tasks of watching over those who believed in him. Thus, the angels are in the service of your salvation. They were assigned to the Son of God to follow him. And among themselves they would say: 'If he has come down into a body what excuse do we have for remaining idle? Let us all descend from heaven too.' It was thus that a great multitude of the heavenly host was to be found praising and glorifying God at the moment of his birth in Bethlehem. The world is filled with Angels!" [328]

What excuse do we have for remaining idle? As you prepare to celebrate Christ dwelling with us, ask your angel what task he has assigned to you.

December 23

ANGELS APPEAR IN LIGHT

In a commentary on the Gospel reading for Midnight Mass, Saint Bede (627–735) said that the appearance of angels differed between the Old and New Testaments. "Nowhere in the whole course of the Old Testament do we find that the angels, who so dutifully ministered to the holy men of old, had ever appeared in light. This privilege was rightly reserved for the days when 'to the righteous a light is risen in darkness' (Psalm 112:4). At the birth of Christ, an angel of the Lord appeared to lowly shepherds watching their flocks, and the 'brightness of God shone round about them' (Luke 2:9)." [329]

The shepherds were fearful in the presence of the angel, "but when fear came upon them, the angel banished it. Not only does he banish fear, but he fills them with joy of spirit." [330]

December 24

THE SUPERLATIVE JOY OF THE ANGELS

 Thomas Merton (1915–1968) was known simply as Father Louis in the Trappist Abbey of Gethesmani near Louisville, Kentucky. In his journal, he described the profound experience of Christmas in the monastery. "What an atmosphere of expectation and joy there is in a Cistercian monastery when the monks get up [at midnight] on Christmas.... The night office begins with a solemn and stately invitatory that nevertheless rocks the church with cadences of superlative joy; from then on it is as though the angels themselves were singing their *Gloria in Excelsis* and showering upon the earth from the near stars, the stars that seem to have become close and warm, their message and promises of peace, peace." [331]

Thomas Merton represented the modern quest for God and for human solidarity and peace. He said, "We are not at peace with others because we are not at peace with ourselves, and we are not at peace with ourselves because we are not at peace with God." [332]

THE ANGELS' CHRISTMAS CAROL

The Gospel of Luke gives us the first Christmas carol — sung by angels: "Glory to God in the highest and on earth peace to those on whom his favor rests" (Luke 2:14). So sang the heavenly hosts of angels in Bethlehem on the night Jesus was born. Angels are messengers of the Word and the will of God. Since Jesus is the Word of God, it was understandable that the angels would tell the world about him. What joyful news! The angels couldn't help but sing about it! If you happily joined others in singing carols today or during the weeks before Christmas, you've been in good company — the company of angels!

"Peace is the first thing the angels sang."

— Pope Saint Leo the Great

Pray for peace on this Christmas day, and then imitate the angels! Sing to praise and glorify God!

December 26

Saint Stephen (First Century)

FACE OF AN ANGEL

 Saint Stephen, one of the first deacons of the Church, was also the first Christian martyr. He reminded Jewish leaders that Israel often failed to obey or understand God's law and prophets. But even Stephen's enemies saw that he was heaven's messenger. "All those who sat in the Sanhedrin looked intently at him and saw that his face was like the face of an angel" (Acts 6:15). For his "blasphemy," Stephen was stoned outside Jerusalem about the year 34. Jesus, God's Son, surrendered his life without resistance. So did Stephen. Like Jesus in his last moments, Stephen asked God to forgive those who were taking his life.

Saint Stephen's face looked like the face of an angel because he had completely surrendered to the service of love and truth. During this Christmas season, try to surrender a bit of your comfort, your money, your time, and your personal desires — for the sake of love and truth.

December 27

Saint John, Apostle and Evangelist (First century)

WHISPERING OF AN ANGEL

 A sixteenth-century Russian icon, Saint John the Theologian in Silence, shows us the elderly Apostle with downcast eyes holding the Gospels. An angel whispers into John's ear, apparently dictating God's Word. The brother of Saint James the Greater and Zebedee's son was the youngest Apostle. Known as the "beloved disciple," John didn't abandon Jesus when he was arrested. John was at the foot of the cross when Jesus asked him to care for Mary and told Mary that John would be a son for her. John's Gospel was the last written and completely original. Instead of retelling Christ's life, John shared the meaning of the Savior's life. John's insight was born out of prayerful silence and attention to an angel's whispered words. [333]

In the beginning was the Word, and the Word was with God, and the Word was God. (John 1:1)

In these first words of his Gospel, John talks about God's loving plan for creation — the plan to send Jesus to our world. On this second day of Christmas, remember that God's plan for creation was perfect — and always included you.

December 28

The Holy Innocents

THE ANGELS' COUNTRY MUSIC HIT

 At Christmas in 1993, Alabama, a country music band, released a song that quickly became a country music favorite. "Angels among Us," by Don Goodman and Becky Hobbs, tells of a little boy lost in the woods in winter who's led home by a kind old man. "Mama couldn't see him," the song says, "oh but he was standing there. And I knew in my heart, he was the answer to my prayers." The song says that angels appear in time of trouble, bringing comfort and hope. In 2012, several weeks after the shooting deaths of twenty elementary school children and six staff members in Newtown, Connecticut, singer Demi Lovato rerecorded the song to memorialize the victims. [334]

Holy Innocents, like the infants massacred by King Herod's soldiers, have been slain many times and in various places throughout history. Hopefully, the bereaved can trust that their children were comforted, embraced, and led home to God by "Angels among Us."

December 29

The Angels Appeared Only Once

 Have you ever thought about what became of the shepherds after that extraordinary first Christmas night? Elizabeth Stuart Phelps thought that "the shepherds went back to their sheep. They had seen their only angels. The next night, the next year, brought no more. They talked all their lives about this one great experience. Did they search the skies midnight upon midnight? Did they tell their children's children how the splendid zenith burst that only time? How the soft winter wind broke into articulate speech? How he looked — the mighty one, who was Gabriel of the heavenly host? And how they found that the angels spoke the truth? For there was the Child and the manger." [335]

Why do we long to see angels? Is it easier to seek the messenger than to heed the message? If God has given you only one angel, what is the truth that angel brings to you?

December 30

The Song of the Angels

 "Let All Mortal Flesh Keep Silence" is a beautiful hymn for any time of the year. The ancient Liturgy of Saint James, written during the fourth century, used the hymn at the presentation of the bread and wine at the offertory. The Eastern Orthodox Church sings it on the Saturday of Holy Week, using the Divine Liturgy of Saint Basil. Orthodox Christians in Jerusalem recite it on the Sunday after Christmas, or as part of the Christmas Eve service. The hymn summons us to stand in awe as the King of kings and Lord of lords descends with an escort of angels.

Let all mortal flesh keep silence
And with fear and trembling stand...
Christ our God to earth descends
Our full homage to demand.

Rank on rank the host of Heaven
Spreads its vanguard on the way...
That the powers of Hell may vanish
As the darkness clears away [336]

THE ANGELS' LOUD HOSANNAS

 The life and prayer of the Holy Family Sisters are steeped in the intimate union of Jesus, Mary, and Joseph. They meditate on Christ's birth through the eyes of a family. "The Inn of Bethlehem is crowded with guests, and so, out into the night they go until they find a grotto where they can share the straw with the beasts. The Holy Family has none of the good things of life.... Angels, it is true, sang their songs of triumph and loud hosannas rang through the court of Heaven and, encircling the throne of God, found echo among the hills of Bethlehem; but with the exception of a few humble shepherd lads, the event made no impression on the world at the time.... When the shepherds went over to Bethlehem, they found Joseph and Mary and the Infant, a family group — the Holy Family. The greatest mystery of God's dealings with the world took outward form in this simple and familiar setting." [337]

Comfort and wealth and fine clothes and all that the modern mind-sets value on are not essential to the home. A family can be supremely happy in a stable, provided their hearts respond to love for one another, sanctified by love for God.

This Reading and Reflection for December 31 bring us to the end of your year spent with "The Angels of the Lord." It is not, by any means, the end of your journey. As you begin a new year, "trust the past to God's mercy, the present to God's love and the future to God's providence" (Saint Augustine of Hippo).

Appendix of Angel Prayers

THE ANGELUS

Traditionally prayed at 6 a.m., noon, and 6 p.m. When prayed in groups, a leader recites the verse (V.) and all others recite the response (R.) and the Hail Marys.

V. The Angel of the Lord declared unto Mary,
R. And she conceived of the Holy Spirit.

Hail Mary …

V. Behold the handmaid of the Lord.
R. Be it done unto me according to Your Word.

Hail Mary …

V. And the Word was made flesh,
R. And dwelt among us.

Hail Mary …

V. Pray for us, O holy Mother of God.
R. That we may be made worthy of the promises of Christ.

Let us pray:

Pour forth, we beseech You, O Lord, Your grace into our hearts; that we, to whom the incarnation of Christ, Your Son, was made known by the message of an angel, may by His Passion and Cross, be brought to the glory of His Resurrection, through the same Christ Our Lord.

Amen.

AVE REGINA CAELORUM (HAIL QUEEN OF HEAVEN)

Hail, Queen of Heaven, beyond compare
To whom the angels homage pay;
hail, root of Jesse, gate of light,
that opened for the world's new day.
Rejoice, O Virgin unsurpassed,
in whom our ransom was begun,
for all your loving children pray
to Christ, our Savior and your Son.

EVENING PRAYER OF SAINT ALPHONSUS LIGUORI (1696–1787)

Jesus Christ my God, I adore you and thank you for all the graces you have given me this day. I offer you my sleep and all the moments of this night, and I ask you to keep me from sin. I put myself within your sacred side and under the mantle of our Lady. Let your holy angels stand about me and keep me in peace. And let your blessing be upon me. Amen. [338]

NIGHT PRAYER OF SAINT AUGUSTINE (354–430)

Watch, O Lord,
with those who wake, or watch, or weep tonight,
and give your Angels and Saints charge over those who sleep.
Tend your sick ones, O Lord Jesus,
Rest your weary ones.
Bless your dying ones.
Soothe your suffering ones.

Pity your afflicted ones.
Shield your joyous ones.
And all for your love's sake.
Amen.

PRAYER TO SAINTS MICHAEL, GABRIEL, AND RAPHAEL, ARCHANGELS

Heavenly King, You have given us archangels
to assist us during our pilgrimage on earth.
Saint Michael is our protector;
I ask him to come to my aid,
fight for all my loved ones,
and protect us from danger.
Saint Gabriel is a messenger of the Good News;
I ask him to help me
clearly hear Your voice
and to teach me the truth.
Saint Raphael is the healing angel;
I ask him to take my need for healing
and that of everyone I know,
lift it up to Your throne of grace
and deliver back to us the gift of recovery.
Help us, O Lord,
to realize more fully the reality of the archangels
and their desire to serve us.

Holy angels, pray for us.
Amen. [339]

PRAYER OF COMMENDATION

(prayed for those approaching death)

Go forth, Christian soul, from this world
in the name of God the almighty Father,
who created you,
in the name of Jesus Christ, the Son of the living God,
who suffered for you,
in the name of the Holy Spirit,
who was poured out upon you.
Go forth, faithful Christian!…
May you return to [your Creator]
who formed you from the dust of the earth.
May holy Mary, the angels, and all the saints
come to meet you as you go forth from this life….
May you see your Redeemer face to face.
*[Toward your soul as it goes forth from the body,
there hastens the glorious company of angels.]*

IN PARADISUM

May God the Father look on you with love,
and call you to himself in bliss above.
May God the Son, good Shepherd of the sheep,
stretch out his hand and waken you from sleep.
May God the Spirit breathe on you his peace,
where joys beyond all knowing never cease.

May flights of angels lead you on your way,
to paradise, and heaven's eternal day!

May martyrs greet you after death's dark night,
and bid you enter into Zion's light!
May choirs of angels sing you to your rest
with once poor Lazarus, now forever blest.

PRAYER FOR THE DEAD

Come to his [her] assistance, you saints of God;
Meet him [her], O angels of the Lord.
Receive his [her] soul, and present it in the sight of the Most High.
May Christ, who called you, receive you;
And may the angels lead you into the bosom of Abraham.
Receive his [her] soul and present it in the sight of the Most High.

AN ANGEL PRAYER FOR THE HOME

O Lord, we ask you to visit this home
And drive from it all the snares of the enemy.
Let your holy angels dwell here, to preserve us in peace;
And may your blessing be upon us forever,
Through our Lord Jesus Christ. Amen. [340]

PRAYER TO SAINT MICHAEL
THE ARCHANGEL

Saint Michael the Archangel, defend us in battle,
Be our protection against the wickedness and snares of the devil;
May God rebuke him, we humbly pray.
And do thou, O prince of the heavenly host,
by the power of God,
cast into hell Satan and all evil spirits

who prowl through the world seeking the ruin of souls. Amen.

— Pope Saint Leo XIII (1810–1903)

PRAYER TO OUR HOLY
GUARDIAN ANGELS

Heavenly Father, Your infinite love for us has chosen a blessed angel in heaven and appointed him our guide during this earthly pilgrimage. Accept our thanks for so great a blessing. Grant that we may experience the assistance of our holy protector in all our necessities. And you, holy, loving angel and guide, watch over us with all the tenderness of your angelic heart. Keep us always on the way that leads to heaven, and cease not to pray for us until we have attained our final destiny, eternal salvation. Then we shall love you for all eternity. We shall praise and glorify you unceasingly for all the good you have done for us while here on earth. Especially be a faithful and watchful protector of our children. Take our place, and supply what may be wanting to us through human frailty, short-sightedness, or sinful neglect. Lighten, O you perfect servants of God, our heavy task. Guide our children, that they may become like unto Jesus, may imitate Him faithfully, and persevere till they attain eternal life. Amen. [341]

EUCHARISTIC PRAYER I

In humble prayer we ask you, almighty God:
command that these gifts be borne
by the hands of your holy Angel
to your altar on high

in the sight of your divine majesty,
so that all of us, who through this participation at the altar
receive the most holy Body and Blood of your Son, may be
filled with every grace and heavenly blessing.
(Through Christ our Lord. Amen.)

PRAYER TO ASK YOUR GUARDIAN ANGEL
TO HELP OTHERS IN NEED

Guardian angel, watch over those whose names you can read in
my heart. Guard them with every care and make their way easy
and their labors fruitful. Dry their tears if they weep; sanctify their
joys; raise their courage if they weaken; restore their hope if they
lose heart, their health if they be ill, truth if they err, repentance if
they fail. Amen.[342]

FROM THE PRAYER KNOWN AS
"THE BREASTPLATE OF SAINT PATRICK"

May the strength of God pilot us.
May the power of God preserve us.
May the wisdom of God instruct us.
May the hand of God protect us.
May the way of God direct us.
May the shield of God defend us.
May the angels of God guard us
  — against the snares of the evil ones
  — against the temptations of the world.[343]

GRATITUDE PRAYER TO
YOUR GUARDIAN ANGEL

Oh most holy angel of God, appointed by God to be my guardian, I give you thanks for all the benefits that you have ever bestowed on me in body and in soul. I praise and glorify you that you condescended to assist me with such patient fidelity, and to defend me against all the assaults of my enemies. Blessed be the hour in which you were assigned me for my guardian, my defender, and my patron. In acknowledgement and return for all your loving ministries to me, I offer you the infinitely precious and noble heart of Jesus, and firmly purpose to obey you henceforward, and most faithfully to serve my God. Amen.

— Saint Gertrude the Great (1256–1302)

PADRE PIO'S DAILY PRAYER TO
HIS GUARDIAN ANGEL

Angel of God,
my guardian,
to whom the goodness
of the Heavenly Father entrusts me.
Enlighten,
protect and guide me
now and forever.
Amen.

— Saint Pio of Pietrelcina (1887–1968) [344]

TO MY GUARDIAN ANGEL,
BY SAINT THÉRÈSE OF LISIEUX

Glorious Guardian of my soul, You who shine in God's beautiful
Heaven

As a sweet and pure flame near the Eternal's throne,

You come down to earth for me, and enlightening me with your
splendor,

fair Angel, you become my Brother, my Friend, my Consoler!…

Knowing my great weakness, You lead me by the hand,

And I see you tenderly remove the stone from my path

Your sweet voice is always inviting me to look only at Heaven.

The more you see me humble and little, the more your face is
radiant.

O you! Who travel through space more swiftly than lightning,

I beg you, fly in my place. Close to those who are dear to me.

With your wing dry their tears. Sing how good Jesus is.

Sing that suffering has its charms, and softly, whisper my name….

During my short life I want to save my fellow sinners.

O Fair Angel of the Homeland, Give me holy fervor.

I have nothing but my sacrifices and my austere poverty.

With your celestial delights, offer them to the Trinity.

For you the Kingdom and the Glory, the Riches of the King of kings.

For me the ciborium's humble Host. For me the cross's treasure.

With the Cross, with the Host,

With your celestial aid,

In peace I await the other life, The joys that will last forever. [345]

— Saint Thérèse of Lisieux (1873–1897)

Seven archangels stand glorifying the almighty and serving the hidden mystery.

Michael, the first, Gabriel the second, Raphael the third — symbol of the Trinity, Surael, Sakakael, Sratael, and Ananael. These are the shining ones, the great and pure ones, who pray to God for mankind. The cherubim, the seraphim, the thrones, dominions, powers, and the four living creatures bearing the chariot of God. The twenty-four elders in the Church of the Firstborn, praise Him without ceasing, crying out and saying, "Holy is God; heal the sick. Holy is the Almighty; give rest to the departed. Holy is the Immortal; bless Thine inheritance. May Thy mercy and Thy peace be a stronghold unto Thy people. Holy, holy, holy, Lord of Hosts. Heaven and earth are full of Thy glory. Intercede for us, O angels, our guardians, and all heavenly hosts, that our sins may be forgiven.

PRAYER TO A GUARDIAN ANGEL,
BY SAINT MACARIUS OF EGYPT (300–391)

Yes, holy angel, God has given you charge of me. Take my hand and bring me to the path that leads to salvation. Forgive every deed of mine that has ever offended you; forgive the sins I have committed today. Protect me during the night and keep me safe. Intercede for me with the Lord; ask him to make me love him more and more, and to enable me to give him the service his goodness deserves. Amen. [346]

GUARDIAN ANGEL PRAYER

Angel of God, my Guardian dear,
To whom God's love commits me here,
Ever this day be at my side,
To light and guard, to rule and guide.
Amen.

PRAYER TO SAINT RAPHAEL THE ARCHANGEL

Glorious Archangel Saint Raphael, great prince of the heavenly court, you are illustrious for your gifts of wisdom and grace. You are a guide of those who journey by land, or sea, or air, consoler of the afflicted, and refuge of sinners. I beg you, assist me in all my needs and in all the sufferings of this life, as once you helped the young Tobias on his travels. Because you are the "medicine of God" I humbly pray to you to heal the many infirmities of my soul and the ills that afflict my body. I especially ask of you the favor (here mention your special intention), and the great grace of purity to prepare me to be the temple of the Holy Spirit. Amen. [347]

USHERERS OF MERCY

Usherers of mercy, usher in our [plea for] mercy, before the Master of mercy, You who cause prayer to be heard, may you cause our prayer to be heard before the Hearer of prayer, You who cause our outcry to be heard, may you cause our outcry to be heard, before the Hearer of outcry, You who usher in tears, may you usher in our tears, before the King Who finds favor through tears. Exert yourselves and multiply supplication and petition before the King, God, exalted and most high. [348]

Notes

1. http://w2.vatican.va/content/francesco/en/angelus/2013/documents/papa-francesco_angelus_20130726_gmg-rio.html.

2. St. Basil the Great, Hom. in Ps 33:5–6.

3. Msgr. Joseph B. Code, *Daily Thoughts of Mother Seton* (Emmitsburg, MD: Chronicle Press, Inc. 1960), July 8.

4. Valentine Long, O.F.M., *The Angels in Religion and Art* (Chicago: Franciscan Herald Press, 1970), 143.

5. https://www.holycrossusa.org/about/saint-andre-bessette/; http://www.catholic.org/saints/saint.php?saint_id=18.

6. http://www.brainyquote.com/quotes/keywords/angels_5.html#VQWHfC3VIL9RxLvm.99.

7. John Henry Cardinal Newman (1801–1890): *Parochial and Plain Sermons*, Vol. 4, 12.

8. Angelo Maria D'Anghiari, O.F.M. Cap., *The Authenticity of the Holy House* (Loreto: Congregzione Universale della Santa Casa, 1967), 58–59.

9. Barbara Romanowski, "Homeles Angel," used with permission of Catholic Online, Saints & Angels, Angel Encounters, http://www.catholic.org/saints/angelstories/?page=0&story=9937.

10. Ladislaus Boros, *Angels and Men* (New York: Crossroad Book, Seabury Press, 1977), 125–126.

11. "Poll: Nearly 8 in 10 Americans believe in angels" (CBSNews), http://www.cbsnews.com/news/poll-nearly-8-in-10-americans-believe-in-angels/.

12. A. Souter, tr., *Tertullian's Treatises Concerning Prayer and Baptism*, http://www.tertullian.org/articles/souter_orat_bapt/souter_orat_bapt_04baptism.htm.

13. *The Summa Theologica*, http://www.ccel.org/a/aquinas/summa/FP/FP050.html#FPQ50OUTP1.

14. Esther Beilenson, *Angels Are Forever* (White Plains, NY: Peter Pauper Press, 1994), 60–61.

15. Benedicta Ward, S.L.G., *The Sayings of the Desert Fathers, The Alphabetical Collection* (Kalamazoo, MI: Cistercian Publications, 1975), 1.

16. http://www.americancatholic.org/Features/Saints/Saint.aspx?id=1263.

17. http://www.catholic.org/saints/saint.php?saint_id=51; http://www.americancatholic.org/Features/Saints/saint.aspx?id=1270.

18. http://www.catholictradition.org/Saints/saintly-quotes2.htm.

19. Jean Danielou, *The Angels and Their Mission*, translated edition (Westminster: Newman Press, 1953), 81.

20. *Blades of Grass*, http://www.templeemanuel.com/blades-grass.

21. http://www.catholic.org/saints/saint.php?saint_id=21; http://www.marypages.com/AngelaMerici.htm.

22. http://ursulinesmsj.org/_uploads/SaintAngelaMericiwritings.pdf, (*Counsels*, Prologue, 10–11).

23. "St. Thomas Aquinas" — *Saints & Angels* — Catholic Online, http://www.catholic.org/saints/saint.php?saint_id=2530.

24. "We are like children, who stand in need of masters…" (Beliefnet), http://www.beliefnet.com/Quotes/Angel/S/St-Thomas-Aquinas/We-Are-Like-Children-Who-Stand-In-Need-Of-Masters.aspx.

25. Mike Aquilina, *Angels of God: The Bible, the Church and the Heavenly Hosts* (Cincinnati: Servant Books, 2006), 54.

26. Ladislaus Boros, *Angels and Men* (New York: Crossroad Book, Seabury Press, 1977), 35.

27. Archbishop Fulton Sheen, *The Integrated Catholic Life*, http://www.integratedcatholiclife.org/tag/archbishop-fulton-sheen/.

28. "St. John Bosco" — *Saints & Angels* — Catholic Online, http://www.catholic.org/saints/saint.php?saint_id=63.

29. F. Forrester Church and Terrence J. Mulry, eds., *The Macmillan Book of Earliest Christian Prayer* (New York: Macmillan Publishing, 1988), 117.

30. Jane Hirshfield, Ed, *Women in Praise of the Sacred: 43 centuries of Spiritual Poetry by Women* (New York: Harper Collins 1994), 187.

31. Valentine Long, O.F.M., *The Angels in Religion and Art* (New Jersey: St. Anthony Guild Press, 1970), 24.

32. https://www.catholicculture.org/culture/liturgicalyear/calendar/day.cfm?date=2004-02-05.

33. F. Forrester Church, *Entertaining Angels* (New York: Harper & Row, 1987), 106.

34. *Padre Pio Newsletter*, Issue 49 page 4, www.saintpio.org.

35. "St. Scholastica" — *Saints & Angels* — Catholic Online, http://www.catholic.org/saints/saint.php?saint_id=240.

36. "St. Bernadette Soubirous" — *Saints & Angels* — Catholic Online, http://www.catholic.org/saints/saint.php?saint_id=1757.

37. Patricia A. McEachern, *A Holy Life: The Writings of St. Bernadette of Lourdes* (San Francisco: Ignatius Press, 2005), 29.

38. "The truth about angelic beings: What does the Bible really teach about angels?" (ANGELS), http://www.christiananswers.net/q-acb/acb-t005.html#3.

39. Joan Wester Andersen, *Where Angels Walk: True Stories of Heavenly Visitors* (New York: Ballantine Books, 1992), 130–132.

40. "History of St. Valentine," http://www.catholiceducation.org/en/culture/catholic-contributions/history-of-st-valentine.html, "St. Valentine" — *Saints & Angels* — Catholic Online.

41. Mary Cholmondeley, *Red Pottage* (Adelaide, South Australia: The University of Adelaide ebooks@adelaide, 1899), chapter 20.

42. In Ps. Qui Habitat, Sermo XII.

43. F. Forrester Church and Terrence J. Mulry, eds., *The Macmillan Book of Earliest Christian Prayer* (New York: Macmillan Publishing, 1988), 99.

44. Mary William, "An Angel without Wings," used with permission of Catholic Online, Saints & Angels, Angel Encounters, http://www.catholic.org/saints/angelstories/?story=5280.

45. Letters III, *Padre Pio Newsletter*, issue 49, page 2.

46. C. S. Lewis, *The Screwtape Letters* (New York: Macmillan Publishing Company, 1952), Preface.

47. Giorgio Vasari, *The Lives of the Artists* (New York: Oxford University Press, 1998), 176.

48. F. Forrester Church, *Entertaining Angels* (New York: Harper & Row, 1987), 106.

49. http://www.catholic.org/saints/saint.php?saint_id=7252.

50. Dom Donald's Blog: *All Angels, A sermon by John Henry Newman,* http://nunraw.blogspot.com/2011/09/all-angels-sermon-by-john-henry-newman.html.

51. "Newman Reader" — *Parochial & Plain Sermons* 4 — Sermon 13 (Newman Reader — *Parochial & Plain Sermons* 4 — Sermon 13), http://www.newmanreader.org/works/parochial/volume4/sermon13.html.

52. "St. Polycarp" | *Saint of the Day* | AmericanCatholic.org, http://www.americancatholic.org/Features/Saints/saint.aspx?id=1300; "St. Polycarp" — *Saints & Angels* — Catholic Online, http://www.catholic.org/saints/saint.php?saint_id=99.

53. https://www.christianhistoryinstitute.org/study/module/polycarp/.

54. Pascal P. Parente, *The Angels* (St. Meinrad, IN: Grail Publications, 1958), 3.

55. Gabriel Awards — "About the Gabriels," https://gabrielawards.nonprofitcms.org/a/page/about.

56. "Belief in Angels" (*The Religion of Islam*), http://www.islamreligion.com/articles/41/belief-in-angels.

57. The Koran (iz Quotes), http://izquotes.com/quote/291424.

58. W. Heywood, tr., *Fioretti The Little Flowers of Saint Francis* (Assisi: Casa Editrice Francescana, 1949), 203–204.

59. Lucius Eugene Chittenden, *Recollections of President Lincoln and His Administration* (New York: Harper & Brothers, 1904), 258–260.

60. Jan Judge, "Jan's Story — St. Katharine Drexel Sent Me an Angel," Not Over Till the Fat Lady Sings.com. Widebertha, Sept. 20, 2005.

61. Catholic News Agency. "The 'angel' of Guatemala: 12-year-old chose death over gang violence." July 16, 2015.

62. M. F. Toal, ed., *The Sunday Sermons of the Great Fathers*, Vol. II (Chicago: Henry Regnery Co., 1958), 34.

63. Pascal P. Parente, *The Angels* (St. Meinrad, IN: Grail Publications, 1958), 125.

64. Ladislaus Boros, *Angels and Men* (New York: Crossroad Book, Seabury Press, 1977), 125.

65. *Ante-Nicene Fathers*, Vol. 3. (Buffalo, NY: Christian Literature Publishing Co., 1885), 4:1.

66. *Apparitions of Angels and Demons in the Lives of the Saints*, "Saint John of God," http://www.therealpresence.org/eucharst/misc/Angels_Demons/ANGES_johngod.pdf.

67. "40 Martyrs of Sebaste," http://www.ewtn.com/library/MARY/40MAR.htm; "Full of Grace and Truth: The Holy Forty Martyrs of Sebaste," http://full-of-grace-and-truth.blogspot.com/2010/03/holy-forty-martyrs-of-sebaste.html.

68. Robert McAfee Brown, *Spirituality and Liberation: Overcoming the Great Fallacy* (Westminster: John Knox Press, 1988), 136.

69. Jacob Epstein (1880–1959) (*Jacob Epstein: Modern Sculptor*, Biography), http://www.visual-arts-cork.com/sculpture/jacob-epstein.htm; "COVENTRY CATHEDRAL" Death and Resurrection, http://www.know-britain.com/churches/coventry_cathedral_1.html.

70. Billy Graham, *Angels: God's Secret Agents* (Nashville: Thomas Nelson Publishers, 1975), 1.

71. "St. Patrick" — *Saints & Angels* — Catholic Online, http://www.catholic.org/saints/saint.php?saint_id=89; "St. Patrick" | *Saint of the Day* | AmericanCatholic.org, http://www.americancatholic.org/Features/Saints/saint.aspx?id=1325.

72. F. Forrester Church and Terrence J. Mulry, eds., *The Macmillan Book of Earliest Christian Prayers* (New York: Macmillan Publishing, 1988), 113.

73. St. Cyril of Jerusalem, Catechetical Lecture 23, "On the Sacred Liturgy and Communion," 6, 14.

74. Benedicta Ward, S.L.G., *The Sayings of the Desert Fathers, The Alphabetical Collection* (Kalamazoo, MI: Cistercian Publications, 1975), 117.

75. *Padre Pio Newsletter*, issue 49, page 2, www.saintpio.org.

76. Blessed John Newman, *Discourses to Mixed Congregations,* Discourse 5.

77. Megan McKenna, *Angels Unawares* (Maryknoll, NY: Orbis Books, 1995), 17–18.

78. Mike Aquilina, *Angels of God: The Bible, the Church and the Heavenly Hosts* (Cincinnati: Servant Books, 2006), 72.

79. Anne Rice, *Christ the Lord: The Road to Cana* (New York: Knopf, 2008), 200.

80. "Father Patrick Dowling and the 'Missouri Miracle'" (*National Catholic Register*), http://www.ncregister.com/daily-news/father-patrick-dowling-and-the-missouri-miracle.

81. Cavan Sieczkowski, "Mystery 'Angel' Priest Appears At Missouri Car Crash, Performs 'Miracle,' Then Disappears" (UPDATE) (*The Huffington Post*), http://www.huffingtonpost.com/2013/08/08/mystery-angel-priest-car-crash-_n_3725992.html.

82. C. S. Lewis, *The Screwtape Letters* (New York: Macmillan Publishing Company, 1952), Preface, vii.

83. Henri-Marie Boudon, *Devotion to the Nine Choirs of Holy Angels, translated edition* (Potosi, WI: St. Athanasius Press, 2009), 67.

84. Basilea Schlink, *The Unseen World of Angels and Demons* (London: Marshall Pickering, 1985), 132–133.

85. Hermas, *The Shepherd,* Commandment 6, chapter 2, http://www.newadvent.org/fathers/02012.htm.

86. Hermas, *The Shepherd*, Commandment 12, 5 and 6; http://www.newadvent.org/fathers/02012.htm.

87. Priscilla Throop, *Isidore of Seville's Etymologies* (Charlotte, VT: MedievalMS, 2005), Book VII, 5.2.

88. Saint Isidore of Seville, *Book of Maxims*, http://catholicsaints.info/saint-isidore-of-seville/.

89. William Newton, "Àngel Custodi," *Catholic Barcelona,* April 1, 2014, http://catholicbarcelona.com/2014/03/01/angel-custodi/.

90. "Saint Julie Billiart," *Saints Stories for All Ages,* Loyola Press, Chicago, 2013, http://www.loyolapress.com/saints-stories-for-kids.htm?cId=403509.

91. M. F. Toal, ed. *The Sunday Sermons of the Great Fathers*, Vol. II (Chicago: Henry Regnery Co, 1958), 242.

92. "St. Gemma Galgani" — *Saints & Angels* — Catholic Online, http://www.catholic.org/saints/saint.php?saint_id=225; "Who Was Saint Gemma Galgani?" (About.com, Religion & Spirituality), http://angels.about.com/od/MiraclesReligiousTexts/p/Who-Was-Saint-Gemma-Galgani.htm.

93. http://www.usccb.org/prayer-and-worship/bereavement-and-funerals/prayers-for-death-and-dying.

94. Megan McKenna, *Angels Unawares* (Maryknoll, NY: Orbis Books, 1995), 169.

95. "President Lincoln dies" (History.com), http://www.history.com/this-day-in-history/president-lincoln-dies.

96. "St. Benedict Joseph Labre" | *Saint of the Day* | AmericanCatholic. org, http://www.americancatholic.org/Features/Saints/saint.aspx?id=1356; "St. Benedict Joseph Labré" — *Saints & Angels* — Catholic Online, http:// www.catholic.org/saints/saint.php?saint_id=1728.

97. http://bedejournal.blogspot.com/2010/01/dancing-with-angels. html.

98. http://orthodoxwiki.org/Cherubic_Hymn.

99. Robert James Laws, III, *The Biblical Foundations of the Spirituality of Dom Hélder Câmara*, padreroblaws.files.wordpress.com/2013/02/ thebiblicalcamara.pdf.

100. http://angels-angelology.com/jacobs-ladder.

101. "Saint Anselm," *Stanford Encyclopedia of Philosophy*, Dec 21 2015; *De Veritate* (On Truth) and *De casu diaboli* (On the Fall of the Devil), http://plato.stanford.edu/entries/anselm/#FreSin.

102. *Cur Deus Homo* (Why God Became Man), Book 1.

103. M. F. Toal, D.D., *The Sunday Sermons of the Great Fathers*, Vol. II (Chicago: Henry Regnery Co., 1958), 436.

104. Megan McKenna, *Angels Unawares* (Maryknoll, NY: Orbis Books, 1995), 70.

105. Shakespeare borrowed the line from the *In Paradisum*, which is sung at the conclusion of the funeral Mass.

106. Peter Kreeft, *Angels and Demons: What Do We Really Know about Them?* (San Francisco: Ignatius Press, 1995), 86–87.

107. http://www.marypages.com/SienaEng.htm; http://www. therealpresence.org/eucharst/misc/Angels_Demons/ANGES_siena.pdf.

108. Judith Lang, *The Angels of God, Understanding the Bible* (Hyde Park, NY: New City Press, 1997), 232, 233.

109. Pascal P. Parente, *The Angels* (St. Meinrad, IN: Grail Publications, 1958), 126–127.

110. PL 54, Sermo, 73, *De Ascensione Domini* IV.

111. Judith Lang, *The Angels of God, Understanding the Bible* (Hyde Park, NY: New City Press, 1997), 165.

112. http://www.catholictradition.org/Angels/angels3f.htm.

113. "Saint Michael's Cave: Gargano, Italy" (Mont Saint Angelo, Italy, St Michael's Cave), http://www.thecatholictravelguide.com/MonteSantAngelo.html.

114. Valentine Long, O.F.M., *The Angels in Religion and Art* (Chicago: Franciscan Herald Press, 1970), 102.

115. "St. John of Ávila" — *Saints & Angels* — Catholic Online, http://www.catholic.org/saints/saint.php?saint_id=3944.

116. Georges Huber, *My Angel Will Go Before You* (Dublin: Four Courts Press, 1983), 105; "Saint Peter Faber (Favre)," http://www.loyolapress.com/blessed-peter-favre.htm.

117. Dag Hammarskjöld, *Markings*, translated by Leif Sjöberg and W. H. Auden (New York: Alfred A. Knopf, 1986), 12.

118. Georges Huber, *My Angel Will Go Before You* (Dublin: Four Courts Press, 1983), 111.

119. "St. Juliana of Norwich" — *Saints & Angels* — Catholic Online, http://www.catholic.org/saints/saint.php?saint_id=4124.

120. "Angels exist but have no wings, says Catholic 'angelologist'" (*The Telegraph*), http://www.telegraph.co.uk/news/worldnews/europe/italy/10530177/Angels-exist-but-have-no-wings-says-Catholic-angelologist.html.

121. "Past Forward: Inspirational Quotes on ANGELS," http://www.healpastlives.com/pastlf/quote/quangels.htm.

122. Valentine Long, O.F.M., *The Angels in Religion and Art* (Chicago: Franciscan Herald Press, 1970).

123. M. F. Toal, ed., *The Sunday Sermons of the Great Fathers*, Vol III (Chicago: Henry Regnery Co, 1959), 206.

124. Peter Kreeft, *Angels and Demons: What Do We Really Know about Them?* (San Francisco: Ignatius Press, 1995), 56–57.

125. Meister Eckhart, *Selected Sermons—True Healing,* Christian Classics Ethereal Library (www.ccel.org), IV, 42.

126. http://www.padrepio.catholicwebservices.com/ENGLISH/Guard.htm 10/7/2014.

127. "Saint Humility," CatholicSaints.Info., May 17, 2015, Web. 8 August 8, 2015.

128. Blessed Charles de Foucauld, *Spiritual Writings* (Rome: Citta Nuova, 1974), 77.

129. Benedicta Ward, S.L.G., *The Sayings of the Desert Fathers, The Alphabetical Collection* (Kalamazoo, MI: Cistercian Publications, 1975), 79.

130. http://idioms.thefreedictionary.com/on+the+side+of+the+angels.

131. Joan Wester Anderson, *Where Angels Walk: True Stories of Heavenly Visitors* (New York: Ballantine Books, 1992), 136–138; "Loretto Chapel miraculous staircase — Santa Fe, New Mexico," http://www.lorettochapel.com/staircase.html.

132. "St. Augustine of Canterbury" | *Saint of the Day* | AmericanCatholic.org, http://www.americancatholic.org/Features/Saints/saint.aspx?id=1396; "A mission to the (Christian History Project)," http://www.christianhistoryproject.org/the-sword-of-islam/gregory-the-great/augustine-of-canterbury.

133. Mortimer J. Adler, *The Angels and Us* (New York: MacMillan Publishing Co., 1982), 5.

134. "Joan of Arc Quotes about Angels" | *A–Z Quotes* (A–Z Quotes), http://www.azquotes.com/author/501-Joan_of_Arc/tag/angel.

135. Justin Martyr, *Apologia I, 6* (Pascal P. Parente, *The Angels* [St. Meinrad, IN, Grail Publications, 1958]), 140–41.

136. Augustine, *De Vera Religione, 35* (Pascal P. Parente, *The Angels* [St. Meinrad, IN: Grail Publications, 1958]), 142.

137. Valentine Long, O.F.M., *The Angels in Religion and Art* (Chicago: Franciscan Herald Press, 1970), 132, 139.

138. http://www.premontre.org/chapter/cat/people/perpetual-calendar-of-order-saints-and-blesseds/st-norbert-june-6/.

139. http://angels-angelology.com/angels-in-the-kitchen; http://www.sandiegohistory.org/journal/88winter/year1588.htm; http://digitallibrary.usc.edu/cdm/ref/collection/p15799coll65/id/18279.

140. Joan Wester Anderson, *Where Angels Walk: The Stories of Heavenly Visitors* (New York: Ballantine Books, 1993), 88–91.

141. http://catholicharboroffaithandmorals.com/Index.html.

142. http://www.yenra.com/catholic/passages/saintjanefrancesdechantalonprayer.html.

143. http://www.yenra.com/catholic/passages/saintjanefrancesdechantalonprayer.html.

144. Benedicta Ward, S.L.G, *The Sayings of the Desert Fathers, The Alphabetical Collection* (Kalamazoo, MI: Cistercian Publications, 1975), 93.

145. BarbE, "Miracle," used with permission of Catholic Online, Saints & Angels, Angel Encounters, http://www.catholic.org/saints/angelstories/?page=0&story=10531.

146. Gregg Allison, *Historical Theology: An Introduction to Christian Doctrine* (Grand Rapids, MI: Zondervan, 2011), 301.

147. "Exorcism conference trains priests in 'ministry of love'" (Catholic News Agency), http://www.catholicnewsagency.com/news/exorcism-conference-trains-priests-in-ministry-of-love/.

148. http://www.beliefnet.com/Inspiration/Angels/2006/07/William-Blake-A-Life-Among-The-Angels.aspx?p=2#DFFqE89gAQypBxeo.99.

149. Northrop Frye, *Fearful Symmetry: A Study of Willam Blake* (Princeton, NJ: Princeton University Press, 2013), 21.

150. Georges Huber, *My Angel Will Go Before You,* translated edition (Dublin: Four Courts Press, 1983), 18–19.

151. Michael Patella, *Angels and Demons: A Christian Primer of the Spiritual World* (Collegeville, MN: Liturgical Press, 2012), 64–69.

152. Quasten, Burghardt and Lawler, *Ancient Christian Writers: Letters of Paulinus of Nola*, Vol. 1 (Mahwah, New Jersey: Paulist Press, 1966), Letter 11, # 21.

153. Gitta Mallasz, *Talking with Angels* (Zurich: Daimon Verlag, 1992), 44, http://www.dialogues-ange.fr/talking_with_angels/gitta_mallasz_en.html.

154. http://www.catholictradition.org/Angels/angels3f.htm.

155. Mike Aquilina, *Angels of God: The Bible, the Church and the Heavenly Host* (Cincinnati: Servant Books, 2009), 50–51; https://www.osv.com/.../catholic-persecution-in-the-spanish-civil-war.asp.

156. http://www.americancatholic.org/Features/Saints/saint.aspx?id=1427; http://www.catholic.org/saints/saint.php?saint_id=616.

157. Irenaeus, *Against Heresies* (Book IV, chapter 20, #1), gnosis.org/library/advh4.htm.

158. *L'Osservatore Romano*, English Edition, February 9, 1987, 6.

159. http://www.catholicnewsagency.com/saint.php?n=501.

160. http://articles.latimes.com/2005/mar/26/local/me-name26; http://www.thequeenofangels.com/mary-the-queen/our-lady-of-the-angels/.

161. http://www.sacred-destinations.com/italy/assisi-santa-maria-degli-angeli.

162. J. Armitage Robinson, *Two Glastonbury Legends: King Arthur and St. Joseph of Arimathea, 1926* (Whitefish, MT: Kessinger Publishing, LLC, 2003), 33, "St Thomas Receiving the Virgin Mary's Girdle at Her

Assumption," *Dimus*, no. 17 (April 2008), http://everything.explained.today/Thomas_the_Apostle/.

163. www.constitution.org/fed/federa51.htm.

164. http://www.mariagoretti.org/alessandrobio.htm.

165. http://sf.thedailydigest.org/2015/05/18/lost-in-translation-pope-misquoted-in-angel-of-peace-comment-to-abbas/.

166. Judith MacNutt, *Angels Are for Real: Inspiring, True Stories and Biblical Answers* (Minneapolis: Chosen Books, 2012), 63–65.

167. http://english.pravda.ru/society/anomal/14-06-2011/118195-angels-0/.

168. F. Forrester Church and Terrence J. Mulry, eds., *The Macmillan Book of Earliest Christian Prayers* (New York: Macmillan Publishing, 1988), 96.

169. http://w2.vatican.va/content/benedict-xvi/en/audiences/2010/documents/hf_ben-xvi_aud_20100317.html.

170. Dorothy Day, *From Union Square to Rome* (New York: Orbis Books, 2006), chapter 1, http://www.pbslearningmedia.org/resource/arct14.soc.qgdayi/other-voices-dorothy-day/.

171. http://www.traditioninaction.org/ProgressivistDoc/A_049_GuittonJP2.htm, from *L'Osservatore Romano,* March 21–22, 1983 cited in Maria Pia Giudici, *The Angels: Spiritual and Exegetical Notes* (New York: Alba House 1993), 149.

172. http://www.ignatianspirituality.com/ignatian-voices/20th-century-ignatian-voices/karl-rahner-sj, Karl Rahner, "Angels," in Karl Rahner (ed.), *Encyclopedia of Theology: The Concise Sacramentum Mundi* (London and New York: Continuum International Publishing Group, 1975), 116, 123.

173. http://thevalueofsparrows.com/2912/10/02/angels-the-angels-a-homily-by-karl-rahner.

174. "Dietrich Bonhoeffer," http://www.christianitytoday.com/ch/131christians/martyrs/bonhoeffer.html; "Dietrich Bonhoeffer Quote" (*A–Z Quotes*), http://www.azquotes.com/quote/1216493.

175. *The Prophecies and Revelations of Saint Bridget of Sweden*, Book VIII, 56.

176. http://www.therealpresence.org/eucharst/misc/Angels_Demons/ANGES_bridgetsweden.pdf.

177. "Prayers of Jews to Angels and Other Intermediaries during the First Centuries of the Common Era," http://oodegr.co/english/istorika/israil/jewish_prayers_angels.htm.

178. http://www.catholic.org/saints/saint.php?saint_id=22.

179. Benedicta Ward, S.L.G., *The Sayings of the Desert Fathers, The Alphabetical Collection* (Kalamazoo, MI: Cistercian Publications, 1975), 21–22.

180. James Russell Lowell, "On the Death of a Friend's Child," in *Lowell: The Poetical Works* (Boston: James R. Osgood, 1877), 88.

181. F. Forrester Church, *Entertaining Angels* (New York: Harper & Row, 1987), 11.

182. https://www.goodreads.com/work/quotes/2940316-meditations-from-mechthild-of-magdeburg-living-library.

183. http://www.catholic.org/saints/saint.php?saint_id=464; http://catholicharboroffaithandmorals.com/St.%20Peter%20Chrysologus.html.

184. Dag Hammarskjöld, *Markings,* translated by Leif Sjöberg and W. H. Auden (New York: Alfred A Knopf, 1986), 140.

185. "Rules for the Fuller Discernment of Spirits, VII," from *The Spiritual Exercises of Saint Ignatius Loyola.*

186. Virginia Smith, "Angel in the Rearview Mirror," used with permission of Catholic Online, Saints & Angels, Angel Encounters, http://www.catholic.org/saints/angelstories/?story=10283.

187. David P. McAstocker, S.J., *Speaking of Angels* (Milwaukee: Bruce Publishing Company 1946), 77.

188. Judith Lang, *The Angels of God, Understanding the Bible* (Hyde Park, NY: New City Press, 1997), 227–228.

189. F. Forrester Church, *Entertaining Angels* (New York: Harper & Row, 1987), 11.

190. *Angels in the Writing of the Saints*, https://www.opusangelorum. org/angels_saints/angels_saints. html.

191. Dom Anscar Vonier, O.S.B., *The Angels* (New York: Macmillan, 1928), 36–39.

192. Dom Anscar Vonier, O.S.B., *The Angels* (New York: Macmillan, 1928), 25.

193. Sr. Patricia Suchalski, S.B.S., President, National Shrine of Saint Katharine Drexel, Saint Katharine's Circle, *Quarterly Newsletter*, Sisters of the Blessed Sacrament, National Shrine of Saint Katharine Drexel, Vol. 1 #1, 2014.

194. http://www.therealpresence.org/eucharst/misc/Angels_Demons/ ANGES_guzman.pdf.

195. *Our Lady of Mercy* (Quotes by St. Teresa Benedicta of the Cross), http://www.olmlaycarmelites.org/quote/teresa-benedicta.

196. *Saint Quotes* (Prayer), http://saintquotes.blogspot.com/2009/05/ prayer.html.

197. *A Year of Prayer: 365 Rosaries* (August 12: Saint Jane Frances de Chantal), http://365rosaries.blogspot.com/2010/08/august-12-saint-jane-frances-de-chantal.html.

198. "Defend Us in Battle: Benedict XVI and Pope Francis Consecrate the Vatican to Michael the Archangel," Catholic Online, http://www. catholic.org/news/international/europe/story.php?id=51602.

199. Basilea Schlink, *The Unseen World of Angels and Demons* translated edition (London: Marshall Pickering, 1985), 104.

200. M. F. Toal, D.D., *The Sunday Sermons of the Great Fathers*, Vol IV (Chicago: Henry Regnery, 1963), 426.

201. http://orthodoxwiki.org/Seraphim_of_Sarov, "Conversation with Nicholas Motovilov," http://orthodoxinfo.com/praxis/wonderful.aspx.

202. Kestutis A. Trimakas, S.J. trans., *Mary Save Us* (New York: Paulist Press, 1960), 33.

203. Peter J. Kreeft, *Angels (and Demons): What Do We Really Know About Them?* (San Francisco: Ignatius Press, 1995), 70.

204. Dorothy Day, *The Long Loneliness*, http://www.azquotes.com/quote/705102.

205. http://www.catholictradition.org/Angels/angels3f.htm.

206. Benedicta Ward, S.L.G., *The Sayings of the Desert Fathers, The Alphabetical Collection* (Kalamazoo, MI: Cistercian Publications, 1975), 73.

207. Dom Anscar Vonier, O.S.B., *The Angels* (New York: Macmillan Company, 1928), 63.

208. *Douay-Rheims* Bible, published 1609.

209. "Sainte-Chapelle, Paris, France," http://www.discoverfrance.net/France/Cathedrals/Paris/Sainte-Chapelle.shtml; http://old.post-gazette.com/travel/20000806chapel6.asp; http://www.visual-arts-cork.com/architecture/sainte-chapelle.htm.

210. Billy Graham, *Angels: God's Secret Agents* (Nashville: Thomas Nelson, 1975), xiii–xiv.

211. "St. Monica" — *Saints & Angels* — Catholic Online, http://www.catholic.org/saints/saint.php?saint_id=1; *The Mother of Saint Augustine* (translation of Her Life [i.e., of L. V. E. Bougaud's *Histoire de Sainte Monique*]), by Lady Herbert (Google Books), https://books.google.com/books.

212. "St. Augustine of Hippo" — *Saints & Angels* — Catholic Online, http://www.catholic.org/saints/saint.php?saint_id=418; "Augustine legends — 01" (Augustine legends), http://www.augnet.org/?ipageid=1390.

213. "Saint Augustine Quotes" (BrainyQuote), http://www.brainyquote.com/quotes/authors/s/saint_augustine.html.

214. Judith MacNutt, *Angels Are for Real: Inspiring True Stories and Biblical Answers* (Minneapolis: Chosen Books, 2012), 137–138.

215. "'Angel Tree' on Mississippi Gulf Coast saved 3 lives during Hurricane Katrina" (jacksonville.com), http://jacksonville.com/sports/outdoorsoutside/2014-08-30/story/angel-tree-mississippi-gulf-coast-saved-3-lives-during.

216. HUMANI GENERIS (HUMANI GENERIS), http://www.papalencyclicals.net/Pius12/P12HUMAN.HTM.

217. "Catholics vs. Protestants: What Do They Believe About Angels?" (Beliefnet), http://www.beliefnet.com/Inspiration/Angels/2009/03/Catholics-Protestants-Angels.aspx.

218. *What Luther Says*, S64, Ewald M. Plass.

219. John Cardinal Wright, *The Angels: Companions and Helpers* (New Rochelle, NY: Scepter Booklets, 1972), 1208; "The Angelic Mind (The Holy Angels)," https://theholyangels.wordpress.com/the-angelic-mind/.

220. http://angelsandsaintsandus.blogspot.com/2012/03/angels-in-disguise.html.

221. "The Life of Saint Gregory the Great" (Catholicismorg), http://catholicism.org/gregory-great.html.

222. "St. Hilary of Poitiers" — *Saints & Angels* — Catholic Online, http://www.catholic.org/saints/saint.php?saint_id=55.

223. A quote by Saint Hilary (Goodreads), http://www.goodreads.com/quotes/718208-everything-that-seems-empty-is-full-of-the-angels-of.

224. www.azquotes.com › Authors › M › Mother Teresa.

225. http://www.healpastlives.com/pastlf/quote/quangels.htm.

226. "The Alexander Column (in St. Petersburg, Russia)," http://www.saint-petersburg.com/monuments/alexander-column/.

227. Eckhart: Sermon 9, *The Reading and Preaching of the Scriptures in the Worship of the Christian Church* (1999), by Hughes Oliphant Old, ch. 9: "The German Mystics," p. 449.

228. Valentine Long, O.F.M., *The Angels in Religion and Art* (Chicago: Franciscan Herald Press, 1970), 14.

229. Jean Danielou, *The Angels and Their Mission* (Westminster: The Newman Press, 1956), viii.

230. Dom Anscar Vonier, O.S.B., *The Angels* (New York: Macmillan, 1928), 34–35.

231. Valentine Long, O.F.M., *The Angels in Religion and Art* (Chicago: Franciscan Herald Press, 1970), 206.

232. http://www.azquotes.com/author/21940-Saint_John_Chrysostom/tag/heaven.

233. Maria Boulding, O.S.B., tr., *Augustine: The Confessions* (Hyde Park NY: New City Press, 1997), Book VIII, 29, 206–207.

234. http://www.azquotes.com/author/21940-Saint_John_Chrysostom/tag/heaven.

235. W. Heywood, tr., *Fioretti: The Little Flowers of Saint Francis* (Assisi: Casa Editrice Francescana, 1949), 210–212.

236. Memorial of Our Lady of Sorrows — September 15, 2014 — LiturgicalCalendar, https://www.catholicculture.org/culture/liturgicalyear/calendar/day.cfm?date=2014-09-15.

237. "International Society of Hildegard von Bingen Studies," http://www.hildegard-society.org/2014/10/o-gloriosissimi-lux-vivens-angeli-antiphon.html.

238. Mark A. Scott, O.C.S.O., *At Home with Saint Benedict: Monastery Talks* (Collegeville, MN: Cistercian Publications, 2011), 93.

239. "On Angels," by Lawrence S. Cunningham, O'Brien Chair of Theology Emeritus, University of Notre Dame (YouTube), https://www.youtube.com/watch?v=PVJ7PJuJZeE — *Saturday with the Saints*.

240. Carroll Eugene Simcox, *A Treasury of Quotations on Christian Themes* (New York: Crossroad, 1973), 27.

241. "Fulton Sheen," https://www.fultonsheen.com/.

242. Joan Wester Anderson, *In the Arms of Angels: True Stories of Heavenly Guardians* (Chicago: Loyola Press, 2004), 171–176.

243. "Padre Pio's Love for the Holy Angels" (Catholic Caucus), http://www.freerepublic.com/focus/f-religion/2839675/posts.

244. http://te-deum.blogspot.com/2013/09/st-padre-pios-july-15-1913-letter.html.

245. Ladislaus Boros, *Angels and Men* (New York: Crossroad Book, Seabury Press, 1977), 53.

246. Hilary of Poitiers Tract. Super Ps. 128:7, cited in Maria Pia Giudici, *The Angels: Spiritual and Exegetical Notes* (New York: Alba House, 1993), 104, footnote.

247. Mike Celizic, "Did Angel Save Dying Girl in Hospital?" NBCNews.com, 12/23/2008.

248. Lourdes Duarte, "The Angels of Lower Wacker," WGN, Jan. 14, 2015.

249. Origen, *Contra Celsum*, V, 5.

250. http://www.nga.gov/content/ngaweb/Collection/art-object-page.46151.html.

251. John Clarke, O.C.D., tr., *Story of a Soul, the Autobiography of Saint Thérèse of Lisieux, Third Edition* (Washington, DC: ICS Publications, 1996), 86.

252. *Poems = PN 5, 12* (CJ 7/17/1897), https://www.opusangelorum.org/English/Littleflower.html.

253. http://www.catholicnewsagency.com/news/be-like-children-believe-in-your-guardian-angel-pope-says-55343/.

254. Pope Saint John XXIII, *Journal of a Soul* (New York: McGraw Hill, 1965), 58.

255. Mother Theodore Guerin, *Journals and Letters of Mother Theodore Guerin* (Saint Mary-of-the-Woods, IN: The Sisters of Providence, 2005), 167.

256. W. Heywood, tr., *Fioretti: The Little Flowers of Saint Francis* (Assisi: Casa Editrice Francescana, 1949), 19–20.

257. Maria Faustina Kowalska, *Diary of Saint Maria Faustina Kowalska: Divine Mercy in My Soul* (Stockbridge, MA: 2005), 418–419, https://liturgicalyear.files.wordpress.com/2012/10/divine-mercy-in-my-soul.pdf.

258. http://www.moscow.info/kremlin/churches/cathedral-archangel.aspx; http://rbth.com/travel/2014/02/07/the_cathedral_of_archangel_michael_the_kremlins_royal_shrine_33975.html.

259. On the Confraternity of the Holy Rosary, Sept. 12, 1897.

260. http://angelsandsaintsandus.blogspot.com/2014/10/angels-and-rosary.html.

261. http://www.angelofthenorth.org.uk/.

262. Marilyn K., "Guardian Angel," used with permission of Catholic Online, Saints & Angels, Angel Encounters, http://www.catholic.org/saints/angelstories/?story=10152.

263. Georges Huber, *My Angel Will Go Before You* (Dublin: Four Courts Press, 1983), 22–25.

264. Peter Kreeft, *Angels and Demons: What Do We Really Know about Them?* (San Francisco: Ignatius Press, 1995), 88–90.

265. Teresa of Ávila (Wikiquote), https://en.wikiquote.org/wiki/Teresa_of_%C3%81vila; "St. Teresa of Ávila" — *Saints & Angels* — Catholic Online, http://www.catholic.org/saints/saint.php?saint_id=208.

266. "St. Ignatius of Antioch" — *Saints & Angels* — Catholic Online, http://www.catholic.org/saints/saint.php?saint_id=677.

267. Melaine Ryther, "Saint John Bosco and the Big Gray Dog," *Angels, Saints ... and the Rest of Us*, January 31, 2012, http://angelsandsaintsandus.blogspot.com.

268. E. B. Tylor, *Primitive Culture*, cited in T. H. Gaster and J. G. Frazer, *Myth, Legend and Custom in the Old Testament* (London: Harper, 1961), 213.

269. http://www.therealpresence.org/eucharst/misc/Angels_Demons/ANGES_paulcross.pdf.

270. http://www.poetseers.org/spiritual-and-devotional-poets/christian/hildegard-of-bingen/hildp/angels/index.html.

271. http://www.holy-transfiguration.org/library_en/lord_trinity_rublev.html; http://www.sacredheartpullman.org/Icon%20explanation.htm; http://www.wellsprings.org.uk/rublevs_icon/rublev.htm.

272. Henri Nouwen, S.J., *Behold the Beauty of the Lord: Praying with Icons* (Notre Dame, IN: Ave Maria Press, 1987), 20–22.

273. Matthew Bunson, *John Paul II's Book of Saints* (Huntington, IN: Our Sunday Visitor, 1999), 170–171.

274. Pascal P. Parente, *The Angels* (St. Meinrad, IN: Grail Publications,1958), 3.

275. Irma Vela, "Three Saved by An Angel," used with permission of Catholic Online, Saints & Angels, Angel Encounters, http://www.catholic.org/saints/angelstories/?story=5340.

276. Joan Wester Anderson, "Angels at the Door," *In the Arms of Angels: True Stories of Heavenly Guardians* (Chicago: Loyola Press, 2004), pp. 197-201.

277. "On Angels," by Lawrence S. Cunningham, O'Brien Chair of Theology Emeritus, University of Notre Dame (YouTube), https://www.youtube.com/watch?v=PVJ7PJuJZeE — *Saturday with the Saints*.

278. "Marc Chagall Quotes" (BrainyQuote), http://www.brainyquote.com/quotes/authors/m/marc_chagall.html.

279. Peter Kreeft, *Angels and Demons: What Do We Really Know about Them?* (San Francisco: Ignatius Press, 1995), 27.

280. Dom Anscar Vonier, O.S.B., *The Angels* (New York: Macmillan, 1928), 53–55, in Johan., XIX, 4; http://www.catholictradition.org/Angels/angels3g.htm.

281. http://newtheologicalmovement.blogspot.com/2010/10/october-2-nd-feast-of-guardian-angels.html.

282. Fr. F. X. Schouppe, S.J., *Purgatory: Explained by the Lives and Legends of the Saints* (Charlotte, NC: TAN Books), 16–19.

283. Suarez, *De Angelis*, VI, 19, cited in Pascal P. Parente, *Beyond Space*, (New York: St. Paul Publications, 1961), 129–130.

284. Saint Clement of Rome, *"Epistle to the Corinthians,"* XXXIV, *The Early Christian Fathers,* ed. and trans. Henry Bettenson, Geoffrey Cumberledge (Oxford: Oxford University Press, 1956), 47.

285. Dom Hélder Câmara, *Through the Gospel with Dom Hélder Câmara* (Maryknoll, New York: Orbis Books, 1986), 10–11.

286. https://padreroblaws.files.wordpress.com/2013/02/thebiblicalcamara.pdf.

287. Comte Paul Biver, *Père Lamy*, trans., Monsignor John O'Connor (Charlotte, NC: Tan Books and Publishers, 2009), 37.

288. Fr. Robert Barron on The Devil (YouTube), https://www.youtube.com/watch?v=IED3S-vJ5AU, "Pope Francis Appoints Fr. Robert Barron Auxiliary Bishop of Los Angeles" | Word on Fire | http://www.wordonfire.org/resources/blog/pope-francis-appoints-fr-robert-barron-auxiliary-bishop-of-los-angeles/4832/.

289. "SAINTLY QUOTES," http://www.catholictradition.org/Saints/saintly-quotes14.htm.

290. Sulpicius Severus, *On the Life of St. Martin. A Select Library of Nicene and Post-Nicene Fathers of the Christian Church*, 1894, chapter 3, http://www.users.csbsju.edu/~eknuth/npnf2-11/sulpitiu/lifeofst.html, http://www.newadvent.org/fathers/3501.htm.

291. https://en.wikipedia.org/wiki/Smiling_Angel; http://www.abelard.org/france/germans_in_france-reims.php; http://www.healpastlives.com/pastlf/quote/quangels.htm.

292. F. Forrester Church, *Entertaining Angels* (New York: Harper & Row, 1987), 33.

293. http://catholicism.org/first-canonized-cabrini.html.

294. Ellen Muehlberger, *Angels in Late Ancient Christianity* (Oxford University Press, 2013), 176–202.

295. Saint Gregory the Great, *Dialogues*, 4.60.3.

296. http://opcentral.org/resources/2015/01/27/albert-the-great-the-mission-of-st-albert-and-st-thomas-by-sr-m-albert-hughes-o-p/.

297. http://breviariumsop.blogspot.com/2013/11/november-15-st-albert-great-b-c-d-op-ii.html.

298. http://www.catholictradition.org/Angels/angels3f.htm, D. Gilbert Dolan, O.S.B., *Saint Gertrude the Great* (London: Sands & Co., 1913), 30.

299. "A Meditation on the Feast of the Presentation of Mary," http://campus.udayton.edu/mary/meditations/Nov21.html.

300. http://www.catholictradition.org/Angels/angels3f.htm.

301. http://www.angelicwarfareconfraternity.org/about/ record of canonization of Saint Thomas Aquinas.

302. *Medieval Sourcebook: The Life of St. Columban, by the Monk Jonas (7th Century)* (Mabillon: *Acta Sanctorum Ordinis S. Benedicti*, Vol. I, Venice, 1733), pp. 3–26 (Latin), http://legacy.fordham.edu/halsall/basis/columban.asp.

303. Alexander Schmemann, *For the Life of the World* (Crestwood, NY: St. Vladimir's Seminary Press, 1973), 106.

304. Anselm Gruen, *Angels of Grace* (New York: Crossroad Publishing Company, 1998), 43.

305. Joan Wester Anderson, *In the Arms of Angels: True Stories of Heavenly Guardians* (Chicago: Loyola Press, 2004), 165–167.

306. Clide S. Kilbey, editor, *A Mind Awake: An Anthology of C. S. Lewis* (San Diego, London, & New York: A Harvest Book, Harcourt, Inc., 1968), 103.

307. http://dorothydayguild.org/.

308. Pope Saint John XXIII, *Journal of a Soul* (New York: McGraw Hill, 1965), 38.

309. "ANGELS" (ANGELS), http://www.catholictradition.org/Angels/guardians18.htm.

310. https://www.ewtn.com/library/MARY/AMBROSE.HTM.

311. Alexander Schmemann, *For the Life of the World* (New York: St. Vladimir's Seminary Press, 1973), 86–87.

312. M. F. Toal, *The Sunday Sermons of the Great Fathers*, Vol. I (Chicago: Henry Regnery Co., 1955), 151.

313. http://www.gratefulness.org/resource/joy-fra-giovanni/.

314. http://www.scborromeo.org/saints/zita.htm.

315. http://www.olgaustin.org/symbolism.shtml; http://www.virginmotherofguadalupe.com/, http://www.olgaustin.org/symbolism.shtml.

316. http://www.theotokos.org.uk/pages/approved/words/wordguad.html.

317. Thomas Merton, *Conjectures of a Guilty Bystander* (New York: Doubleday& Company, 1966), 141.

318. http://www.catholic.org/saints/saint.php?saint_id=65.

319. "In the Bleak Midwinter" (Poetry Foundation), http://www.poetryfoundation.org/poem/238450.

320. "My Guardian Angel," http://www.battleofthebulgememories.be/stories26/32-battle-of-the-bulge-us-army/743-my-guardian-angel.html.

321. Stichera by Patriarch Anatolios on "O Lord, I have cried unto Thee," http://www.orthodoxchristian.info/pages/Christmas_hymns.html.

322. Chrysostom: Homily 141: *A Sermon on the Incarnation of Christ.*

323. "Shepherds' Field" (See The Holy Land), http://www.seetheholyland.net/shepherds-field/; "Shepherd's Field and Grotto," http://www.custodia.org/default.asp?id=1888.

324. "Padre Pio's Love for the Holy Angels" (Catholic Caucus), Jan. 29, 2012, http://www.freerepublic.com/focus/f-religion/2839675/posts.

325. *Tract. Super Ps.* 124 (PL 9, 682 BC).

326. M. F. Toal, D.D., *The Sunday Sermons of the Great Fathers*, Vol. I (Chicago: Henry Regnery Co., 1955), 104, 107.

327. M. F. Toal, D.D., *The Sunday Sermons of the Great Fathers*, Vol. I (Chicago: Henry Regnery Co., 1955), 107.

328. Thomas P. Scheck*, Origen: Homilies 1–14 on Ezekiel* (Mahwah, NJ: Paulist Press, 2010), 1:7, 36.

329. M. F. Toal, D.D., *The Sunday Sermons of the Great Fathers*, Vol. I (Chicago: Henry Regnery Co, 1955), 104.

330. *Geometer in the Catena Aurea of Saint Thomas Aquinas.*

331. Thomas P. McDonnell, ed., *A Thomas Merton Reader, Revised Edition* (New York: Doubleday, 1989), 155.

332. http://www.brainyquote.com/quotes/authors/t/thomas_merton.html.

333. *John the Apostle | The Theologian in Silence (A Readers Guide to Orthodox Icons),* https://iconreader.wordpress.com/2012/05/07/john-the-apostle-the-theologian-in-silence/334.

334. https://www.youtube.com/watch?v=b1xK_wKIQ-Y.

335. Alfred Fowler, D.D., *Our Angel Friends in Ministry and Song* (Washington, DC: Library of Congress, 1903), 316.

336. https://songsandhymns.org/hymns/detail/let-all-mortal-flesh-keep-silence; https://wedgewords.wordpress.com/2013/01/02/12-days-of-christmas-carols-let-all-mortal-flesh-keep-silence/.

337. Rev. D. J. Kavanagh, S.J., *The Holy Family Sisters of San Francisco* (San Francisco: Gilmartin Co., 1922), 59–61.

338. www.catholicity.com/prayer/prayer-before-sleep.html.

339. http://www.catholicdoors.com/prayers/english4/p02940.htm.

340. Mike Aquilina, *Angels of God: The Bible, the Church and the Heavenly Hosts* (Cincinnati: Servant Books, 2006), 104, adapted from "Night Prayer," available at www.catholic-forum.com.

341. http://www.communityofhopeinc.org/Prayer%20Pages/Guardian%20Angels.html.

342. http://angels.about.com/od/AngelsReligiousTexts/f/What-Are-Some-Catholic-Guardian-Angel-Prayers.htm.

343. F. Forrester Church and Terrence J. Mulry, eds., *The Macmillan Book of Earliest Christian Prayers* (New York: Macmillan Publishing, 1988), 113.

344. http://padrepiodevotions.org/prayers-of-padre-pio/.

345. https://opusangelorum.org/English/Littleflower.html.

346. F. Forrester Church and Terrence J. Mulry, eds., *The Macmillan Book of Earliest Christian Prayers* (New York: Macmillan Publishing, 1988), 99.

347. http://www.straphaeloil.com/prayers/.

348. "Prayers of Jews to Angels and Other Intermediaries during the First Centuries of the Common Era," http://oodegr.co/english/istorika/israil/jewish_prayers_angels.htm.

ABOUT THE AUTHORS

CATHERINE M. ODELL is a writer and editor whose primary professional experience has been in the religious press. A native of South Bend, Indiana, Odell was born, grew up, and was educated in the shadow of Notre Dame's "Golden Dome." A freelance journalist, curriculum writer, and editor, she is also the author of three books for children and nine trade books for adults, including Our Sunday Visitor's *Those Who Saw Her: Apparitions of Mary, Faustina: Apostle of Divine Mercy, Solanus Casey: The Story of Father Solanus*, and *Praying the Rosary for Intercession*. Odell has also enjoyed teaching on the elementary and junior high levels. She is married, has two grown children, and is a committed organic gardener, baker, walker, and reader.

MARGARET A. SAVITSKAS writes religion textbooks and teacher guides, as well as a wide variety of children's books and resources for Catholic students, teachers, and parents. Savitskas also served as parish director of catechesis and sacramental formation for many years. Her interest in the saints and angels began when she was ten and found *The Lives of the Saints* in her grandmother's bedroom. From those first sneak peeks to her master's work in theology, through personal and professional joys and challenges, her familiarity and love of the saints and angels has enriched and guided her life. Savitskas enjoys spending time with her family, traveling, and reading.